Pelican Island National Wildlife Refuge

Comprehensive Conservation Plan

U.S. Department of the Interior
Fish and Wildlife Service
Southeast Region

September 2006

Submitted by: _~Signed~_____ Date: _4/10/06_
  Paul Tritaik, Refuge Manager
  Pelican Island NWR

Concur: _~Signed~_____ Date: _7/20/06_
  Elizabeth Souheaver, Refuge Supervisor
  Southeast Region

Concur: _~Signed~_____ Date: _7/21/06_
  Jon Andrew, Regional Chief
  Southeast Region

Approved by: _~Signed~_____ Date: _7/24/06_
  Sam Hamilton, Regional Director
  Southeast Region

PELICAN ISLAND NATIONAL WILDLIFE REFUGE

COMPREHENSIVE CONSERVATION PLAN

U.S. Department of the Interior
Fish and Wildlife Service

Southeast Region
Atlanta, Georgia

September 2006

TABLE OF CONTENTS

SECTION A. COMPREHENSIVE CONSERVATION PLAN

SECTION B. APPENDICES

LIST OF FIGURES

LIST OF TABLES

I. BACKGROUND

INTRODUCTION

Pelican Island National Wildlife Refuge in Sebastian, Florida, is the birthplace of the National Wildlife Refuge System (Figure 1). What happened on this tiny island that made it so important, that it became a catalyst for what is now the world's largest network of lands and waters managed for fish and wildlife–the National Wildlife Refuge System? By the end of the 1800s, plume hunters, egg collectors, and vandals had nearly exterminated all the egrets, herons, and spoonbills from Pelican Island proper (i.e., the original 5.5-acre rookery island). Paul Kroegel (who was to later become the first Refuge Manager) protected the last nesting brown pelicans on the east coast of Florida and petitioned ornithologists and naturalists to help him. At the urging of researchers, concerned citizens, the Audubon Society, and the American Ornithologists' Union, President Theodore Roosevelt signed an Executive Order that set aside Pelican Island as a preserve and breeding ground for native birds on March 14, 1903, thus establishing the first national wildlife refuge (originally 5.5 acres) and the National Wildlife Refuge System.

Pelican Island is both the name of the refuge and the name of the original 5.5-acre rookery island. While Pelican Island proper (i.e., the original rookery island) eroded by more than half from 5.5 acres in 1943 to 2.2 acres in 1996, the refuge has grown to encompass ±5,445 acres (as of September 30, 2002). Within the ±6,184-acre acquisition boundary (Figure 2), the Fish and Wildlife Service owns ±363 acres and leases or otherwise manages the bulk of the refuge (i.e., ±5,062 acres), while remaining inholdings total ±409 acres. (This leaves ±330 acres unaccounted. These acres are most likely part of the lease with the State of Florida.)

Located in the Indian River Lagoon on the east coast of Florida, Pelican Island National Wildlife Refuge now supports important bird rookeries, key fish spawning sites, and a globally important juvenile sea turtle nursery. Primarily comprised of lagoonal waters, the refuge includes aquatic, transitional, and upland habitats supporting a diversity of species, including 14 federally listed threatened and endangered species. This complex ecological system also supports hundreds of species of birds, fish, plants, and mammals. When the refuge was established at the beginning of the 20th century, as many as 10,000 brown pelicans occupied the tiny 5.5-acre Pelican Island as a last stronghold for this species along the east coast of Florida. Today, the number of brown pelicans using the Island has dwindled in magnitude to less than 100 nesting pairs. And today at least 16 different bird species nest on Pelican Island proper, including brown pelicans, wood storks, egrets, herons, ibises, anhingas, oystercatchers, and cormorants. Beyond the tiny rookery of Pelican Island proper, over 130 species of birds use the refuge as a rookery, roost, feeding ground, and/or loafing area. Further, federally protected West Indian manatees and sea turtles inhabit the lagoonal waters of the refuge, alongside some 30,000 annual boaters. A growing human population, along with ongoing development and other human activities, currently threaten the fragile, but highly productive waters of the Indian River Lagoon and the refuge.

Figure 1. Refuge location and acquisition boundary

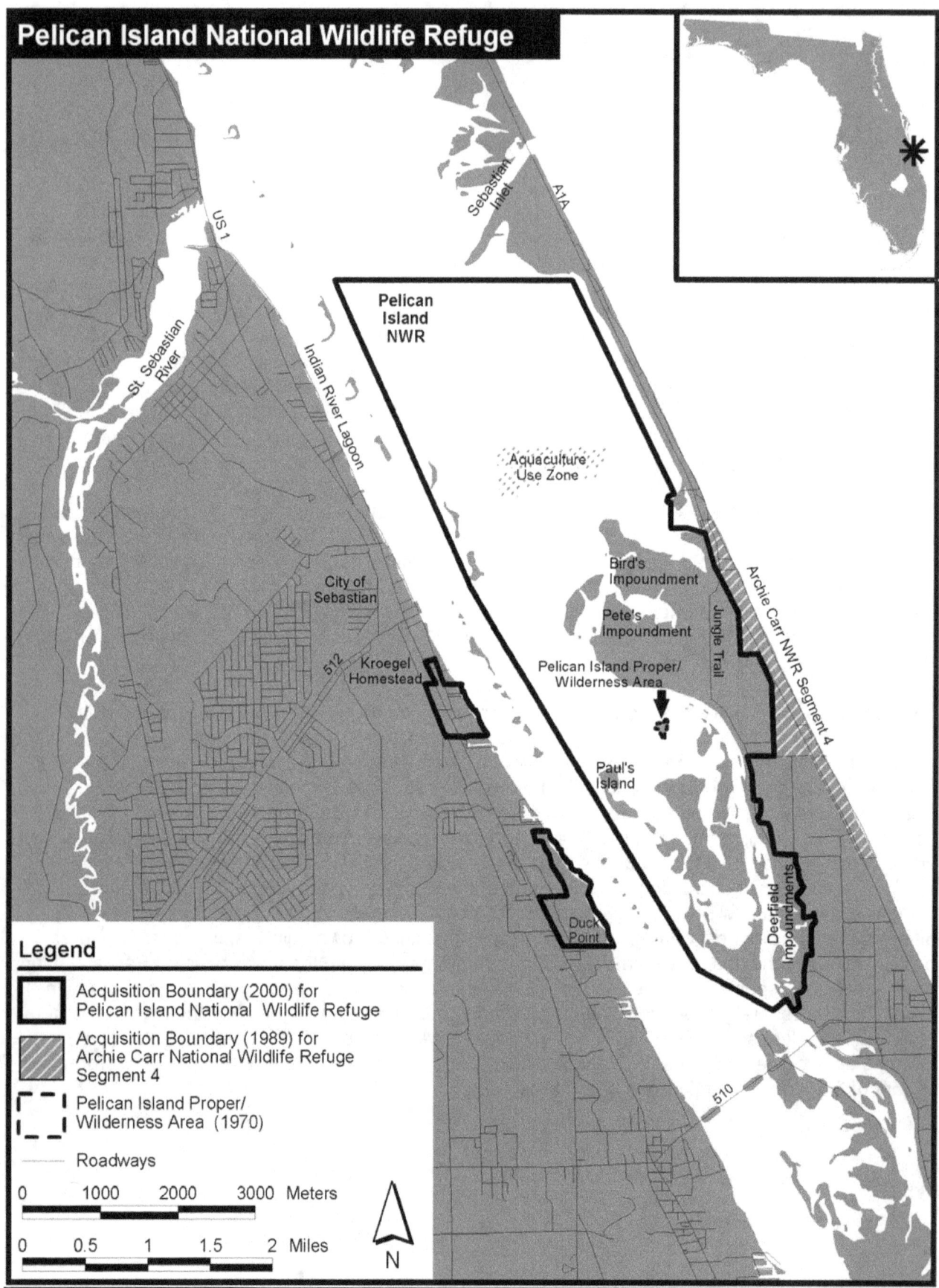

Figure 2. Status map (as of October 2003)

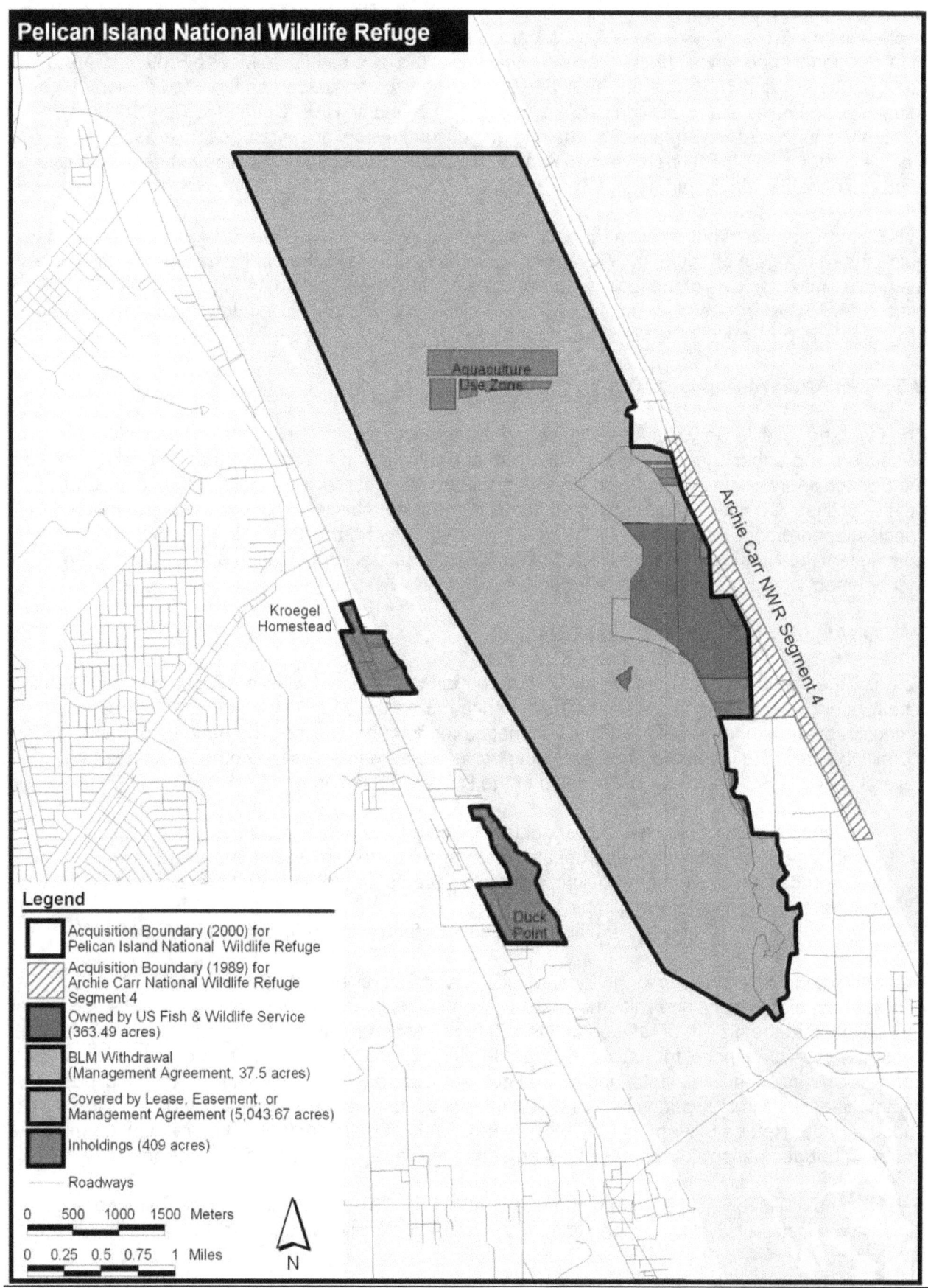

Pelican Island National Wildlife Refuge

Aquaculture Use Zone

Archie Carr NWR Segment 4

Kroegel Homestead

Duck Point

Legend

Acquisition Boundary (2000) for Pelican Island National Wildlife Refuge

Acquisition Boundary (1989) for Archie Carr National Wildlife Refuge Segment 4

Owned by US Fish & Wildlife Service (363.49 acres)

BLM Withdrawal (Management Agreement, 37.5 acres)

Covered by Lease, Easement, or Management Agreement (5,043.67 acres)

Inholdings (409 acres)

Roadways

0   500   1000   1500   Meters

0   0.25   0.5   0.75   1   Miles

N

Beyond being the birthplace of the National Wildlife Refuge System, the refuge is also designated as a National Historic Landmark (1963), one of the smallest units of the National Wilderness Preservation System (with a 5.5-acre Wilderness Area encompassing Pelican Island proper) (1970), and a Wetland of International Importance (1993). The refuge is also listed as a candidate Marine Protected Area (2000). Beginning in 2001, facilities have been and are being constructed on the eastern side of the refuge on the barrier island through partnerships (e.g., with Indian River County) to view the historic Pelican Island rookery and interpret the natural and cultural history of the refuge, the area, and the Refuge System. Another currently active partnership activity is focused on refuge habitat restoration efforts with the Florida Department of Environmental Protection and Indian River County.

This Comprehensive Conservation Plan for Pelican Island National Wildlife Refuge was prepared to guide future refuge management. A planning team developed a range of alternatives that best met the goals and objectives of the refuge. Following a public review and comment period on the draft plan, a final decision was made by the Fish and Wildlife Service that will guide refuge management programs and projects over a 15-year planning period.

U.S. FISH AND WILDLIFE SERVICE

The Fish and Wildlife Service is the primary federal agency responsible for the conservation, protection, and enhancement of the Nation's fish and wildlife populations and their habitats. Although the Service shares some conservation responsibilities with other federal, state, tribal, local, and private entities, it has specific trustee obligations for migratory birds, threatened and endangered species, anadromous fish, and certain marine mammals. As part of its mission, the Service administers the National Wildlife Refuge System, a national network of lands and waters for the management and protection of these resources.

NATIONAL WILDLIFE REFUGE SYSTEM

To date, the Refuge System is comprised of more than 540 national wildlife refuges and over 3,000 small waterfowl breeding and nesting sites covering more than 95 million acres, the world's largest collection of lands and waters specifically managed for fish and wildlife. The majority of these lands, 77 million acres, are in Alaska. The remaining acres are spread across the other 49 states and several island U.S. territories. The mission of the Refuge System is:

> "...to administer a national network of lands and waters for the conservation, management, and where appropriate, restoration of the fish, wildlife and plant resources and their habitats within the United States for the benefit of present and future generations of Americans."
> - National Wildlife Refuge System Improvement Act of 1997

The wildlife and habitat vision for national wildlife refuges stresses that wildlife come first; that ecosystems, biodiversity, and wilderness are vital concepts in refuge management; that refuges must be healthy; that the growth of refuges and the Refuge System must be strategic; and that the Refuge System serves as a model for habitat management with broad participation from others. This broad participation includes local, state, and federal government partners; organizations; the local business communities; individuals; and volunteers. Volunteers continue to be a major contributor to the success of the Refuge System and in 1999, some 36,000 of them contributed more than 1.3 million hours on refuges nationwide, representing an economic value of more than $20 million.

The National Wildlife Refuge System Improvement Act of 1997 established, for the first time, a clear legislative mission of wildlife conservation for the National Wildlife Refuge System. Activities were initiated in 1997 to complement the direction of this new legislation, including an effort to complete 15-year management plans (i.e., comprehensive conservation plans) for all refuges. These plans, which are conducted with full public involvement, help guide the future management of refuges, including providing management direction for natural resources and recreation and education programs. The Improvement Act states that each refuge shall be managed to:

- fulfill the mission of the Refuge System;
- fulfill the individual purposes of each refuge;
- consider the needs of fish and wildlife first;
- fulfill the requirement of developing a comprehensive conservation plan for each unit of the Refuge System and fully involve the public in the preparation of these plans;
- maintain the biological integrity, diversity, and environmental health of the Refuge System; and
- recognize that wildlife-dependent recreation activities, including hunting, fishing, observing wildlife, photographing wildlife, and participating in environmental education and interpretation, are legitimate and priority public uses of national wildlife refuges.

The National Wildlife Refuge System hosts over 35 million annual visitors. Economists found that these refuge visitors contribute more than $400 million annually to local economies. In 2001, on conservation lands throughout the nation, approximately 37.8 million people participated in wildlife-related activities, most to observe wildlife in their natural habitats. These visitors represented nearly 40 percent of the country's adults who spent $108 billion on wildlife-related pursuits in 2001, according to the National Survey of Fishing, Hunting, and Wildlife-Associated Recreation (U.S. Department of Interior, Fish and Wildlife Service and U.S. Department of Commerce, U.S. Census Bureau 2002). As visitation continues to grow on conservation lands and waters in general and specifically on refuges, adjacent local communities are realizing important economic benefits.

LEGAL POLICY CONTEXT

Administration of national wildlife refuges is guided by the mission and goals of the National Wildlife Refuge System, Congressional legislation, Presidential executive orders, and international treaties. Policies for management options of refuges are further refined by administrative guidelines established by the Secretary of the Interior and by policy guidelines established by the Director of the Fish and Wildlife Service. Management options are guided by a refuge's establishing authorities; Public Law 104, Stat. 2957 (§108, H.R. 3338); and the National Wildlife Refuge System Improvement Act of 1997 (see Appendix III for more information on legal and policy guidance for the operation of national wildlife refuges).

Key guidance and direction can be found in:

- National Wildlife Refuge System Administration Act of 1966;
- Refuge Recreation Act of 1962;
- Title 50 of the Code of Federal Regulations;
- U.S. Fish and Wildlife Service Manual; and
- National Wildlife Refuge System Improvement Act of 1997.

Since refuges must be managed for wildlife first, lands and waters within the National Wildlife Refuge System are closed to public uses unless specifically and legally opened under specified conditions allowing compatibility with the refuges' purposes. All programs and uses of a refuge must be evaluated based on mandates set forth in the National Wildlife Refuge System Improvement Act, including those that:

- contribute to ecosystem goals, as well as to refuge purpose(s) and goals;
- conserve, manage, and restore fish, wildlife, and plant resources and their habitats;
- monitor the trends of fish, wildlife, and plants;
- manage and ensure compatible wildlife-dependent visitor uses as those uses which benefit the conservation of fish and wildlife resources and which contribute to the enjoyment of the public (these uses include hunting, fishing, observing wildlife, photographing wildlife, and participating in environmental education and interpretation); and
- ensure that visitor activities are compatible with refuge purpose(s).

ECOSYSTEM CONTEXT

Pelican Island National Wildlife Refuge is part of the South Florida Ecosystem (Figure 3). Comprising one of the 52 ecosystems around the country, the Fish and Wildlife Service's South Florida Ecosystem encompasses more than 26,000 square miles, 19 southern Florida counties, and over 7 million people. The South Florida Ecosystem has undergone numerous human disturbances, including alteration of hydroperiod, fire history, and drainage patterns. Developing and dredging the canal system and expanding agricultural operations have eliminated and diminished natural systems. Exotic species such as Old World climbing fern, melaleuca, Australian pine, and Brazilian pepper are further contributing to wildlife population and habitat declines. Over the last 50 years, the South Florida Ecosystem has undergone dramatic changes, which are largely attributed to various human activities and growth.

Despite the ongoing landscape alteration and rapidly expanding population, the scrub, hardwood hammocks, cypress swamps, salt marshes, mangrove islands, coral reefs, and seagrass beds of south Florida support one of the most ecologically diverse systems on the planet. The majority of the remaining wildlife and habitats of the South Florida Ecosystem are found on national interest lands, including sixteen national wildlife refuges, three national parks, one national preserve, and one national marine sanctuary. Despite tremendous human development, the South Florida Ecosystem supports more than 600 rare or imperiled species, where 68 are federally listed as threatened or endangered, including 8 mammals, 13 birds, 10 reptiles, 2 invertebrates, and 35 plants.

RELATIONSHIP TO STATE PARTNERS

The Fish and Wildlife Service is committed to encouraging and maintaining partnerships with others to improve the environmental health of ecosystems and the National Wildlife Refuge System. Partnerships are recognized by the Service as vital to fulfill our mission and help share our advocacy for fish and wildlife resources. Some of our current partners include federal and state agencies, environmental organizations, outdoor sporting groups, industry, local governments, and private landowners.

A provision of the National Wildlife Refuge System Improvement Act of 1997 and subsequent agency policy provide that the Service shall ensure timely and effective cooperation and collaboration with other federal agencies and state fish and wildlife agencies during the course of acquiring and managing refuges. For Pelican Island Refuge, state fish and wildlife management is administered by the Florida Fish and Wildlife Conservation Commission (http://www.floridaconservation.org/) and the Florida Department of Environmental Protection (http://www.dep.state.fl.us/). These state agencies

Figure 3. South Florida Ecosystem

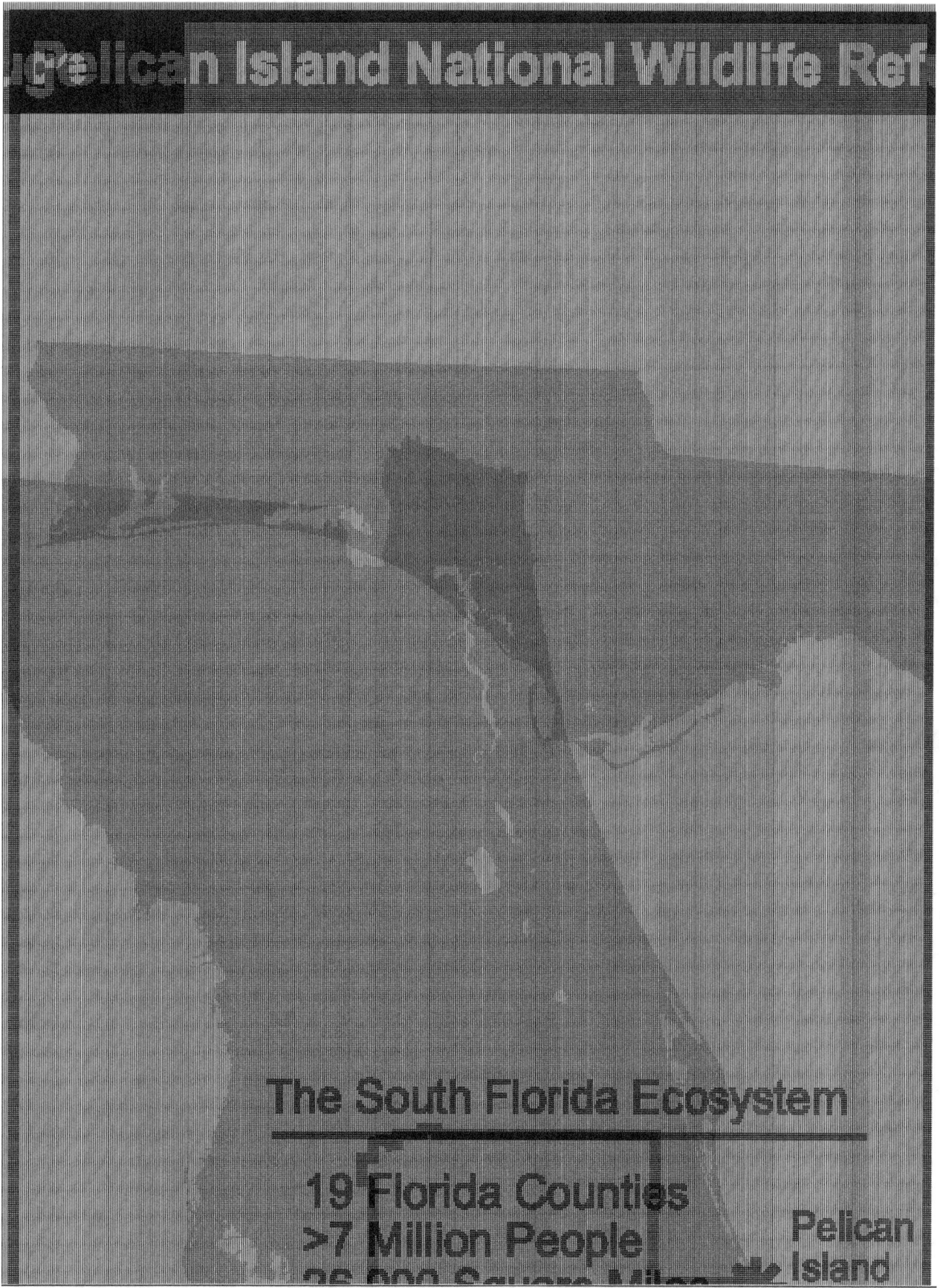

The South Florida Ecosystem

19 Florida Counties
>7 Million People

Pelican
Island

are charged with enforcement responsibilities relating to migratory birds, trust species, and fisheries, as well as with management of natural resources of the state. Both the Florida Fish and Wildlife Conservation Commission and the Florida Department of Environmental Protection manage state lands and waters. The Florida Fish and Wildlife Conservation Commission manages 4.3 million acres of public lands and 220,000 acres of private lands for recreation and conservation purposes. The Florida Department of Environmental Protection manages 150 state parks covering nearly 600,000 acres and 57 coastal and aquatic managed areas, totaling over 5 million acres of submerged lands and coastal uplands.

Since the 1960s, the State of Florida has been an important partner with the Service at Pelican Island Refuge (by leasing open waters and islands of the state to the Service, comprising the majority of property within the refuge). The State of Florida has helped champion the refuge through various efforts, including participation in the Pelican Island Working Group, an active working group comprised of a variety of public and private partners dedicated to improving the refuge and the resources it protects. For example, the Florida Department of Environmental Protection and Indian River County have been invaluable partners in securing and funding habitat restoration activities on the refuge. Various agencies within the state government have also participated in a mix of other refuge projects, including the planning process to develop a 15-year management plan for the refuge. The State of Florida's participation and contribution throughout this comprehensive conservation planning process provide for ongoing opportunities and open dialogue to improve the ecological sustainment of fish and wildlife in Florida. An integral part of the comprehensive conservation planning process is integrating common mission objectives, where appropriate.

II. The Refuge

INTRODUCTION

Part of the South Florida Ecosystem, Pelican Island National Wildlife Refuge is located within the southern Indian River Lagoon (Figure 1). The Indian River Lagoon is located along a transition zone between the warm-temperate climate to the north and a more subtropical climate to the south. The area of the Lagoon surrounding the refuge is the focus of the planning study (Figure 1). The Lagoon's location, combined with its large size and other physical characteristics, make it the most diverse estuary in North America.

PURPOSES AND DESIGNATIONS OF THE REFUGE

Currently over 5,400 acres, Pelican Island National Wildlife Refuge was established in 1903 on 5.5 acres "as a preserve and breeding ground for native birds" through an unnumbered Executive Order and expanded in 1909 by Executive Order 1014. The Pelican Island Refuge "shall be administered by him (the Secretary of the Interior) directly or in accordance with cooperative agreements and in accordance with such rules and regulations for the conservation, maintenance, and management of wildlife, resources thereof, and its habitat thereon" [16 USC §664 (Fish and Wildlife Coordination Act)]. The refuge shall "conserve fish, wildlife, and plants, including those which are listed as endangered species or threatened species" [16 USC §1534 (Endangered Species Act)]. Further, the refuge serves "...the development, advancement, management, conservation, and protection of fish and wildlife resources... [16 USC §742(f)(a)(4) (Fish and Wildlife Act)] ...for the benefit of the United States Fish and Wildlife Service, in performing its activities and services..." [16 USC §742(f)(b)(1) (Fish and Wildlife Act)].

Later, the Refuge Recreation Act was also applied to the refuge "...for (1) incidental fish and wildlife-oriented recreational development, (2) the protection of natural resources, (3) the conservation of endangered species or threatened species...." [16 USC §460k-1 (Refuge Recreation Act)]. The existence of the refuge serves the "...conservation, management, and restoration of the fish, wildlife, and plant resources and their habitats for the benefit of present and future generations of Americans...." [16 USC §668dd(a)(2) (National Wildlife Refuge System Administration Act)]. Finally, the Pelican Island Wilderness Area "...shall be administered for the use and enjoyment of the American people in such manner as will leave them (wilderness areas) unimpaired for future use and enjoyment as wilderness, and so as to provide for the protection of these areas, the preservation of their wilderness character, and for the gathering and dissemination of information regarding their use and enjoyment as wilderness...." [16 USC 1 1 21 (note) (Wilderness Act)].

On October 23, 1970 under Public Law 91-504, the 5.5-acre Pelican Island became one of the smallest wilderness areas in the National Wilderness Preservation System. All management activities occurring within the original 5.5-acre wilderness boundary must meet the standards and criteria set forth in the Wilderness Act. Currently, about 3.3 acres of the wilderness area are submerged due to the erosion of Pelican Island proper.

The refuge is also designated as a National Historic Landmark, a Wetland of International Importance, and a candidate Marine Protected Area. Because of its status as the first federal area set aside specifically to protect wildlife, the refuge was designated a National Historic Landmark by the Secretary of the Interior in 1963. Thirty years later in 1993, Pelican Island Refuge was recognized by the Ramsar Convention on Wetlands as a Wetland of International Importance for its support of endangered species and large assemblages of migratory birds, as well as for its support of species at critical stages in their biological development. In 2000, the refuge was listed as a candidate Marine Protected Area for its protection of estuarine waters.

ECOLOGICAL THREATS AND PROBLEMS

Pelican Island National Wildlife Refuge is in a critical location to serve and support biological diversity in the Indian River Lagoon and South Florida. Human impacts and underlying causes and threats to biological diversity include:

- the direct loss of habitat due to development and other human activities;
- the simplification and degradation of remaining habitats, including habitat alteration and fragmentation;
- the loss and decline of species and biological diversity;
- the effects of constructing navigation and water diversion facilities;
- the introduction and spread of exotic, nuisance, and invasive species;
- the lack of environmental regulation and enforcement; and
- the cumulative effects of land and water resource development projects.

As a result of these causes and threats, many species endemic to the southern Indian River Lagoon have become extinct, endangered, or threatened under the Endangered Species Act. The refuge supports at least 14 federally threatened or endangered species. Further, the refuge also supports 45 species listed by the State of Florida as either threatened, endangered, special concern, or commercially exploited; 54 species listed by the Florida Committee on Rare and Endangered Plants and Animals; 54 species, 3 communities, and 2 sites listed by the Florida Natural Areas Inventory; and 11 species listed by the Audubon WatchList for Florida. (See Appendix IV for a complete listing of these species.) Nationally, 1,262 species are federally listed, with 986 listed as endangered (388 animals and 598 plants) and 276 listed as threatened (129 animals and 147 plants). Further, 257 species are listed as candidates for federal listing.

Habitats in and around the refuge serve a variety of species and are highly important in this developed landscape. A number of biodiversity hotspots are located in and around the refuge. These hotspots are areas with a high degree of overlap for 54 kinds of declining wildlife species with known occurrences of flora, fauna, and natural communities (Cox, Kautz, Maclaughlin, and Gilbert 1994). St. Sebastian River State Buffer Preserve (including impoundments and wetlands), seagrass beds in and around the refuge, and privately owned mangrove islands south of Wabasso bridge are hotspots identified as the most critical. Adjacent conservation lands are also critical to many species of wildlife that also use the refuge (Figure 4).

The high productivity and biological diversity of Pelican Island Refuge have been altered by people, which, in turn, have altered the way the Indian River Lagoon functions. The refuge faces ongoing threats from contaminated air, soil, and water; erosion and sedimentation; and cumulative habitat impacts from land and water resource development activities. Rapid population growth and development have resulted in long-term negative effects to the Pelican Island Refuge. By the year 2010, about one million people will reside in the Indian River Lagoon area. Terrestrial habitats that once dominated upland areas include hardwood hammocks, which are very important for mammals and migratory birds. Urbanization and agricultural operations (e.g., large citrus groves) now dominate land uses in upland areas. Stormwater inputs, saltwater exchange through fortified ocean inlets, pollution, habitat destruction, and continual land and water use practices are constant threats to fish and wildlife.

Figure 4. Conservation lands

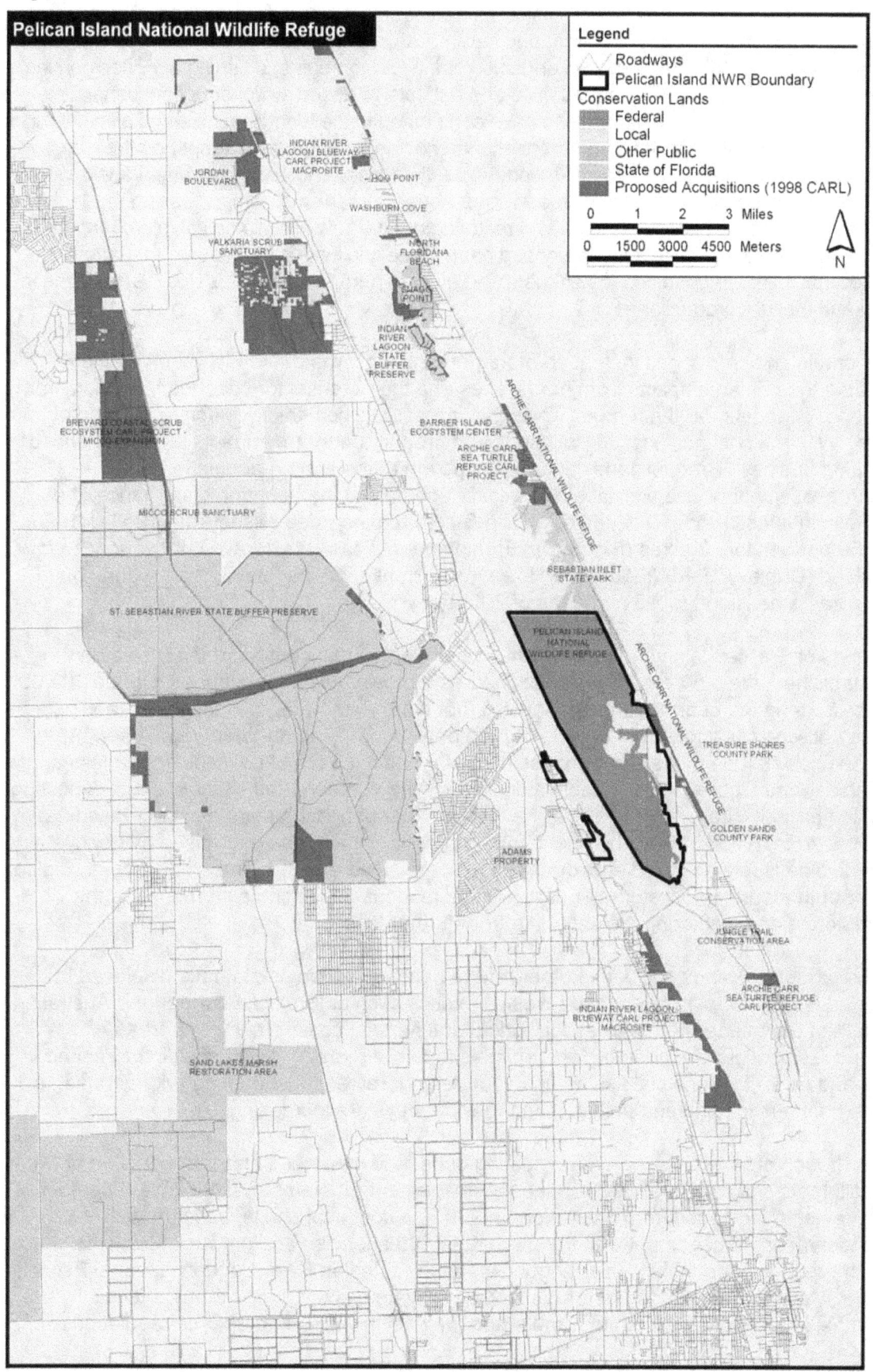

The reduction of ecological function and connection is a major problem in areas where the modification of inland waterways has caused major declines in fisheries and aquatic resource productivity. Beaches, seagrass beds, salt marshes, mangrove islands, and hammocks are subject to further loss or elimination. Causeways, the Intracoastal Waterway, beach and shoreline development, and fishing activities dominate aquatic uses in transitional and aquatic communities and habitats. Causeway construction, canal dredging, and commercial agricultural operations have contributed to the long-term loss and elimination of aquatic resources and habitats. Wetlands (former salt marshes and mangrove swamps) on the refuge were converted and managed to aid in mosquito control. Until recently, these impoundment areas were cut off from the rest of the Lagoon, isolating fish and other aquatic organisms from accessing this highly productive area. Reconnecting impoundments and restoring natural flow and biological interchange, while maintaining mosquito control and migratory bird habitat, are challenges to resource managers. As water quality declines in the Lagoon due to sediment and nutrient runoff, seagrasses decline, resulting in declines in fish and mollusk production.

Erosion of Pelican Island proper has increased management concerns of the Fish and Wildlife Service regarding the primary impacts from boat wakes and the potential for secondary impacts from dredging a deeper channel near the refuge. The rapid increase in coastal development is also of major concern. With the continual loss of Pelican Island proper, long-term impacts are experienced by many declining species. Predominantly due to the growth of the human population and the associated increases in public use activities and wildlife and habitat impacts and disturbance, the land base of Pelican Island proper (i.e., the original 5.5-acre rookery) decreased from 1943 to 1996 by more than 50 percent to 2.2 acres (Figure 5). Erosion predictions show grave consequences for this rookery island (Dunlevy 1996) (Figure 6). However, current shoreline stabilization efforts have increased the size of the Island to 2.8 acres (as of 2004).

Habitat conditions on Pelican Island have been changing over the last century. In 1903, when the refuge was established, the 5.5-acre Island functioned as a brown pelican rookery with some 10,000 pelicans counted during the peak nesting season. At that time, Paul Kroegel focused on keeping market hunters and egg collectors from decimating the population. One hundred years later, more than a dozen species nest on the Island with less than 100 nesting pairs of pelicans on the Island in the spring. Table 1 and Figure 7 clearly show a decline for the numbers and types of species nesting on Pelican Island proper. From 1910 to 1999, the total number of nesting pairs has decreased nearly 94 percent. Even from 1995 to 1999, the total number of nesting pairs has decreased by nearly 44 percent. This decline is related to the erosion of the rookery island and the general decline of wildlife species in the South Florida Ecosystem. Today, managers focus on limiting disturbance to the rookery and restoring and stabilizing the shoreline from further loss.

On many of the lagoonal islands and within other refuge habitats, exotic plants have displaced the majority of the native species. Problem and invasive exotics such as Brazilian pepper and Australian pine cover much of the refuge. Citrus trees for agricultural harvest cover other large areas. Commercial and residential development, feral animals and free roaming pets (including feral and domestic cats and dogs), commercial fishing and shell fishing, recreational boating and marinas, as well as elevated nutrient loading and pollution on the waterways are increasing.

Continual disturbance of fish spawning areas, nesting birds, and manatees and the reduction of water quality from pollutants and watercraft are continual management problems. With a limited number of full-time staff (i.e., staff increased from one to four in 2001), a continual challenge is the ability to coordinate conservation management with the more than 100 agencies and organizations who share responsibility of managing the Indian River Lagoon watershed (Indian River Lagoon National Estuary Program 1996). Management overlap of refuge lands and waters is shared by many agencies. The refuge was set aside for conservation, yet without adequate levels of staff to enforce regulations.

Figure 5. Pelican Island proper erosion over time

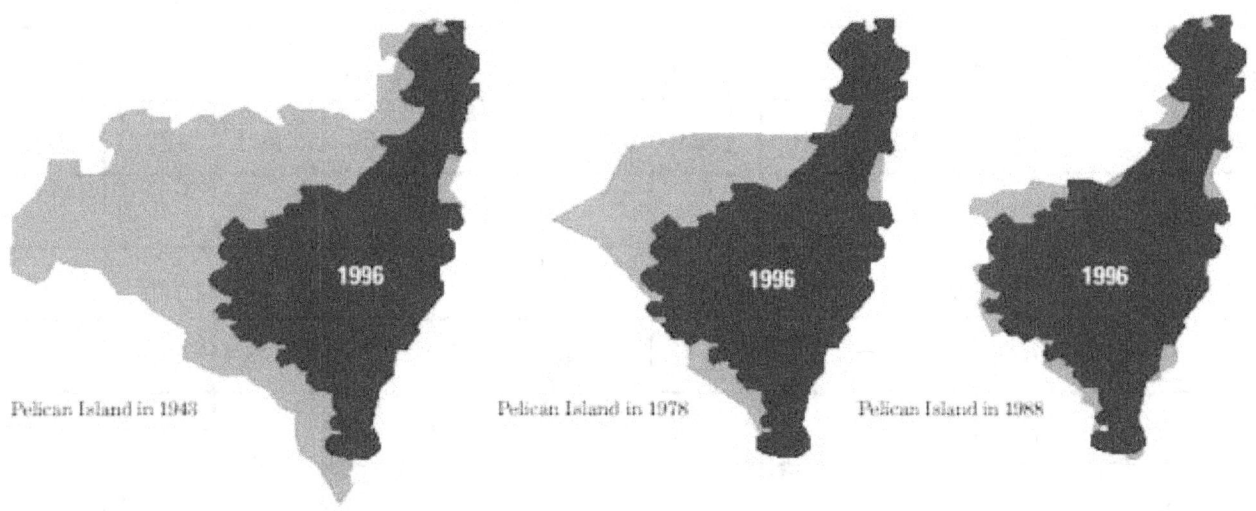

Pelican Island in 1943   Pelican Island in 1978   Pelican Island in 1988

Figure 6. 2010 and 2020 Pelican Island proper erosion predictions

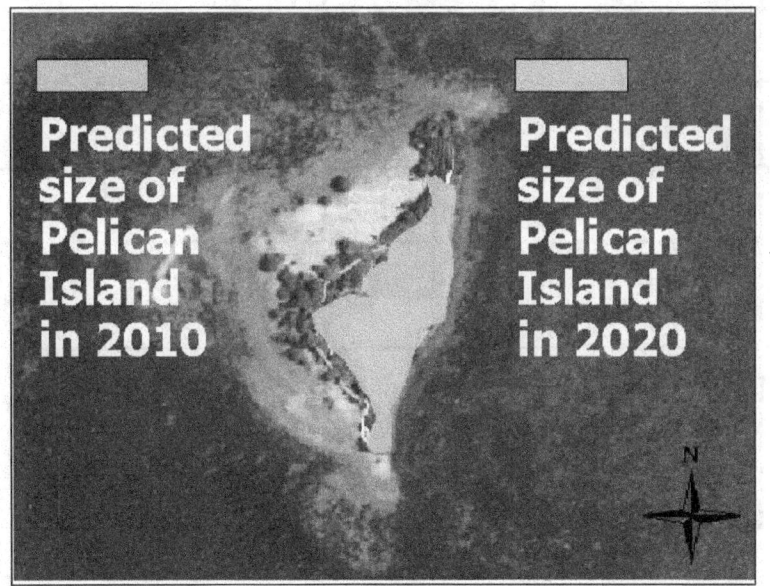

Predicted size of Pelican Island in 2010

Predicted size of Pelican Island in 2020

1996 Pelican Island Shoreline

Jack Knife Predictions for 2010 and 2020

Dunlevy 1996

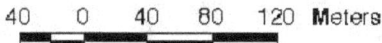

40   0   40   80   120   Meters

N

Table 1. Number of nesting pairs and types of species found on Pelican Island proper

Species	Number of Nesting Pairs								
	1910	1920	1941	1965	1976	1986	1995	1999	2004
Brown Pelican	5,000	800	500	300	300	200	153	80	47
Wood Stork				200	250	150	220	135	167
Great Blue Heron				100	20	25	15	10	24
Tri-colored Heron			500	50		45	15	3	10
Little Blue Heron			300	50		5	5	1	1
Black-crowned Night Heron			25	25	4	4	10	3	1
Great Egret			25	150	50	48	50	15	10
Snowy Egret			500	200		40	35	20	6
Cattle Egret				10		400	5	5	9
Cormorant				75	125	50	50	40	25
Anhinga			4			20	0	0	3
Reddish Egret						2	4	4	3
American Oystercatcher						1	1	1	0
Green-backed Heron					2	2	1	0	0
Total	5,000	800	1,854	1,160	751	992	564	317	306

Figure 7. Decline of colonial nesting birds on Pelican Island proper

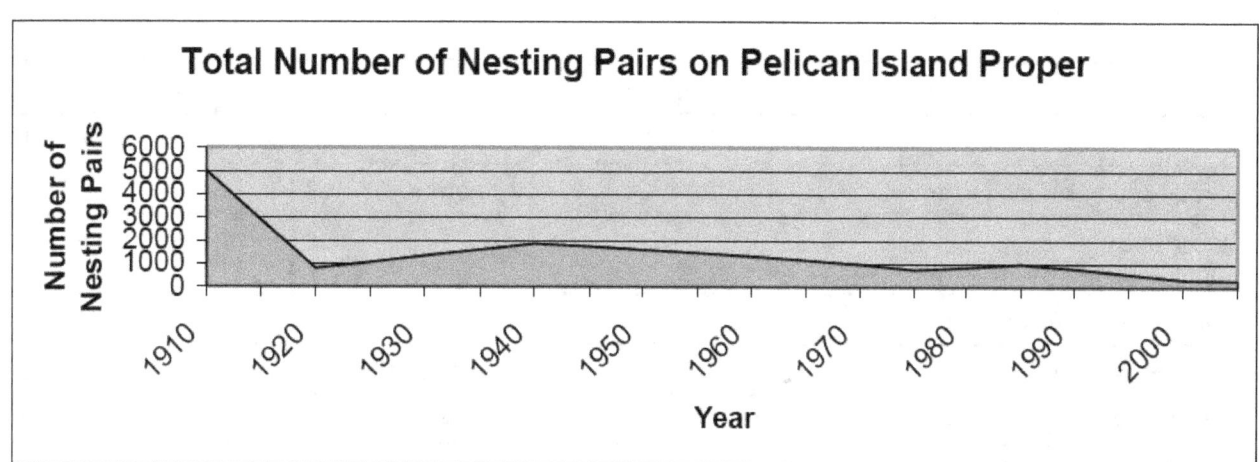

Today, the lagoonal portion of the refuge is being utilized primarily for recreation. Lagoonal islands in and around the refuge are overrun with exotic plants, trash, and debris, but thanks to the efforts of several private groups and the Florida Department of Environmental Protection, some of the islands of the Indian River Lagoon are being restored and protected.

The lack of Service ownership of most of the refuge presents a difficult management challenge (i.e., the Service owns ±363 acres and leases the bulk of the over 5,400 acres from the State of Florida). Current long-term lease and management agreements between landowners with properties within the approved refuge acquisition boundary tend to favor stipulations and mission requirements of the owner, making it difficult for the Service to fulfill its mission, the refuge's purposes, and trust responsibilities. For instance, the management agreement between the State of Florida and the Service stipulates that many activities, including boating, sun bathing, commercial and sport fishing, and shell fishing would continue to be allowed within most of the refuge boundary. These traditional activities continue to contribute to a diverse economy and provide recreational opportunities to its residents, but at a cost to fish and wildlife resources. To manage in support of fish and wildlife conservation (e.g., to regulate activities to protect colonial nesting birds, juvenile fish, and threatened and endangered populations), refuge managers need additional authority to protect fish and wildlife resources to meet agency mission and legal requirements.

REFUGE ENVIRONMENT

Pelican Island National Wildlife Refuge is located along the southeast coast of Florida in the most productive estuary in the country--the Indian River Lagoon. The Lagoon has more species of plants and animals than any other estuary in North America, including over 2,200 animal species and over 2,100 plant species. Since it is located where the temperate and tropical zones overlap and located within the Indian River Lagoon at the confluence of freshwater and saltwater sources, the refuge is uniquely situated to support a wide variety of resident and migratory species.

Although Pelican Island Refuge was established in 1903, land purchases did not begin until 87 years later in 1990. To date, only ±351 acres have been acquired. As of September 30, 2002, the refuge manages over 5,400 acres of the ±6,184-acre acquisition boundary. Table 2 summarizes the Service-owned and managed lands and waters within the refuge, while Figure 2 delineates these areas.

Table 2. Service-owned and managed lands and waters within the refuge's acquisition boundary (as of October 31, 2003)

Entity	Method	Acreage
USFWS	ownership	363.493
Bureau of Land Management	withdrawal	37.500
Orchid Island Golf and Country Club	easement	127.280
Windsor (27.19 acres total)	easement	19.161
Indian River County	Management agreement	122.480
State of Florida (Pelican Island NWR lease)	Lease	4,737.540
State of Florida (Archie Carr NWR leases)	Leases	37.210
Total Acreage under Pelican Island NWR Management (as of October 31, 2003)		5,444.664

Management efforts from 1903 until 2002 focused on coordinating with partners controlling exotic and invasive species; securing staff to operate the refuge; managing volunteers; and initiating conservation programs that benefit migratory birds and federally endangered and threatened species. During this planning process, in 2001, the refuge expanded its staff from one to four. Two more positions were also added during this planning process in 2002. The now six-person staff addresses a variety of refuge projects, including recent conservation management projects such as:

- recruiting and training staff and volunteers;
- developing visitor facilities;
- coordinating shoreline stabilization and restoration of Pelican Island proper;
- coordinating habitat restoration and facility improvements on the barrier island to showcase Refuge System Centennial events (in March 2003) and to provide opportunities for on-site wildlife viewing, environmental education, and cultural history interpretation;
- removing exotic, invasive, and nuisance species; and
- contributing to the recovery of federally threatened and endangered species (e.g., by posting refuge boundary signs and conducting patrols).

FISH, WILDLIFE, AND PLANT POPULATIONS

Pelican Island Refuge serves as a critical repository of gene pools, species, and communities that is very important to the overall contribution and health of the Indian River Lagoon and the South Florida Ecosystem. Named after the original pelican rookery that currently occupies a 2.8-acre lagoonal island and that serves as the focal point of the refuge, Pelican Island Refuge provides an important ecological niche for fish, wildlife, and plant species. The Service manages refuge resources and coordinates with neighboring land managers and agencies to conserve biological diversity in the Indian River Lagoon region.

The refuge serves as an important site for the recovery of federal and state listed threatened and endangered species. The refuge's location and habitat features are important for the future of 14 federally listed threatened and endangered species, as well as for the future of 45 species listed by the State of Florida (see Appendix IV). Restoration efforts on the refuge, coupled with a combination of protected and managed public and private lands, could provide the necessary conditions for endangered species to live with minimal disturbance, despite the high level of human development and use in and around the refuge. Beyond the 14 federally listed species and despite limited data, the refuge is known to support hundreds of species of birds, mammals, reptiles and amphibians, fish, invertebrates, and plants, with many more species suspected to occur on the refuge.

Avian species are highly important wildlife resources identified on the refuge with more than 140 species of birds using the refuge as a nesting, roosting, feeding, or loafing area. At least 16 different species of birds nest on Pelican Island proper. And at least 39 bird species using the refuge are listed by federal or state governments, Florida Committee on Rare and Endangered Plants and Animals, Florida Natural Areas Inventory, or Audubon WatchList. (Refer to Appendix IV for a listing of these birds.) The federally endangered wood stork is of special interest to Service managers. Wood stork populations have declined sharply in Florida, from 60,000 in the 1930s to 5,000 pairs today. Wood storks have been nesting on Pelican Island proper since 1950. The Pelican Island colony has been one of the most consistently active rookeries in the State of Florida (Rogers, Wenner, and Schwikert 1987). Currently, between 90 and 150 pairs of wood storks nest on Pelican Island proper each year.

At least 18 mammals are known to occur on the refuge: short-tailed shrew, least shrew, nine-banded armadillo, opossum, bobcat, river otter, eastern wood rat, cotton mouse, southeastern beach mouse, raccoon, black rat, gray squirrel, hispid cotton rat, spotted skunk, marsh rabbit, eastern cottontail, West Indian manatee, and bottlenose dolphin. The Lagoon is used extensively by Atlantic bottlenose dolphins and West Indian manatees and both are commonly seen on the refuge.

And 27 reptiles and amphibians are known to occur on the refuge: eight snakes, eight frogs and toads, five sea turtles, and three lizards, as well as the gopher tortoise, diamondback terrapin, and American alligator. As a juvenile sea turtle nursery, the lagoonal waters of the refuge serve critical needs for threatened and endangered sea turtles.

A variety of fish species also utilize the refuge. One hundred and six different fish species were identified in 1897 during the first fisheries survey ever conducted in the Lagoon (Evermann and Bean). Surveys conducted in 1994 (Gilmore 1995) listed 782 fish species for east central Florida, with at least half of this amount occurring at some point of their life history in the Indian River Lagoon. Over 200 fish species are known to occur on the refuge. One federally endangered fish species occurs on the refuge: smalltooth sawfish. In addition, the refuge supports 10 fish species listed by the State of Florida, Florida Committee on Rare and Endangered Plants and Animals, or Florida Natural Areas Inventory, including sturgeon, pipefish, goby, rivulus, and snook. Other fish using the refuge include tarpon, spotted sea trout, flounder, black mullet, red and black drum, ladyfish, mackerel, and bluefish. The American eel also occurs on the refuge and is currently under consideration as a candidate for listing under the Endangered Species Act. And, although not federal or state listed, fat snook and tarpon snook are included in Florida's Wildlife Legacy Initiative as part of Florida's species of greatest conservation needs. Fish species within the refuge are important not only to commercial and recreational interests, but also to the ecology of the area. Important fish habitat, such as fish spawning and fish larvae settlement sites in the refuge, must be protected to ensure healthy, sustainable fish populations.

A wide variety of marine, freshwater, and terrestrial invertebrates are found within the refuge's boundary. For example, the mangrove crab is found on the refuge and is listed by the Florida Committee on Rare and Endangered Plants and Animals. Some of the more common invertebrates include conchs, snails, oysters, land crabs, dragonflies, butterflies, and cicadas.

Beyond wildlife species, the refuge supports an estimated 300 plant species, including 18 species listed by the federal government, State of Florida, Florida Committee on Rare and Endangered Plants and Animals, and/or Florida Natural Areas Inventory: giant leather fern, Curtiss' milkweed, hand fern, Christmas berry, butterfly orchid, beach creeper, Johnson's seagrass, crested coralroot, pineland lantana, Simpson stopper, shell mound prickly pear cactus, cinnamon fern, pepper, inkberry, inflated wild pine, giant wild pine, coastal vervain, and Tampa vervain.

HABITATS

The primary habitats of the refuge fall into three categories: aquatic communities, transitional communities, and upland communities. Lagoonal waters, including estuarine waters, seagrasses, drift algae, and exposed bottoms, cover over 75 percent of the refuge (see Lucode = 5400 in Table 3). The remaining habitats of the refuge include agriculture (i.e., citrus groves), hardwood forest, Australian pine, lakes, mangrove swamps, forested wetlands, scrub-shrub wetlands, non-vegetated wetlands, rural land in transition (e.g., former citrus groves that are currently in early successional stages), spoil areas, and roadways. Existing land uses within the refuge's acquisition boundary, but not currently part of the refuge, include residential, commercial, and agricultural uses, as well as roadways. See Table 3 and Figure 8 for a breakdown of the land use/land cover types within the refuge's acquisition boundary. (The land use/land cover types were obtained from the St. Johns River Water Management District and represent 1995 conditions. Habitat surveys on the refuge may yield slightly different results.) See Table 4 for the characteristics of the main habitat types of the refuge.

Aquatic communities of the refuge are in a mix of habitats, including lagoonal waters (e.g., exposed bottoms, drift algae, seagrasses, and open estuarine waters) and the open water portion of the impoundments. Exposed bottoms and oyster bars provide cover for invertebrates and small fish, providing a forage base for a variety of wildlife along the food chain (this habitat supports key species such as segmented worms, brittle stars, clams, oysters, stingrays, and flounders). Drift algae is free drifting algae that collects in response to wind, water currents, and bottom topography and which contributes to the primary productivity, and overall complexity of the Lagoon ecosystem (this habitat supports key species such as juvenile green sea turtles). With seven species found in this area, seagrasses are a key habitat of the Lagoon system, playing a prominent role as a nursery (key species supported in this habitat include manatees, red drum, spotted sea trout, sea horses, blue crabs, clams, shrimp, sea urchins, and wading and diving birds). In seagrass meadows, 214 fish species have been identified, with 87 percent of the species in a juvenile stage. Providing a transition from fresh water to salt water, the open estuarine water of the Lagoon provides the basis for the diversity of wildlife found on the refuge (this habitat supports key species such as manatees, bald eagles, sea turtles, ospreys, dolphins, pelicans, cormorants, waterfowl, black skimmers, terns, and a variety of fish).

Aquatic communities adjoin a variety of transitional communities on the refuge, including high salt marsh, mangrove swamp, mud flat, perennial and ephemeral freshwater wetlands, and impounded wetlands. Salt marshes are areas of salt tolerant wetland vegetation, often containing ponds, natural depressions, and creeks that are utilized by fish, crabs, and shrimp. Other key species in salt marshes include diamondback terrapins, fiddler crabs, marsh rabbits, Atlantic salt marsh snakes, clapper rails, and wood storks. In mangrove swamps and fringes, mangroves trap and collect sediment to help stabilize shorelines and reduce flood damage. Over 100 fish species and shellfish are dependent on mangroves. Key animal species found in this habitat include mangrove water snakes, river otters, raccoons, mangrove crabs, snook, pelicans, wood storks, herons, egrets, shorebirds, periwinkle snails, and juvenile and predatory fish. Freshwater wetlands created with water control structures that ultimately connect to the Lagoon could allow for anadromous fish migration, benefiting pipefish, snook, and gobies. This could result in the recruitment of 10 fish species unique to this area. Seasonally fluctuating ponds would benefit frogs, salamanders, crayfish,

Table 3. Land use/land cover within the refuge's acquisition boundary

Primary Land Use/ Cover Code (Lucode)	Secondary Land Use/ Cover Code (Lucode2)	Land Use/Land Cover Code Description	Estimated Acreage
1100	0	Residential, low density, <2 dwelling units per acre	55.7
1200	0	Residential, medium density, 2-5 dwelling units per acre	2.2
1300	0	Residential, high density, >5 dwelling units per acre	8.1
1400	0	Commercial and services	6.8
1850	0	Parks and zoos	3.8
1900	0	Open land	6.2
2210	4370	Agriculture, citrus groves, Australian pine	380.4
2430	0	Agriculture, ornamentals	4.3
3300	0	Mixed rangeland (old field, cabbage palm)	5.7
4200	0	Upland hardwood forest	6.3
4250	4220	Temperate/tropical hardwood (maritime hammock), Brazilian pepper	69.1
4370	4220	Australian pine, Brazilian pepper	106.7
5100	0	Streams and waterways	0.9
5200	0	Lakes	31.8
5340	0	Reservoirs <10 acres	8.1
5400	0	Bays and estuaries	3,697.5
5400	6450	Bays and estuaries, submerged aquatic vegetation	879.1
6120	4370	Mangrove swamps, Australian pine	2.5
6120	6420	Mangrove swamps, saltwater marshes	737.3
6120	6500	Mangrove swamps, Non-vegetated wetland	3.3
6300	0	Wetland forested mixed	18.1
6410	0	Freshwater marsh	1.1
6420	0	Saltwater marsh	56.6
6460	0	Mixed scrub-shrub wetland (predominantly willow and wax myrtle)	65.5
6500	0	Non-vegetated wetland	16.0
7430	0	Spoil areas	4.7
8140	0	Roads and highways	6.2
Total acreage within the refuge's acquisition boundary			6,184.0

Figure 8. Land use/land cover of the refuge

Table 4. Characteristics of the main habitat types of the refuge

Community	Habitat Type	Characteristics	Key Species
Aquatic	Exposed Bottoms	Exposed bottoms lack rooted plants, yet support algae communities. Oyster bars are another important component of this community. Both areas provide cover for invertebrates and small fish (which provide a forage base for a variety of wildlife along the food chain).	Segmented Worms, Brittle Stars, Clams, Oysters, Conch, Stingrays, and Flounders
	Drift Algae	Drifting red, green, and brown algae collect in response to wind, water currents, and bottom topography and contribute to the primary productivity and overall complexity of the Lagoon ecosystem.	Juvenile Green Sea Turtles
	Seagrasses	Seagrasses are flowering plants that live underwater (submerged aquatic vegetation). The depth in which these plants can grow is limited by water clarity and sunlight penetration. Seven species of seagrasses are found in this area, each occupying a different ecological niche. Seagrasses play a prominent role as a nursery and are a key habitat of the Lagoon system. In grass meadows, 214 fish species have been identified. Of these, 87 percent (i.e., 187) is juveniles.	Manatees, Redfish, Spotted Seatrout, Sea Horses, Blue Crabs, Clams, Conch, Shrimp, Sea Urchins, and Wading and Diving Birds
	Open Estuarine Waters	The refuge is part of the Indian River Lagoon system, which is fed by several freshwater rivers, creeks, and canals. The transition from freshwater to saltwater provides the basis for the diversity of wildlife found in this area.	Manatees, Bald Eagles, Sea Turtles, Ospreys, Dolphins, Pelicans, Cormorants, Waterfowl, Black Skimmers, Terns, and a Variety of Fish
Transitional	High Salt Marsh	Bordering the Lagoon between the mean daily high tide and the annual high tide line, salt marshes are areas of salt tolerant wetland vegetation. Salt marshes often contain ponds, natural depressions, and creeks that are utilized by fish, crab, and shrimp.	Diamondback Terrapins, Fiddler Crabs, Marsh Rabbits, Atlantic Salt Marsh Snakes, Clapper Rails, Roseate Spoonbills, and Wood Storks

Community	Habitat Type	Characteristics	Key Species
Transitional (Cont'd)	Mangrove Swamps	Mangrove swamps are found below the mean high tide line. A mangrove fringe is found along the developed shorelines of the Lagoon. Mangrove detritus is a critical source of estuarine productivity. Further, mangroves trap and collect sediment to help stabilize shorelines, as well as reduce flood damage. Over 100 fish species and shellfish are dependent upon mangroves.	Mangrove Water Snakes, River Otters, Mangrove Crabs, Snook, Pelicans, Wood Storks, Herons, Egrets, Periwinkle Snails, and Juvenile and Predatory Fish
	Impoundments	During the 1950s and 1960s, impoundments were created by constructing a low earthen dike around a salt marsh. This allowed for the regulation of water levels for the control of mosquitoes.	Herons, Egrets, Shorebirds, Waterfowl, Reptiles, River Otters, Wood Storks, Ibises, Peregrine Falcons, and Bald Eagles
Uplands	Islands	Lagoonal islands provide environmental, recreational, and aesthetical qualities. Natural islands are typically low in elevation and are colonized by mangroves. Spoil islands are higher and include more upland plants, including exotics such as the Australian pine.	Wood Storks, Ibises, Egrets, Herons, Ospreys, Brown Pelicans, and Shorebirds
	Hammocks	Coastal hammocks occur on the barrier islands where the air temperatures are moderated by the surrounding waters. Hammocks are dominated by live oaks and cabbage palms, but include an understory with a diverse assemblage of tropical and temperate plants.	Neotropical Migratory Birds, Woodrats, Eastern Indigo Snakes, Land Crabs, and Bobcats
	Citrus Groves	Existing and former citrus groves of the refuge serve as habitat for a variety of species. These are characterized by sandy soils, herbaceous cover, and early successional vegetation.	Ground Doves, Marsh Rabbits, Painted Buntings, Indigo Buntings, Loggerhead Shrikes, and Hawks

land crabs, rivulus, red-bellied sliders, mud turtles and snapping turtles. The created freshwater wetlands would provide foraging grounds for nesting and wintering birds. Restoration is planned on the barrier island near Jungle Trail to mimic the natural conditions once found in this area. Beyond these natural and restored aquatic habitats, the refuge also manages impounded wetlands. Under a management agreement, Bird's and Pete's impoundments are actively managed for mosquito control by the Indian River Mosquito Control District. In addition, the refuge currently coordinates with the Indian River Mosquito Control District to regulate the water levels in Pete's and Bird's impoundments on an alternative rotation schedule for wading bird feeding. The North and South Deerfield impoundments are breached and therefore function according to the natural rhythms of the Indian River Lagoon. Key species supported by these impoundments include herons, egrets, shorebirds, waterfowl, reptiles, river otters, wood storks, ibises, peregrine falcons, and bald eagles.

Finally, transitional communities give way to upland communities on the refuge, including lagoonal islands, spoil islands, coastal hammock, citrus groves, refugia habitat, and developed and interpretative lands.

The refuge manages three spoil islands and 23 natural islands and islets. While both the natural and spoil islands have natural and exotic vegetation, the spoil islands tend to be dominated by exotic plants. Many of the spoil islands off the refuge are used for recreational activities such as day use and overnight camping and these uses tend to spill over onto the spoil islands managed by the refuge, which are managed under the lease agreement with the State of Florida and which are open to the traditional public uses specified in the lease agreement. The most well known natural island of the refuge is Pelican Island proper. From 1943 to 1996, Pelican Island proper eroded to less than half its original size (i.e., from 5.5 acres to about 2.2 acres) (see Figure 5). However, recent shoreline stabilization efforts have restored the Island to 2.8 acres in 2004. The total number of nesting pairs of birds on this historic rookery has declined nearly 94 percent since 1910 (Figure 7). In an effort to combat these losses, shoreline stabilization efforts began as a multi-partner effort in 2000 to protect Pelican Island proper from eroding and losing its functionality as a rookery. Depending on the success of the shoreline stabilization efforts, additional actions to limit erosion may or may not be necessary to protect this historic rookery. These efforts are expected to reduce the loss of lands from erosion, aid in the accretion of sediment, and help in the revegetation of the original 5.5 acres. This loss of land and habitat has led to decreased populations of nesting birds on the Island, including brown pelicans, wood storks, herons, and egrets. The mangroves which provide prime nesting substrate are also declining.

To provide a buffer to the historic rookery, the refuge is acquiring lands within the acquisition boundary on the barrier island, including citrus groves. Dependent upon available Service, partner, and grant funds, the refuge plans to restore existing and acquired citrus groves to mimic natural conditions and hydrology. Coastal hammocks represent much of the native habitats that previously existed on the barrier island. Coastal hammocks are dominated by live oaks and cabbage palms, and include an understory with a diverse assemblage of tropical and temperate plants. Key wildlife species in coastal hammocks of the refuge are neotropical migratory birds, woodrats, eastern indigo snakes, land crabs, and bobcats. In general, and especially within the Indian River Lagoon, tropical hardwood hammocks have been greatly reduced by conversion to other land uses (from historically agricultural uses to predominantly urban and suburban uses), fragmentation, and increased distance between forest patches, resulting in the decline of breeding birds. Tropical hardwood hammocks are severely threatened by invasions of non-indigenous animal species (Snyder, Herndon, and Robertson 1990). Established non-indigenous animal species in tropical hardwood hammocks include 7 mammals, 30 birds, 4 amphibians, and 25 reptiles (Snyder, Herndon, and Robertson 1990). As a remnant of former agricultural operations, an old field habitat exists on the refuge. Although not a native habitat, this old field habitat is managed and maintained by the refuge as refugia habitat for the federally listed southeastern beach mouse. This old field habitat occupies small parts of upland areas and is also valuable for grassland guild migrants such as bobolinks and loggerhead shrikes. By increasing management, this old field habitat will better support southeastern beach mice, ground doves, gopher tortoises, and migrants such as bobolinks and loggerhead shrikes. The refuge contributes to recovery efforts for the southeastern beach mouse by protecting this old field habitat and coordinating with researchers to conduct baseline surveys on the refuge.

Also, non-native habitats, developed, and interpretative lands do occur on the refuge. The refuge is currently involved in habitat restoration and facility development in the Jungle Trail area. Refuge facilities in this area include dike trails, a boardwalk, and observation tower, serviced by county-built and maintained parking areas, a restroom facility, and the Jungle Trail roadway. Proposed, but unfunded facilities include a wildlife drive, additional boardwalks and trails, informational kiosks, a hummingbird/butterfly garden, and other interpretative lands, as well as a visitor center (where four potential sites exist for this facility).

LAND PROTECTION AND CONSERVATION

The Service is involved in a variety of land protection and conservation activities at Pelican Island Refuge, including a lease agreement with the State of Florida, management agreements, conservation easements, partnership land acquisition efforts, and Service land acquisition efforts.

The refuge leases the majority of the lands and waters of the refuge from the State of Florida. So it is important that the refuge and the State of Florida coordinate management to minimize injury, mortality, and disturbance of the West Indian manatee and trust species, as well as native wildlife and habitat in general. Under the current lease agreement, public uses including traditional navigation, boating, bathing, shell fishing, and commercial and sport fishing are not restricted with the exception of a 410-foot buffer zone surrounding Pelican Island proper. (This buffer zone is measured from the mean high water line.) The current lease agreement does not specify control of using personal watercraft and camping on spoil islands, which are currently uncontrolled on the refuge. Beyond this lease agreement, the Service has other agreements addressing refuge management, including agreements with Indian River Mosquito Control District for the impoundments and with Indian River County for 122.5 acres. And a conservation easement with Orchid Island Properties allows the refuge to manage an additional 127 acres.

Beyond existing agreements, the Service is pursuing new agreements and acquisitions, especially for the buffer properties located on the barrier island. Given the ongoing and growing development pressures experienced in this area, acquisition of the buffer for the Pelican Island rookery is already a priority. Without acquisition of these barrier island properties by the refuge and/or its partners and given the growth pressures of the area and current development activities, it is likely that these properties will be developed privately in the near future.

To the west, on the mainland, the Service is working with Indian River County and other partners to pursue acquisition and management of the Kroegel Homestead, since it is an integral piece of the history of the National Wildlife Refuge System and the local community. Ongoing negotiations are underway with the Kroegel family.

EDUCATION AND VISITOR SERVICES

Consistent with the provisions outlined in the National Wildlife Refuge System Improvement Act, the Service can provide high quality compatible wildlife-dependent recreation programs. At Pelican Island Refuge these include fishing, observing and photographing wildlife, and participating in environmental education and interpretation (see Figure 9). These priority public uses provide the public with an opportunity to learn about, enjoy, and appreciate natural resources, but not at the expense of the natural environment. Any allowed use of the refuge, including these priority public uses, must be determined to be compatible with the refuge's purposes and with the mission of the

Figure 9. Current visitor facilities

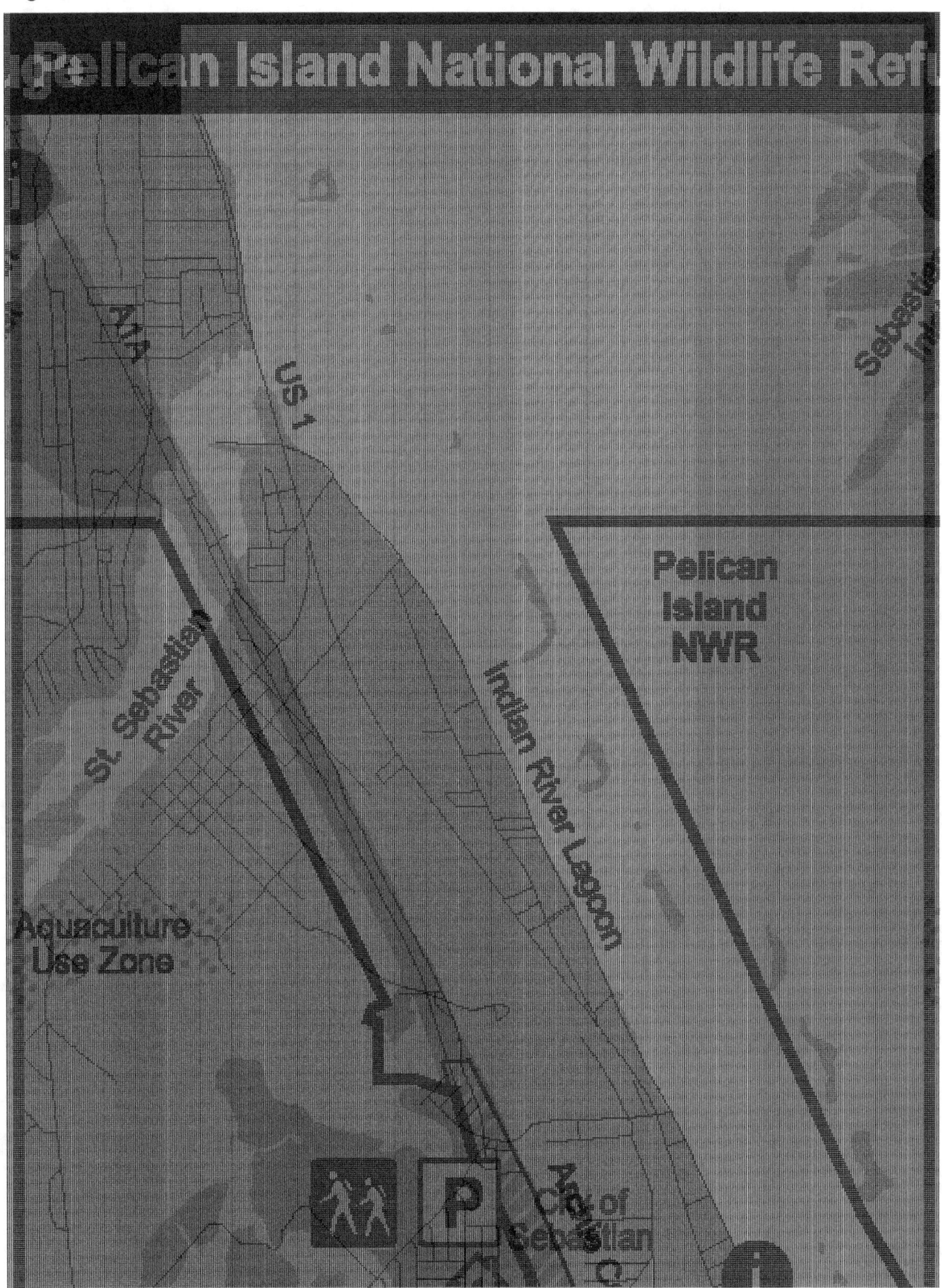

National Wildlife Refuge System (see Appendix V for the compatibility determinations).

Fundamental and supreme to the provision of these uses is the provision of viable and diverse fish and wildlife populations and the habitats upon which they depend. Those uses that do not support the purposes of the refuge, that threaten or disturb fish and wildlife populations, or that are not compatible public uses will be phased out on the refuge.

Priority public use activities currently occurring on the refuge include fishing and observing and photographing wildlife (see Figure 9 for current facilities and facilities under construction). Fishing is permitted in the open water areas of the Indian River Lagoon under the lease agreement with the State of Florida and opportunities exist for catching a variety of sport fish, including redfish, snook, seatrout, mangrove snapper, and Jack Crevalle. Fishing on the refuge includes fishing from a boat, as well as bank and wade fishing in the Indian River Lagoon. State fishing regulations apply. Bank fishing currently occurs in the Indian River Lagoon. However, the locations of these activities are not managed by the Service because of the lack of staff and the conditions of the lease agreement, resulting in wildlife loss and disturbance (e.g., bank fishing can flush nesting birds, leaving the nest and any eggs or young subject to predation and direct sunlight for prolonged periods). Wildlife observation and photography are highly popular activities, with visitors attracted to the area on a year-round basis. Facility development and improvements are underway, including a boardwalk and observation tower off Jungle Trail. Environmental education programs are not offered on the refuge, however, the staff does conduct occasional on-site interpretive programs and off-site outreach activities. The refuge also offers a web site and several brochures describing refuge program activities.

Under the existing lease agreement with the State of Florida, fishing and boating are not restricted by the refuge, except for a narrow buffer area around the 2.2-acre Pelican Island. Current uses include those which are negatively impacting wildlife and habitats (e.g., using personal watercraft and camping on the spoil islands). Also, current boating, personal watercraft use, and camping activities are negatively impacting key bird nesting sites (e.g., these activities flush birds from nests, resulting in nest abandonment and nest predation).

REFUGE ADMINISTRATION

Historically, the refuge was managed by one staff member, a single boat, and a shotgun, or less. For nearly 100 years, the refuge was sustained by the partners, including state and local government agencies and conservation organizations such as the Audubon of Florida, Indian River Area Preservation League, Pelican Island Audubon Society, and the Indian River County Historical Society. Most recently, the refuge has been aided by the efforts of the Pelican Island Preservation Society. The Pelican Island Preservation Society has been instrumental in providing volunteers to increase public awareness and to increase support from local, state, and federal agencies regarding pressing issues. Preservation Society volunteers also provide support for other refuge management activities (e.g., exotic plant control activities). Supplementing the efforts of the volunteers and the partners, refuge staff has grown to six full-time employees.

Numerous research activities by a variety of entities currently occur on the refuge. However, due to the lack of staff, the refuge has historically not managed nor has the refuge been aware of all the research conducted within its boundary, the data collected, or the wildlife and habitat impacts from conducting this research. As a result of this planning process, the refuge began issuing special use permits for research activities in May 2002; however, research activities continue to occur without refuge permits.

Adopted in 1986, the Wilderness Management Plan outlines existing objectives and management actions for the Wilderness Area located on Pelican Island proper. Predominantly utilized by colonial nesting birds, the 2.2-acre Pelican Island Wilderness Area includes an estimated cover of 50 percent red and black mangroves interspersed with smooth cord grass, salt grass, sea oxeye daisy, prickly pear cactus, and Christmas berry. The shallow waters surrounding the Wilderness Area contain beds of widgeon and shoal grasses. The Wilderness Area is closed year-round to the public to protect the variety of colonial nesting birds. Although public use is prohibited within this small wilderness area, wildlife viewing just outside the wilderness boundary is popular.

A survey for soil contaminants was conducted June 15-17, 1999, near the vicinity of the Jungle Trail (on the Kennedy, Surman, and Pryor tracts). Materials such as fertilizers and low levels of copper in localized areas were removed from the soil. The refuge also removed debris and paint cans. As new citrus groves are acquired, the Service will conduct additional contaminant surveys.

CULTURAL RESOURCES

Although the refuge is 100 years old, its history is a bit older. Florida's terrestrial vertebrate life dates back 25 million years (Myers and Ewel 1990); human inhabitation of the Indian River Lagoon region extends back at least 12,000 years; and Indian shell middens throughout the area date from 1,000 BC to 1,000 AD. Since the refuge includes several archaeological sites and since these sites are fairly accessible to disruption, vandalism, and theft, several archaeological surveys have been conducted on the refuge since 1981. The refuge and Indian River County are currently working together to list midden sites in the Florida Master Site File. Some of these sites are eligible for listing in the National Register. In the event that a previously undetected archaeological site is uncovered, activity must stop and the refuge must coordinate with the Service's Regional Archaeologist and Florida's State Historic Preservation Office.

Recognized for its historic significance as the first refuge and the birthplace of the National Wildlife Refuge System, Pelican Island Refuge was designated a National Historic Landmark in 1963. The Kroegel Homestead is locally and nationally historically significant as the home of the first Refuge Manager. Yet, the historic Kroegel Homestead is facing mounting development pressures. The Kroegel Homestead was settled in 1881 and is located directly across the Indian River Lagoon from Pelican Island proper and the rest of the refuge. The refuge and the Kroegel Homestead are integral elements of the local community. Descendants of the Kroegel family are still active in the local community and continue to live on what remains of the original Homestead.

SOCIAL AND ECONOMIC ENVIRONMENT

The refuge is located along the Indian River Lagoon region, which was generally unaffected by human activities until the early 1800s. Early activities included growing citrus, harvesting palmetto berries, and growing pineapple. By the late 1800s, commercial fisheries opened up the Lagoon's resources. With repeated freezes devastating agricultural crops, cattle grazing increased in the region. Various military facilities were developed in the region during World War II. By the 1960s, NASA's space program instigated considerable growth in the area. The modern economy of the Indian River Lagoon is based on tourism and agriculture, as well as on fishing, manufacturing, real estate, services, and government. Today, citrus is a $2.1 billion industry in the Lagoon region (Indian River Lagoon National Estuary Program 1996).

The Indian River Lagoon is renowned for its recreational and ecotourism opportunities. The marsh beds act as nursery grounds that support an $800 million dollar industry to the local economy. Commercial and sport fishing, tourism, and real estate development are the mainstay in this area. In

1995, residents and tourists valued the Indian River Lagoon at more than $733 million, including spending on recreational activities (e.g., rental of fishing boats), commercial fish landings (e.g., seafood sales), and Lagoon-front property (e.g., home purchases) (Apogee 1996). [Of this $733 million, access to the resources, valued at $200 million, is not reflected in market transactions (Apogee 1996).] An estimated $54 million was spent on recreational fishing in the Lagoon in 1990 with an anticipated escalation to $87 million by 2010 (Milon and Thunberg 1993). The Florida Fish and Wildlife Conservation Commission estimates that non-consumptive bird use (e.g., observing, photographing, drawing, and painting) annually generates $477 million in retail sales in Florida (Florida Fish and Wildlife Conservation Commission 2000). The Indian River Lagoon region figures prominently in the Great Florida Birding Trail with over 40 sites throughout the Lagoon region and a main gateway at Merritt Island National Wildlife Refuge. Over 15 percent of Florida's restaurants and hotels are located within the Indian River Lagoon region (Indian River Lagoon National Estuary Program 1996).

In 1990, the Indian River Lagoon region supported a population of about 750,000. By 2010, this population is anticipated to reach 1 million (Indian River Lagoon National Estuary Program 1996). Although a smaller county in the region, Indian River County's population increased by over 25 percent over the last 10 years from 90,208 in 1990 (U.S. Census Bureau 1991) to 112,947 in 2000 (U.S. Census Bureau 2000e). During this same time period, the city of Sebastian grew at a rate of 58.6 percent (U.S. Census Bureau 2000e). Median household income for Indian River County in 1997 was approximately $35,895 (U.S. Census Bureau 2000d). While this value is above the national average, it is estimated that approximately 11.2 percent of the population of Indian River County live at or below the poverty level (U.S. Census Bureau 2000d). Further, in October 2000, the unemployment rate for Indian River County was more than double (i.e., 7.5 percent) either the Florida or the U.S. unemployment rate (i.e., 3.7 percent for Florida and 3.6 percent for the U.S.) (Florida Department of Labor and Employment Security 2000). The county's population continues to be predominantly white and older, with considerable increases in the Hispanic and Asian race categories. The county's median age rose in the 1990s to 47 years of age (Eljera 2001b). The adjacent counties are generally larger than Indian River County: to the north, Brevard County's 2000 population was 476,230; to the south, St. Lucie County's 2000 population was 192,695; and to the west, Osceola County's 2000 population was 172,493 (U.S. Census Bureau 2000e). By 2015, Indian River County's population is forecasted to reach 144,000 (Lenze 2002).

Natural and agricultural lands of the area are increasingly being converted to urban and suburban uses. This rapid growth and its associated impacts dramatically affect the refuge and its resources. This growth even extends to the borders of the refuge. See Figure 10 to view the land use/land cover classifications in and around the refuge (St. Johns River Water Management District 1995). See Figure 11 for an aerial view showing the development surrounding the refuge–image taken in 1999 with 1 meter resolution (Florida Department of Environmental Protection 1999c). To the west of the refuge, across the Indian River Lagoon and the highly utilized Intracoastal Waterway is the City of Sebastian. Development west of the refuge includes residential uses (e.g., single-family homes, condos, and mobile home parks), the City of Sebastian's Riverview Park, commercial uses (e.g., gas stations, restaurants, automobile and boat dealers, and small businesses), minor undeveloped lands (e.g., Duck Point), citrus groves, plant nurseries, and sand mining operations. To the north of the refuge are residential uses, Sebastian Inlet, and the highly utilized Sebastian Inlet State Recreation Area (the annual visitation to the Recreation Area is approximately 750,000). The County Road 510 Bridge (i.e., Wabasso Causeway), the Environmental Learning Center, Disney's Vero Beach Resort, and commercial uses are to the south of the refuge. Residential developments (e.g., towns of Orchid and Windsor), residential lots (up to 3 units per acre), active agricultural operations (i.e., citrus groves), Indian River County beach front parks (e.g., Treasure Shores), and Archie Carr Refuge line the eastern border of the refuge.

Figure 10. Land use/land cover of the area

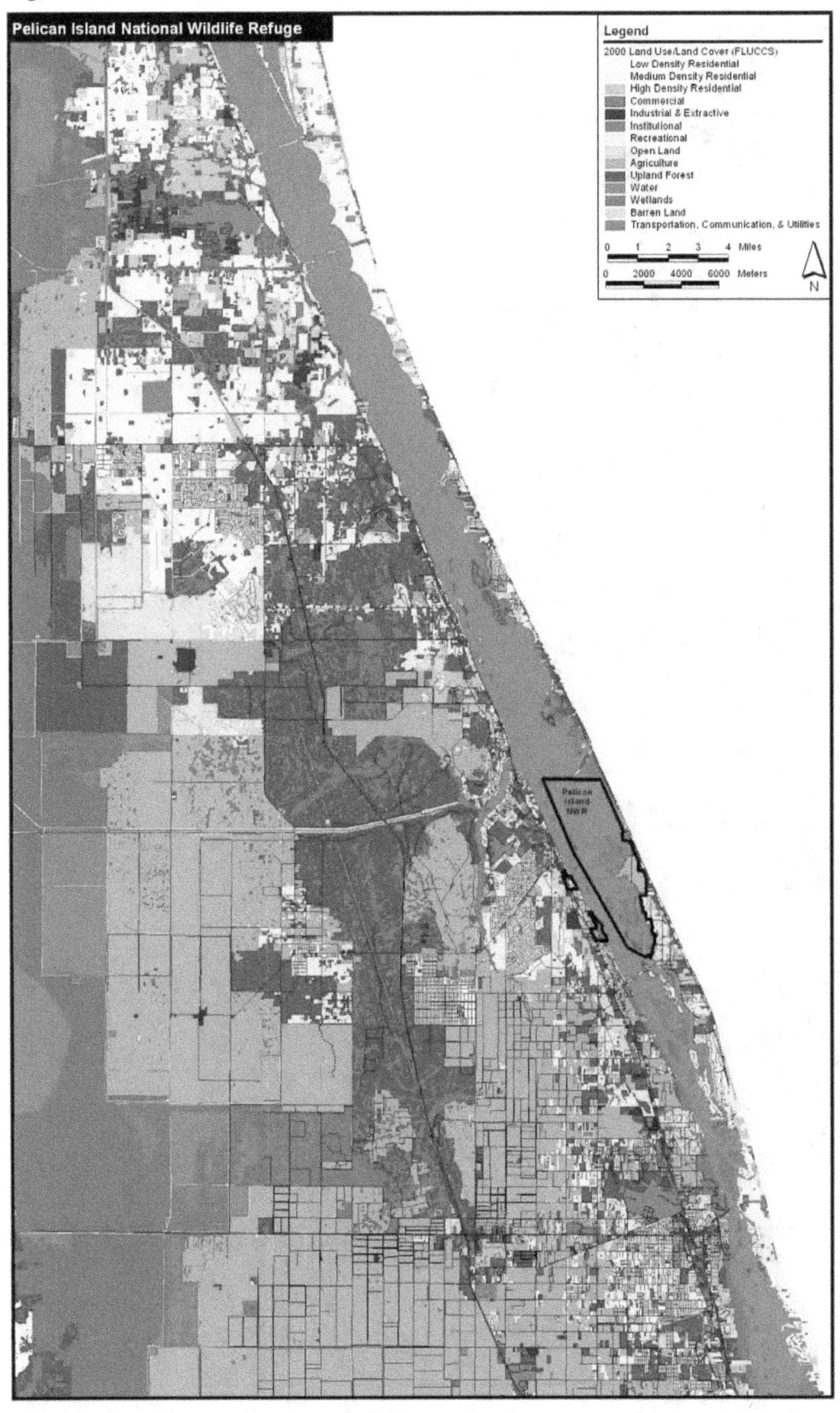

Figure 11. Aerial view of refuge

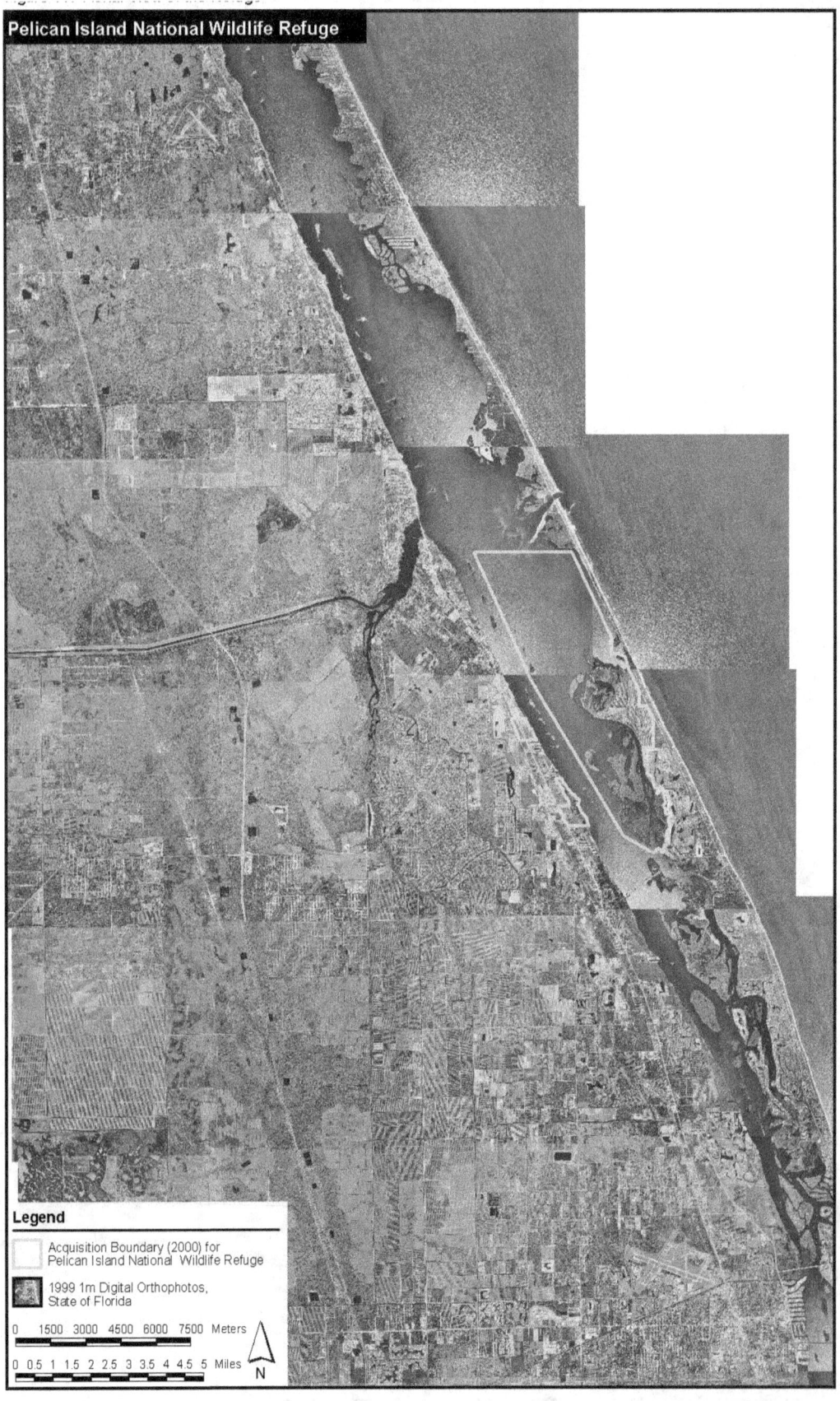

Pelican Island National Wildlife Refuge

PHYSICAL ENVIRONMENT

The climate, topography, geology, air quality, soils, and waterways form the foundation of the physical environment of the refuge.

Pelican Island National Wildlife Refuge's climate is subtropical and temperate. The average temperature is 67 degrees Fahrenheit with long, warm, humid summers and mild winters. Tropical storms impact the area, especially from May through mid-November. Generally, the area averages between 55 to 60 inches of rain annually, mostly in the summer and early fall.

On the refuge, elevation rises east to west sharply from sea level to 15 feet, and then drops more gradually back to below sea level in the Indian River Lagoon. Generally, the elevation of the area between the Lagoon and St. Sebastian River is 20 feet. West of that, the ancient dune elevation rises from 20 to 30 feet.

The surface formations of the Pelican Island Refuge area are of Pleistocene (Glacial) and Holocene (Recent) origin. Previously submerged lands were exposed during the late Pleistocene period, providing for the spread of flora and fauna from the peninsula. Wetlands, salt marshes, mangroves, and other swampy formations lined the margins between uplands and submerged lands. The tropical hammocks and coastal shrubs of the area were most likely nourished by the prevailing West Indies with substantial influences on the flora, birds, and insects from Cuba and the Bahamas (summarized from Myers and Ewel 1990).

The air pollutants of major concern in Florida are carbon monoxide, lead, nitrogen dioxide, ozone, particulate matter and sulfur dioxide (Florida Department of Environmental Protection 1999a). The primary sources of these pollutants are vehicle emissions, power plants, and industrial activities. In 1999, all areas of Florida were air quality attainment areas (Florida Department of Environmental Protection 1999a). The Indian River Lagoon area is considered to have good air quality. However, occasional temperature inversions, lasting up to 48 hours, can temporarily degrade local air quality below acceptable levels.

The general soils of the refuge include Canaveral-Captiva-Palm Beach, which is characterized by gently sloping, somewhat poorly drained to moderately well drained sandy soils with shell fragments, and McKee-Quartzipsamments-St. Augustine, which is characterized by level, somewhat poorly drained soils mixed with sand and shell fragments (Wettstein, Nobel, and Slabaugh 1987). Specific soils found on the refuge include: Canaveral Fine Sand, 0-5 percent Slopes; Quartzipsamments, 0-5 percent Slopes; Captiva Fine Sand; McKee Mucky Clay Loam; and Kesson Muck (Wettstein, Noble, and Slabaugh 1987).

With numerous small rivers, creeks, and canals flowing into it, the narrow estuarine Indian River Lagoon stretches from Ponce de Leon south of Daytona Beach to Jupiter Inlet near West Palm Beach–about 155 miles. The Intracoastal Waterway is the deepest part of the Lagoon. Near the refuge the St. Sebastian River and Turkey Creek contribute fresh water to the brackish Lagoon. The Fellsmere Farms and Sebastian River water control districts feed water through the St. Sebastian River to the Lagoon. The St. Sebastian River flows into the Lagoon nearly opposite of Sebastian Inlet along the northern edge of the refuge. The Lagoon has several identified water quality parameters of concern: cadmium, lead, mercury, nutrients, selenium, thallium, and dissolve oxygen (U.S. Environmental Protection Agency 2000b). Water circulation within the Lagoon is affected by the Intracoastal Waterway (e.g., navigation channel maintenance and boat usage), winds, inlets, and causeways. The water quality within the refuge boundary is generally better quality (with Class II water) than nearby portions of the Lagoon.

III. Plan Development

OVERVIEW

It began at Pelican Island with one man, Paul Kroegel, and a small group of concerned citizens and scientists. From their efforts rose the largest collection of lands and waters for managed wildlife, the National Wildlife Refuge System.

Although the Pelican Island National Wildlife Refuge comprehensive conservation planning effort officially began in 2000, the planning process was preceded by nearly a decade of preplanning activities. In 1993, the first management plan was developed for the refuge. This first plan was 19 pages and outlined limited refuge management actions. In 1996, a public meeting was held to determine the refuge management activities and facilities desired by the public. Subsequent to this meeting, the Pelican Island Planning Group was created to prepare a plan for refuge facilities. A draft plan was completed in 1997. In 1998, building on the success of the Pelican Island Planning Group, the Pelican Island Working Group formed as a subcommittee of the South Florida Ecosystem Team and focused on pressing refuge management issues (e.g., erosion of Pelican Island proper) and on the Centennial of Pelican Island National Wildlife Refuge and the National Wildlife Refuge System. Following a series of meetings, the vision document, "Pelican Island: Honoring a Legacy," was written by existing and former Fish and Wildlife Service employees, with the cooperation of a variety of partners and the public, and published in November 1999. This vision document set the foundation for the comprehensive conservation plan and clearly outlined the steps needed to protect this refuge. The refuge has been and will continue to be sustained by the public and its partners. More recently, the public was involved in an array of refuge activities ranging from conducting shoreline stabilization efforts for the historic Pelican Island rookery to preparing for the 100th anniversary of the refuge and the National Wildlife Refuge System.

As it has over the past 100 years, the public will continue to play an integral role in the refuge over the next 100 years, including being involved in the development of this comprehensive conservation plan. The planning process provides for public involvement in developing a plan for the future management of a refuge. Plans are revised every 15 years, or earlier, if monitoring and evaluation determine that changes are needed to achieve refuge purposes, vision, goals, and/or objectives. The basic steps of the planning process involve gathering information, scoping public input, developing the draft plan, gathering and reviewing public input on the draft plan, developing the final plan, and implementing and monitoring the proposed actions identified in the final plan.

PUBLIC INVOLVEMENT AND PLANNING PROCESS

January 2000 officially began the planning process with preplanning activities such as gathering data and information, meeting with Pelican Island Refuge staff and Merritt Island Refuge Complex staff since the refuge was managed as part of the Merritt Island National Wildlife Refuge Complex until 2002, meeting with intergovernmental partners, visioning, and preparing for the public scoping phase of the planning process. To include the governmental partners in the planning process, an Intergovernmental Coordination Planning Team was formed. Team meetings were conducted on January 20, 2000; February 18, 2000; March 16, 2000; April 12, 2000; and May 4, 2000. The Intergovernmental Coordination Planning Team identified items such as existing and needed data, refuge resources, issues, concerns, affected members of the public, vision ideas, and public participation issues. As a group, this Intergovernmental Team prioritized its top issues to be addressed by the refuge over the 15-year life of the plan.

A Service Core Planning Team was assembled and held a series of meetings in preparation for conducting the planning effort and in advance of public scoping. Public scoping commenced on April 24, 2000, including notices in the *Federal Register* (on April 24, 2000 and May 12, 2000) and in local newspapers (on April 28-30, 2000 and May 19-20, 2000). Additional information about the planning process and public scoping was provided through informational flyers, planning updates, several articles in the local newspapers, and postings on the Fish and Wildlife Service's Internet web sites (http://merrittisland.fws.gov and http://pelicanisland.fws.gov). Given the proximity of the two refuges, several shared issues, and many overlapping interested parties, joint public meetings were held for Pelican Island and Archie Carr refuges.

Utilizing existing public mailing lists of the refuge, as well as public mailing lists from various governmental partners, more than 1,200 informational flyers were initially mailed. This first flyer invited participation in the planning process through a variety of means, including public meetings, letters, faxes, telephone calls, e-mail messages, and personal visits. The flyer also announced the times and locations of the public meetings, provided other information, and described the purposes of the two refuges. Afterwards, three neighborhood meetings were conducted on May 3, May 25, and June 1, 2000. Outlining the planning process and highlighting the issues and concerns raised to date, a June 2, 2000 Planning Update was mailed out to over 2,800 interested parties. Following this Planning Update, two summary, countywide meetings were held on June 14 and June 15, 2000, in Sebastian (Indian River County) and Melbourne (Brevard County).

The public meetings were attended by a total of 90 individuals representing a variety of interests and organizations. Approximately 117 individuals, organizations, and governmental entities submitted comments regarding the plans for Pelican Island and Archie Carr refuges. Letters, faxes, email messages, and phone calls were received from across the country. Comments from the public were submitted by a variety of entities, ranging from a local middle school student to a coalition of six organizations representing more than 700,000 members.

Members of the Service's Core Planning Team met periodically to review public comments, data, and information collected to write the plan. Professional reviews of the refuge were conducted to determine the status, trends, and conditions of refuge resources and facilities. Experts from the Service, State of Florida (including Fish and Wildlife Conservation Commission, Department of Environmental Protection, and St. Johns River Water Management District), Indian River Mosquito Control District, University of Central Florida, and NASA's Kennedy Space Center/Dynamac participated in a 3-day wildlife and habitat management review of the refuge. The information garnered from this review helped the planning team analyze and develop recommendations for the draft plan and environmental assessment. A wilderness review was conducted on August 15, 2000, by Service staff. In review of the federally owned lands within the legislatively defined boundary of the refuge, no additional lands were found suitable for designation as Wilderness at this time. A public use review was conducted on November 7-9, 2000, involving Service public use specialists and outdoor recreation planners. This review focused on existing activities and provided specific recommended actions to improve program development and facilities for sport fishing, wildlife viewing, environmental education and interpretation.

SCOPING OF ISSUES AND CONCERNS

During the preplanning and public scoping phases of plan development, a myriad of issues, concerns, and opportunities were raised by the public, the Service, and other public agencies. Issue identification is a major factor in determining future management goals and objectives, as well as future projects. In addition to the general public scoping meetings, a series of meetings were conducted with federal, state, and local governmental agencies. Coordination with the governmental partners and the public is essential to ensure support for the plan and identified projects. While some of the issues and concerns raised during scoping are important to the future of the refuge, many are not within the Service's management jurisdiction or authority, and some are completely outside of its control. Several opportunities raised during scoping are addressed by the Service in this plan. A Service planning team evaluated the long list of issues raised, identified the priority issues to be addressed over the next 15 years, evaluated steps to rectify these issues and resource needs, and measured the impact of plan implementation. The Core Team then developed a list of goals, objectives, and strategies to shape the management of the refuge for the 15-year life of the plan.

The priority issues are divided into six categories: fish, wildlife, and plant populations; habitats; land protection and conservation; education and visitor services; refuge administration; and cultural resources.

FISH, WILDLIFE, AND PLANT POPULATIONS

Much of the wildlife using the refuge are declining, including threatened and endangered species, neotropical migratory birds, shorebirds, and native wildlife in general. The decline and loss of wildlife and habitats; the fragmentation of habitats; the increase in disturbance to wildlife and habitat; and the spread of exotic, invasive, and nuisance species are negatively impacting the wildlife resources of Pelican Island National Wildlife Refuge.

Wildlife utilizing the rookery on Pelican Island proper are negatively impacted by a variety of factors, including erosion of the Island, loss and decline of the nesting substrate, and ongoing disturbance from public use activities (due to the constraints of the lease agreement and due to a lack of sufficient staff for patrol and enforcement activities). Figure 5 shows the loss of half of Pelican Island proper since 1943. Figure 6 shows the predicted continued loss of Pelican Island proper without intervention. The erosion of the Island is due in large part to wave energy from increased boat traffic in the Intracoastal Waterway. The resultant increased wave energy from Sebastian Inlet may also play a role in the erosion of the Island. In other words, these impacts were man-made. The figures and data portrayed in Figures 5 and 6 spurred the refuge to act. Shoreline stabilization efforts began in February 1996 with the planting of 100 mangrove propagules encased in cut bamboo stalks. The mangroves did not survive a subsequent freeze. A follow-up replanting in August was also unsuccessful due to birds perching on the bamboo stalks. A study by Florida Tech and a partnership with Lewis Environmental Services produced a different strategy for protecting Pelican Island's shoreline. In February 2000, 165 feet of clam and oyster shell, bagged in burlap, were placed by hand on the northeast shoreline of Pelican Island. Operation Save Pelican Island, in February 2001, not only added shell and vegetation to further the shoreline stabilization efforts, but also helped broadcast on a national scale the threats facing this refuge and other refuges around the country. Monitoring must be conducted to ensure that these efforts continue their initial successes at stabilizing and rebuilding the Island. Evaluation of additional activities is also required (e.g., the §1135 alternative for the U.S. Army Corps of Engineers to scrape down and restore specific spoil islands and use that material to raise the bay bottom in a targeted area offshore of Pelican Island proper).

The ongoing increases in human population translate to ongoing increases in human activities and use in and around the refuge. Lethal and sub-lethal impacts to wildlife stem from commercial, residential, and recreational use of the waterway, natural and spoil islands, barrier island, and mainland. Ongoing development of the landscape is consuming and fragmenting remaining off-refuge habitats, which are also used by numerous refuge wildlife (e.g., for feeding, migrating, and dispersing). This development further pollutes area waterways, including on the refuge and increases public use of the refuge, further impacting and disturbing wildlife (e.g., island rookeries are disturbed by shell collecting and picnicking activities). Development also fuels the spread of exotic, invasive, and nuisance species, further impacting wildlife resources (e.g., free roaming pets and feral cats prey on refuge wildlife). If these activities are not controlled, refuge and area wildlife and habitats are in imminent danger of harm.

HABITATS

Refuge habitats are facing increased recreational pressures; negative impacts from disturbance; and the spread of exotic, invasive, and nuisance species. Pelican Island proper has been eroding, which could result in the loss of this historic rookery. The Indian River Lagoon system lost 18 percent or 12,400 acres of seagrass from 1943 to 1992, resulting in an estimated negative economic impact of $120 million per year (St. Johns River Water Management District 1999). The refuge has a mix of stable seagrass, increased seagrass, and lost seagrass, while Indian River County experienced an overall 61 percent gain and southern Brevard County experienced an overall 73 percent loss from 1943 to 1992 (St. Johns River Water Management District 1999).

The majority of the refuge is leased from the State of Florida and is not governed by refuge regulations. High public use of the waterway portion of the refuge is governed by this lease, highly constraining or eliminating the refuge's ability to ensure compatibility of these uses. Consequently, wildlife and habitat impacts and disturbances are occurring. Outstanding shellfish leases still exist within the refuge. This planning process identified the need to investigate and develop methods to ensure better protection of the resources associated with the lands and waters leased from the State of Florida, to investigate strengthening and expanding the lease, and to monitor impacts of aquaculture activities to ensure no adverse impacts are experienced by important resources of the refuge.

Encompassing more than just native habitats, the refuge also includes exotic species and disturbed sites, such as the citrus groves that once covered much of this area of Florida. Of immediate concern are two exotic plant species: Australian pine and Brazilian pepper. Australian pine and Brazilian pepper cover many of the refuge's natural and spoil lagoonal islands and are found throughout the barrier island portion of the refuge. These exotics have direct negative impacts to wildlife by aggressively out-competing native vegetation and growing uncontrollably. Beyond exotic species, citrus groves cover large portions of the refuge. To better serve resident and migratory wildlife, the refuge must remove exotics and must restore native habitats. Current habitat management activities plan for the restoration and creation of mangrove forests, tidal marsh, freshwater wetlands, palm prairies, hydric hammocks, and maritime hammocks. To do this, the water table and topography should be restored to mimic historic, natural conditions.

Through this planning process, management recognized the need to better coordinate with a variety of partners at various landscape scales to address long-term habitat management and restoration. Through this planning process, the refuge delineated the need to restore and manage habitats to benefit native species (e.g., remove exotics and replant with native vegetation; manage impoundments for specific wildlife benefits, especially for wood storks; and restore citrus groves to freshwater marsh and maritime hammock); restore and manage habitats to aid in the recovery of threatened and endangered species; develop and implement data gathering and monitoring programs; restore and manage shorebird nesting habitat; and protect important foraging, loafing, and fish spawning sites.

LAND PROTECTION AND CONSERVATION

The refuge exists in a highly developed landscape with properties within the acquisition boundary of the refuge under serious threat of development, with existing habitat fragmentation, and with limited ocean to river connectivity. Further, the existing lease agreement with the State of Florida restricts refuge management and prevents opportunities for controlling wildlife disturbance and negative habitat impacts.

Urban and suburban developments continue to sprawl across Florida, degrading and destroying wildlife, habitats, and the natural functions of ecosystems. Indian River County grew over 25 percent between 1990 and 2000 to 112,947 (U.S. Census Bureau 2000e). The city of Sebastian grew at a rate of 58.6 percent between 1990 and 2000 to 16,181 (U.S. Census Bureau 2000e). This growth extends to the borders of the refuge and properties within the acquisition boundary (that are not currently part of the refuge) face tremendous development pressures. If the buffer needed to protect Pelican Island proper is not purchased, it is very likely that these lands will be developed. This planning process crystallized the need to acquire the remaining inholding tracts of lands over the next 3-5 years as a buffer for the historic rookery to secure a needed connection between Pelican Island and Archie Carr refuges, providing habitat for migratory birds, threatened and endangered species, and other native wildlife.

EDUCATION AND VISITOR SERVICES

The refuge is facing a variety of negative impacts from public use activities that stem from increased boat traffic along the Intracoastal Waterway and elevated fishing pressure. Further, limited opportunities exist for wildlife observation, photography, and interpretation. Although environmental education activities are conducted in the area by refuge partners, education efforts do not sufficiently address wildlife. These factors hinder the ability of the Service to increase awareness and understanding of wildlife and habitats.

This comprehensive conservation planning process identified the importance of addressing the increasing impacts from human activities and use (e.g., lethal and sub-lethal impacts from boating activities; personal watercraft use; collisions; wildlife disturbances; decreased water quality; erosion; development; and increased pollution, runoff, trash, and illegal access). The refuge must work with its partners to develop solutions such as designating and enforcing waterway speed limits and zones, increasing the presence of law enforcement personnel, and posting signs for the refuge. Further, the planning process identified that the refuge should provide education, outreach, and public use opportunities; create visitor facilities to provide these services to the community and visitors (e.g., visitor center, trails, and observation tower); and showcase the birthplace and tell the story of the National Wildlife Refuge System. Only through education will people change their behaviors. During the public scoping process, the need for environmental education surfaced repeatedly as one of the top concerns of the public, especially for the local schools. Support for the resources and for the refuge will be found through educational programs, outreach efforts, and compatible wildlife-dependent recreational opportunities.

REFUGE ADMINISTRATION

Few staff, funds, facilities, and equipment are available to address the myriad of issues facing refuge management. Further, uncontrolled or unknown research activities on the refuge have the potential for negative wildlife and habitat impacts. Exotic species introduction, global climate change, erosion, and other human activities and influences affect the ecological character and function of the Wilderness Area. A difficult challenge is simply having the resources necessary to administer/restore the natural conditions of the 5.5-acre Wilderness Area, given all the human influences that are beyond the control of the Service. Since 1903, this globally and historically significant refuge has operated with a staff of either one or none. Only in 2001 did the refuge move beyond a single staff member, predominantly due to the upcoming Centennial in 2003, the vision document, and the comprehensive conservation planning process. Funding for this refuge has historically been minimal or nonexistent. Since the 1960s, funds have been diverted from the Merritt Island National Wildlife Refuge Complex and the South Florida Ecosystem Team to cover needed management projects and more recently to cover the salary of the Refuge Manager. Hence, this refuge has been sustained by the public and the partners.

CULTURAL RESOURCES

The refuge has not only been an integral part of the local community, but it has been and continues to be a source of pride and a city symbol. Given the long history of the refuge in the community and given the development pressures of the area, the historical and archaeological resources protected by the refuge are important. Issues to be addressed involving the refuge's historical and archaeological resources include high development pressure facing the historically significant Kroegel Homestead, the home of the first Refuge Manager and the high potential for disturbance, vandalism, and theft from archaeological and cultural sites on the refuge.

IV. Management Direction

INTRODUCTION

The Service manages fish and wildlife habitats considering the needs of all resources in decision-making. However, first and foremost, fish and wildlife conservation assumes priority in refuge management. The National Wildlife Refuge System Improvement Act of 1997 requires the Service to maintain the ecological health, diversity, and integrity of refuges. A refuge is a vital link in the overall function of an ecosystem. Refuges in the South Florida Ecosystem include imperiled coastal areas and lagoonal islands, like those protected at Pelican Island Refuge. To offset the historic and continued loss of habitats within the ecosystem, the Pelican Island Refuge and other public lands and waters provide a biological safety net for native species, trust resources, and federal and state listed species.

VISION

Pelican Island. This is the place where it all started. It began in 1903 with a President named Theodore Roosevelt in a swampland called Florida at a rookery known as Pelican Island. It was at this small island that a promise was made to the American people to preserve wildlife and wild places for their own intrinsic values. Over 100 years later, we are indebted to this President for fulfilling his promise to allow future generations the opportunity to enjoy our wildlife heritage.

The 1999 vision document, "Pelican Island: Honoring a Legacy," sets forth the future for Pelican Island National Wildlife Refuge (U.S. Fish and Wildlife Service 1999b). This future is a haven for pelicans, egrets, herons, wood storks, and other colonial waterbirds; a restored, healthy, and stabilized Pelican Island; a place where manatees and dolphins thrive and where threatened and endangered species are protected; clean lagoonal waters, abundant seagrass beds, open mud flats, thick mangrove islands, sandy shores, freshwater wetlands, managed salt marshes, and lush maritime hammock; a nursery for juvenile sea turtles; a persistent stopover for migratory wildlife; a highly biologically diverse estuary and fishery; a protected and secure wilderness area; and a place for appropriate and compatible research, wildlife-dependent recreation, and environmental education.

Pelican Island is the birthplace and showcase of the National Wildlife Refuge System, the first refuge, the original rookery, the impetus for national wildlife protection. Pelican Island National Wildlife Refuge reminds us of our past and the national legacy originating at this rookery and inspires us to honor that legacy by reaching out to partners for the conservation, protection, and enhancement of wildlife and wild places for current and future generations.

Pelican Island National Wildlife Refuge continues to be protected, conserved, enhanced, and restored, providing high-quality, functional habitats managed to help sustain abundant populations of native species and to help recover threatened and endangered species. As the landscape continues to be developed, the importance of Pelican Island National Wildlife Refuge increases through time, as part of an interconnected system linking the Indian River Lagoon to the Atlantic Ocean through the Archie Carr National Wildlife Refuge, and linking other public lands, habitats, refuges, and nations for global species protection.

GOALS, OBJECTIVES, AND STRATEGIES

The goals, objectives, and strategies delineated are the Service's response to the resource problems, issues, concerns, and needs expressed by the Service, the public, and the governmental partners. They reflect the Service's commitment to achieve the purposes and vision of Pelican Island National

Wildlife Refuge, the mission of the National Wildlife Refuge System, and the mandates of the U.S. Fish and Wildlife Service. The implementation of all goals, objectives, and strategies outlined will follow the refuge's best management practices and will pursue avoidance and minimization of impacts to federally threatened and endangered species, to the extent possible and practicable (see Appendix VI for more information regarding avoidance and minimization). The Service intends to accomplish these goals, objectives, and strategies over the 15-year life of the comprehensive conservation plan.

GOAL A: FISH, WILDLIFE, AND PLANT POPULATIONS

Continue working with the partners to maintain viable populations of those wildlife species endemic to the sub-tropical barrier island and lagoonal system of the refuge, especially sea turtles, West Indian manatee, eastern indigo snake, Atlantic salt marsh snake, wood stork, and other migratory and resident birds.

Discussion: Since the refuge lacks data regarding almost all refuge fish, wildlife, and plant populations, inventory and monitor activities dominate refuge management actions during the 15-year life of the comprehensive conservation plan. Satisfying these data needs will require considerable coordination within the Service and with refuge partners.

Objective A.1: Sea Turtles
Throughout the 15-year life of the plan, contribute to the efforts of the Service's South Florida Ecological Services Office to protect sea turtles and foraging areas through management, enforcement, and scientific research in the lagoonal waters of the refuge. Within 5 years of plan approval, develop baseline data for sea turtles in the lagoonal waters of the refuge.

Discussion: The refuge is a globally important juvenile sea turtle nursery with high catch per unit efforts by researchers. With the addition of staff, the refuge will take a more active role in the recovery of these species. In the past, Kemp's ridley and hawksbill sea turtles have been rare visitors to the protected lagoonal waters of the refuge. Refuge staff will work with the South Florida Ecosystem Team and South Florida Ecological Services Field Office to determine the need for action and to potentially develop and implement recovery plans for these species, if warranted. The refuge will continue to acquire all applicable permits related to management activities regarding federally protected sea turtles. For additional information about the recovery plans for these species, see the South Florida Multi-species Recovery Plan (U.S. Fish and Wildlife Service 1999c).

Disease (fibropapillomatosis) is affecting more than half of the juvenile green sea turtle population (Ehrhart and Redfoot 1995). Sea turtles are also impacted by boat strikes and propellers, discarded nets, discarded monofilament fishing line, plastic bags, balloons, and other litter.

Strategies:

- Continue to gather and encourage research into species and population biology of these sea turtle species.
- Encourage continued and expanded research into the fibropapilloma disease occurring in sea turtles in this area.
- Encourage the investigation of the role of contaminants in disease in juvenile green sea turtles.
- Continue working with the University of Central Florida to research the foraging needs and to study genetic diversity and movement of juvenile green sea turtles on the refuge.

- Document the occurrence and distribution of the Kemp's ridley and hawksbill sea turtles on the refuge and coordinate with area researchers for this documentation, including the University of Central Florida, Florida Institute of Technology, Marine Resources Council, and Hubbs-Sea World Research Institute.
- Coordinate management with the South Florida Ecological Services Field Office and the environmental education partners to increase public awareness and education for sea turtles.

Objective A.2: **West Indian Manatee**

Within one year of plan approval, increase coordination activities with the State of Florida and the Service's South Florida Ecological Services Office to reduce manatee injury, mortality, and disturbance and to increase public awareness of manatees. Within 15 years of plan approval, develop baseline data for manatees in the lagoonal waters of the refuge.

Discussion: With the addition of staff, the refuge will take a more active role in the recovery efforts for the West Indian manatee identified in the South Florida Multi-Species Recovery Plan (U.S. Fish and Wildlife Service 1999c). The refuge will continue to acquire all applicable permits related to management activities regarding the federally protected manatee.

Given the small size of the refuge, the developed character of the surrounding landscape, and the broad boating access to refuge lands and waters in the Indian River Lagoon, the refuge experiences considerable impacts and faces numerous threats from human activities on and around the refuge. Boat strikes and propellers especially impact manatees. Discarded monofilament fishing line, discarded nets, and other litter also impact manatees.

Strategies:

- Coordinate management within the Service, including implementing rules and regulations, law enforcement training (e.g., salvage and necropsy program), and new technologies; installing signs; and improving reporting and investigations.
- Encourage research into the physiology, life history, and ecology of the manatee, as well as research into habitat components.
- Coordinate management with the South Florida Ecological Services Field Office and the environmental education partners to increase public awareness and education for the manatee.
- Evaluate the quality of manatee habitat in the refuge.
- Develop approaches to implement research, identify potential threats, and collect scientific data.
- Develop approaches to limit or eliminate the threats and impacts to manatees (e.g., patrol and enforcement activities).
- Work with the Indian River Lagoon partners to address water quality impacts to manatees.

Objective A.3: **Eastern Indigo and Atlantic Salt Marsh Snakes**

Within five years of plan approval, contribute to federal recovery efforts for eastern indigo snake and Atlantic salt marsh snake populations by encouraging and conducting research, population surveys, and monitoring on the refuge and by conducting environmental education on the refuge and in the local community. Within 10 years of plan approval, develop baseline data for eastern indigo and salt marsh snakes on the refuge.

Discussion: Eastern indigo snakes have been found on the refuge. The Atlantic salt marsh snake has been surveyed near the refuge and intergrades have been sighted on the refuge. With the addition of staff, the refuge will contribute to recovery efforts identified in the South Florida Multi-species Recovery Plan (U.S. Fish and Wildlife Service 1999c), as appropriate. The refuge will continue to acquire all applicable permits related to management activities regarding federally protected indigo and salt marsh snakes.

Strategies:

- Identify, evaluate, and protect against the threats to these species.
- Encourage and manage research on the biology and ecology of the eastern indigo snake.
- Work with the partners to increase awareness of and improve behavior towards the eastern indigo snake.
- Provide informational brochures and lectures regarding both of these species.
- Coordinate with others (e.g., adjacent landowners and Indian River County) to discourage the use of rat poison in and around the refuge.
- Coordinate monitoring and survey protocols with researchers and governmental partners. Design and conduct surveys to determine the presence and relative abundance of these two species on the refuge. Document and monitor the occurrence of these two species.
- If appropriate, direct research into the biology of the Atlantic salt marsh snake and coordinate studies to measure contaminants with partners.

Objective A.4: **Wood Stork**
Within five years of plan approval, evaluate the refuge's role in wood stork recovery, develop baseline habitat information for wood stork foraging areas and roosting sites, and develop and implement appropriate restoration plans.

Discussion: The refuge has served as one of the most consistent wood stork rookeries in Florida. However, wood stork nesting on Pelican Island proper has declined from 900 in 1980 to 85 in 1990. It is currently estimated that a total of 90-150 pairs of wood storks breed on Pelican Island proper. With the addition of staff, the refuge will take a more active role in this recovery plan. The refuge will continue to acquire all applicable permits related to management activities regarding the federally protected wood stork. For additional information about the recovery plan for this species, see the South Florida Multi-Species Recovery Plan (U.S. Fish and Wildlife Service 1999c).

Strategies:

- Work with South Florida Ecological Services Field Office to identify and map wood stork foraging and roosting sites on the refuge.
- Restore wood stork feeding areas and rookeries on the refuge and locate foraging and roosting habitat for wood storks off the refuge.
- Participate in wood stork annual nesting surveys. Locate foraging and roosting habitat for wood storks using the refuge. Utilize standardized census procedures where disturbance is minimal. Contribute to meeting the population goals of the Southeast U.S. Regional Waterbird Conservation Plan.
- Encourage research on the biology and life history of wood storks, including research into productivity of wood stork nesting, survivorship, age structure, movement patterns of fledglings and post-breeding adults, foraging ecology and behavior, importance of roost sites, and impacts of contaminants.

- Encourage research into essential habitat components necessary to trigger successful nesting by wood storks, including research into the densities, species composition, and size classes of fishes necessary and research into the effects of natural and human-caused influences, such as impoundment water levels, on the ecology of the prey base.
- Continue managing the impoundments for multiple objectives, including for wood stork foraging.

Objective A.5: **Migratory and Resident Birds**

Within 10 years of plan approval, develop baseline data and monitoring programs to evaluate the status and trends of migratory and resident bird species on the refuge to support healthy populations of the migratory and resident birds of the Peninsular Florida Physiographic Region.

Discussion: The refuge has collected data for Pelican Island proper (i.e., the original 5.5-acre island) for nearly 100 years, but lacks data coverage for the rest of the refuge. The refuge currently conducts a few bird surveys (i.e., two to three annual roost counts, two to three annual colonial waterbird surveys, and the annual Audubon Christmas Bird Count), but this information is insufficient. Further, the federally listed piping plover and bald eagle occasionally occur on the refuge. With the addition of staff, the refuge will contribute towards recovery efforts for these species as identified in the South Florida Multi-Species Recovery Plan. The refuge will continue to acquire all applicable permits related to management activities regarding migratory and resident birds.

Strategies:

- Coordinate surveys, data collection, and monitoring protocols to determine baseline populations on the refuge as part of the standardized region-wide monitoring protocols for all waterbird groups. Continue to survey brown pelicans, roseate spoonbills, white ibis, reddish egret, little blue heron, and other colonial nesting birds on Pelican Island proper to monitor trends.
- Establish point count stations to determine population changes with emphasis on species of refuge management concern (e.g., those identified on the Audubon Watch List and the Partners-in-Flight Watch List for this area).
- Conduct nest productivity studies and other research for priority species, including monitoring predator disturbance during the nesting season in rookeries, woodlands, hammocks, and citrus groves.
- Develop volunteer training and programs to survey and monitor birds. Encourage partners and volunteers to assist in surveys. Investigate utilizing Sebastian River High School students (to help satisfy their community involvement requirements).
- Monitor bald eagle nesting and foraging activities in the refuge.
- Coordinate management to increase outreach and education opportunities, including increasing public awareness of the habitat related issues that affect the recovery of the bald eagle in South Florida.
- Determine the presence of nesting or wintering painted buntings in coastal hammock habitats on the refuge.
- Manage adequate acreage of shrub communities to reverse declines of priority bird species using the refuge (e.g., painted bunting, indigo bunting, Florida prairie warbler, and eastern towhee).

Objective A.6: **Shorebirds**

Within 10 years of plan approval, evaluate the refuge's role in relation to shorebirds, develop baseline data, and develop and implement appropriate restoration plans.

Discussion: Shorebirds are an important part of coastal refuges. Pelican Island Refuge already provides shorebird habitat (e.g., along the impoundments and along the natural and spoil islands) for a mix of shorebirds. However, data have not been collected regarding the amount of shorebird habitat provided, the quality of shorebird habitat provided, and the quantity of shorebird habitat that could be provided. Further, minimal data have been collected regarding the abundance and diversity of shorebirds using the refuge. The refuge will continue to acquire all applicable permits related to management activities regarding the abundance and diversity of shorebirds.

Strategies:

- Coordinate management with the partners to maintain and restore shorebird habitat.
- Enhance shorebird habitats within the impounded wetlands using existing or additional portable pumps and water control structures [recommended in the U.S. Shorebird Conservation Plan (Fish and Wildlife Service 2000)].
- Monitor habitat used to support local populations of shorebirds. Survey abundance and distribution of shorebirds on and near the refuge. Contribute to meeting population goals of the Southeast U.S. Regional Waterbird Conservation Plan. Evaluate and prioritize those areas that could potentially serve as shorebird habitat.
- Identify the numbers of acres available and being utilized by shorebirds, the number of islands involved, and the types and numbers of shorebirds using the refuge.
- Consider creating least tern and black skimmer nesting habitat in developing an offshore wave break for Pelican Island proper.
- Utilize existing research regarding nesting substrates (e.g., Mallach and Leberg 1999).
- Maintain wash overs, sand flats, and mud flats within the refuge.
- When and where possible, do not immediately attempt to repair hurricane created shorebird habitat.
- Enhance and restore spoil and natural islands for breeding terns, black skimmers, and other shorebirds. Remove exotic vegetation and maintain bare sand or sparsely vegetated conditions on these islands. Determine required elevation of natural gradients and soil types needed. Emphasize black skimmer, least tern, Wilson's plover, and American oystercatcher.
- Evaluate the potential of including seasonal shorebird foraging in the multiple objectives of managing the impoundments.
- Compile management guidelines for wintering piping plovers. Determine the ongoing occurrence and location of wintering sites of piping plovers through annual surveys. Identify factors within the refuge limiting the quantity and quality of piping plover habitat. If applicable, modify the lease with the State of Florida to provide protection for piping plover wintering sites by closing and buffering islands during piping plover use. Implement public information and education programs through partnerships.

Objective A.7: Resident Wildlife

Within the 15-year life of the plan, develop baseline data and monitoring programs to evaluate the status and trends of native wildlife species on the refuge to support healthy populations of resident wildlife.

Discussion: The refuge has collected data for Pelican Island proper (i.e., the original 5.5-acre island) for nearly 100 years, but lacks data coverage for the rest of the refuge. The survey of resident species of wildlife (e.g., woodrats, diamondback terrapins, land crabs, and bobcats) may yield important information essential for the prevention of such species from becoming extirpated.

Strategies:

- Conduct surveys of resident species of wildlife to establish biodiversity baseline data, as well as to determine the relative abundance and range of a variety of species of refuge management concern (e.g., woodrats, diamondback terrapins, land crabs, and bobcats).
- Investigate the presence of species expected, but not yet confirmed on the Refuge (e.g., round-tailed muskrats, rice rats, and bats).
- Work with the partners to evaluate the needs, costs, and benefits of installing wildlife underpasses (e.g., under A1A).

Objective A.8: Exotic Plants

Within the 15-year life of the plan, eliminate exotic plants as the primary land cover type in all refuge uplands habitats.

Discussion: Exotic, invasive, and nuisance species are serious threats to fish and wildlife in Florida. With the addition of staff and through improved coordination with partners and neighbors, the Service will control exotic, invasive, and nuisance species on the refuge that threatened the survival of many species. The refuge provides orientation information to all new employees, volunteers, and contractors involved in controlling and removing exotic plants regarding federally listed species found on the refuge. The refuge will make all efforts possible and practicable to limit wildlife impacts of management activities associated with controlling and removing exotic plants. The refuge will continue to acquire all applicable permits related to exotic plant control activities, including any earthmoving activities, before commencement.

The main exotic, invasive, and nuisance plants of the refuge are Brazilian pepper, Australian pine, and Guinea grass. And citrus groves persist within the refuge and within the acquisition boundary. During implementation of this plan, refuge management aims to eliminate all exotic plants, including citrus, as the primary land cover type in all refuge upland habitats. A primary cover type is defined here as >50% of the land cover of a site. (Existing land use/land cover types are outlined in Figures 8 and 10 and Table 3, while planned refuge habitats are outlined in Figure 12.) Despite the management efforts outlined, Brazilian pepper and other exotics will continue to persist in varying degrees as secondary or tertiary land cover on the refuge throughout the 15-year life of this plan.

Strategies:

- Coordinate with refuge neighbors, including giving talks at meetings of nearby homeowners' associations and providing educational and informational materials regarding exotic, invasive, and nuisance plants (e.g., regarding exotic and ornamental plants).
- Prioritize the eradication of exotic, invasive, and nuisance plants that impact state and federally listed species and other species of management concern and control accordingly.
- Seek supplemental funding (e.g., Florida Department of Environmental Protection's Invasive Upland Plant Removal Program) for removal and treatment activities and for the restoration to native vegetation (through other partnerships and funding sources).
- Annually monitor all treated areas to evaluate the effectiveness and success of eradication efforts.
- Expand the volunteer program to increase exotic plant removal activities (e.g., Moon Vine Crew and Pepper Busters).
- Survey areas with exotic infestation prior to control activities to identify occurrence of wildlife and take measures to limit wildlife impacts.

Objective A.9: **Exotic, Invasive, and Nuisance Species**

Within the 15-year life of the plan, control and eliminate, where feasible, exotic, invasive, and nuisance species found on the refuge and work with the partners and neighbors to control the spread of these species onto refuge lands and waters. Within 10 years of plan approval, develop baseline data regarding the presence and spread of exotic, invasive, and nuisance species throughout refuge habitats.

Discussion: Exotic, invasive, and nuisance species are serious threats to fish and wildlife in Florida. With the addition of staff and through improved coordination with partners and neighbors, the Service will control exotic, invasive, and nuisance species on the refuge that threatened the survival of many species.

Strategies:

- Coordinate with refuge neighbors, including giving talks at meetings of nearby homeowners' associations and providing educational and informational materials regarding exotic, invasive, and nuisance species (e.g., regarding exotic and ornamental plants, free roaming pets, and feral cats).
- Prioritize the eradication of exotic, invasive, and nuisance species that impact state and federally listed species and other species of management concern and control accordingly.
- Seek supplemental funding (e.g., Florida Department of Environmental Protection's Invasive Upland Plant Removal Program) for removal and treatment activities and for the restoration to native vegetation (through other partnerships and funding sources).
- Annually monitor all treated areas to evaluate the effectiveness and success of eradication efforts.
- Prohibit the introduction of non-native fish and shellfish to refuge waters.
- Expand the volunteer program to increase exotic species removal activities (e.g., Moon Vine Crew and Pepper Busters).

GOAL B: HABITATS

Restore and manage the values and functions of refuge habitats characteristic of the southern Indian River Lagoon system to augment opportunities for nesting, resting, foraging, and/or migrating native species.

Discussion: All refuge habitats have been impacted to one degree or another, from changes in water quality to wholesale alteration of native landscapes. Figure 12 and Table 5 outline acreages and areas of primary habitats to be maintained, created, and/or restored during the 15-year life of the plan. During the life of the plan and through acquisition or some type of management agreement, the refuge expects to dramatically lower or eliminate the occurrence of several uses within the refuge's acquisition boundary, including residential, commercial, and agricultural, as well as exotics. Further, the refuge plans to substantially restore and create key habitats, especially upland hardwood forest and maritime hammock. As habitats are created and restored, the refuge's vegetation/habitat map will be updated in conformance to the National Vegetation Classification System.

Objective B.1: **Refugia Habitat**
Within five years of plan approval, restore and maintain ±5.3 acres of old field as refugia habitat for the Southeastern beach mouse, while also providing habitat benefits for ground doves, gopher tortoises, and other native species.

Figure 12. Proposed habitats of the refuge

Table 5. Proposed land use/land cover within the refuge's acquisition boundary in 15 years

Primary Land Use/ Cover Code (Lucode)	Secondary Land Use/ Cover Code (Lucode2)	Land Use/Land Cover Code Description	Estimated Acreage
1100	0	Residential, low density, <2 dwelling units per acre	25.0
1750	0	Governmental (shop, offices)	5.0
1880	0	Historical sites	55.7
1890	0	Other recreational (public access)	9.8
2210	4370	Agriculture, citrus groves, Australian pine	32.9
3300	0	Mixed rangeland (old field, cabbage palm)	5.3
4200	0	Upland hardwood forest	73.0
4250	0	Temperate/tropical hardwood (maritime hammock)	69.1
4250	4220	Temperate/tropical hardwood (maritime hammock), Brazilian pepper	16.2
4250	6410	Temperate/tropical hardwood (maritime hammock), freshwater marsh	339.5
4370	4220	Australian pine, Brazilian pepper	24.7
5100	0	Streams and waterways	0.9
5200	0	Lakes	31.8
5340	0	Reservoirs <10 acres	8.1
5400	0	Bays and estuaries	3,697.5
5400	6450	Bays and estuaries, submerged aquatic vegetation	879.1
6120	6420	Mangrove swamps, saltwater marshes	739.8
6120	6500	Mangrove swamps, Non-vegetated wetland	3.3
6300	0	Wetland forested mixed	18.1
6410	0	Freshwater marsh	0.2
6420	0	Saltwater marsh	56.6
6460	0	Mixed scrub-shrub wetland (predominantly willow and wax myrtle)	65.5
6500	0	Non-vegetated wetland	16.0
7430	0	Spoil areas	4.7
8140	0	Roads and highways	6.2
Total Acreage within the Refuge's Acquisition Boundary			**6,184.0**

Discussion: Although the refuge does not include dune habitat, which is the kind of habitat favored by the Southeastern beach mouse, this species persists in an old field habitat on the refuge. Recent surveys report 1-4 individuals on the refuge. This species previously existed on the adjacent dunes of Segment 4 of Archie Carr National Wildlife Refuge. With the addition of staff, the refuge will contribute to recovery efforts plan for this species, see the South Florida Multi-species Recovery Plan (U.S. Fish and Wildlife Service 1999c). The refuge will continue to acquire all applicable permits related to management activities regarding the federally protected beach mouse.

Strategies:

- Coordinate survey, research, and monitoring activities with the University of Central Florida [e.g., conduct two to three southeastern beach mouse surveys throughout each year to determine the ongoing abundance and distribution, expand this research and monitor the remnant population, develop data and results in consultation with others (e.g., through GIS databases)].
- Pursue a habitat connection to Archie Carr National Wildlife Refuge to support the migration of the southeastern beach mouse and other species (e.g., land crabs).
- Continue the control of feral and free roaming predators through pet owner education, feral predator removal, traps, and humane euthanasia of feral predators.
- Encourage research into the basic biology of the species and on the population viability (through risk assessment) of the species, as well as encourage research into habitat components, minimum patch size, and beneficial habitat management actions.
- Work with research partners, the South Florida Ecological Services Field Office, and environmental education partners to investigate the viability of a captive propagation and reintroduction program and to increase awareness about this species.
- Work with the partners to evaluate the needs, costs, and benefits of installing wildlife underpasses (e.g., under A1A).

Objective B.2: Jungle Trail Habitat Restoration

Within five years of plan approval, restore approximately 356 acres of salt marsh, mangrove swamp, and maritime hammock to mimic natural conditions and natural hydrology and manage about 1,225 acres of these habitats along Jungle Trail to support a diversity of wildlife species characteristic of the refuge's barrier island and lagoonal system.

Discussion: At Pelican Island Refuge, habitat restoration usually begins with the removal and treatment of Brazilian pepper, Australian pine, citrus, and other non-native vegetation. Previous refuge habitat restoration efforts have been limited, but in 2001, the Service joined in partnership with the Florida Department of Environmental Protection (FDEP) and Indian River County to restore refuge habitats in the Jungle Trail area. This partnership included the administration of two million dollars in grant funds by FDEP. To date, FDEP and Indian River County have played invaluable roles in habitat restoration on the refuge. Although Hurricanes Frances (September 4-6, 2004) and Jeanne (September 25-26, 2004) caused flooding and downed trees on the refuge, progress continues on this restoration project. To date, about 100 acres have been restored in the former Surman and Kennedy groves.

Citrus trees and exotic vegetation will be removed from other former groves and restored to support native habitat. The main focus of restoration activities in the Jungle Trail area is on restoring original contours water tables to emulate the natural hydrology of the area. Freshwater lakes and freshwater ephemeral ponds will be excavated in areas where wetlands were once drained. Ditches have been and will continue to be filled. Existing wetlands will be enhanced. Native vegetation will be planted

In each of the restored habitats (e.g., maritime hammock, palm hammock, freshwater wetlands, and tidal wetlands). The refuge will continue to acquire all applicable permits related to restoring habitat and hydrology in the Jungle Trail area. Figure 13 details habitat restoration and facility development for the Jungle Trail area.

Strategies:

- Coordinate partnerships to pursue complete restoration of the Jungle Trail area (i.e., the remaining habitats on the barrier island).
- Coordinate partnerships to pursue habitat links between Pelican Island National Wildlife Refuge and Archie Carr National Wildlife Refuge.
- Assess response of neotropical migratory birds and woodrats to hammock restoration.

Objective B.3: **Pelican Island Proper Rookery**
Within five years of plan approval, protect the Pelican Island proper rookery by stabilizing the shoreline of Pelican Island proper to reduce wave action and erosion and by managing this area to stimulate the natural processes of native plant recruitment and succession, creating a stable environment for shoreline accretion to restore the Island to its original 5.5 acres within the 15-year life of the plan.

Discussion: Pelican Island proper is the original 5.5-acre rookery island, which is also designated as a Wilderness Area (Figure 1) and is closed to the public to protect the rookery management activities conducted within the Wilderness Area must meet the standards and criteria set forth in the Wilderness Act. From 1943 to 1996, Pelican Island proper eroded to less than half its original size (i.e., from 5.5 acres to about 2.2 acres). The total number of nesting pairs of birds on this historic rookery has declined nearly 94 percent since 1910. In an effort to combat these losses, shoreline stabilization efforts began with a mangrove planting in 1996 that proved unsuccessful. A multi-partner effort began in 2000 to protect Pelican Island proper from eroding and losing its functionality as a rookery. Phase 1 was completed in 2000 and involved placing loose shell and shell bags and planting spartina and mangroves along 165 feet of the northern shore of Pelican Island proper. Phase 2 was completed in February 2001 and involved placing loose shell and planting vegetation (i.e., spartina and mangroves) along 930 feet around the north and west shorelines of Pelican Island proper. Depending on the success of the shoreline stabilization efforts, additional actions to limit erosion may or may not be necessary to protect this historic rookery. Recent estimates show the Island at 2.8 acres in 2004. The refuge will continue to acquire all applicable permits related to protecting the Pelican Island proper rookery, including earthmoving activities associated with shoreline stabilization.

During 2000, the refuge negotiated with the State of Florida for an amendment to the lease for a buffer of up to 410 feet for the Pelican Island rookery. However, current studies show that the recommended minimum buffer size for brown pelicans is 549 feet (Rodgers and Schwikert 2000).

Strategies:

Monitor measurable changes to Pelican Island proper (e.g., accretion, sea level changes, and vegetation growth and regrowth) by visiting the Island once a month (in conjunction with the monthly Wilderness Area visit). Supplement shell, where needed. Supplement existing vegetation to ensure the ongoing availability of a nesting substrate on the Island.

- Continue to work with the partners to evaluate the causes of the erosion of Pelican Island proper (e.g., increased boat traffic and speeds and increased wave energy reaching the Island due to Sebastian Inlet) and to develop and implement solutions.

Figure 13. Jungle Trail visitor facilities and restoration project

Implement slow speed areas to reduce wave impacts to Pelican Island proper by working with the State of Florida (e.g., through alteration of the lease agreement) and the partners.

- Expand the buffer of the Pelican Island rookery to one supported by current research. Adapt this minimum buffer size as new data become available.
- Post closed area signs at the buffer. Post closed area and Wilderness Area information and regulations at informational kiosks, city and county boat ramps, and all visitor information facilities.
- Design and implement a program to monitor the effectiveness of the buffer (e.g., monitor the number of times a day the buffer is violated, monitor the numbers of nests, and monitor nest success). Document probable causes of any changes.

Objective B.4: **Natural and Spoil Islands**
Within 10 years of plan approval, manage, maintain, and restore, where necessary, approximately 332 acres of natural and spoil island vegetation characteristic of the southern Indian River Lagoon to benefit breeding terns, shorebirds, and colonial birds and to minimize disturbance to birds utilizing these islands.

Discussion: With the ongoing increases in the human population around the refuge and with the growth of commercial and recreational use of the area, the resources of the refuge are facing increasing disturbances. As the landscape continues to develop and as the locations for wildlife continue to dwindle, it will become more and more important for the refuge to provide disturbance-free or minimal disturbance areas for wildlife to roost, nest, forage, and rest, especially on natural and spoil islands of the Indian River Lagoon. Further, exotic species can be found in almost every refuge habitat, in many cases disturbing and disrupting natural systems. The natural and spoil islands of the refuge are no exception. Measures must be taken to limit and eliminate the growth and spread of exotic species. Utilizing existing studies (e.g., Rodgers and Schwikert 2000) and any new studies, refuge staff will work with the partners to establish buffer zones and closed areas around those islands serving key habitat needs within the refuge to limit wildlife and habitat disturbance. The refuge will continue to acquire all applicable permits related to management activities regarding natural and spoil islands, including prescribed fire activities and earthmoving activities associated with shoreline stabilization and exotic plant control and removal.

Strategies:

- Survey wildlife abundance and distribution on refuge islands and determine baseline populations for shorebirds on these islands.
- Develop outreach materials and educational displays to promote public awareness of fish and wildlife threats on and around refuge islands.
- Coordinate restoration and protection strategies with the partners to limit wildlife disturbances. Work with the partners to develop outreach materials to increase awareness and understanding of the importance of disturbance free areas for wildlife.
- Increase enforcement and patrol of the refuge's waterways and islands and improve coordination with State partners to protect these fish and wildlife communities from disturbance within the refuge's boundary.
- Remove all exotic, nuisance, and invasive species from key spoil islands serving wildlife needs (e.g., Pelican Island and Preacher's Island).
- Eliminate exotic plants as the primary land cover type on all refuge islands.

Objective B.5: **Aquatic Habitats**

Throughout the 15-year life of the plan, maintain over 4,500 acres of lagoonal waters on the refuge (including open estuarine waters, seagrasses, drift algae, exposed bottoms, and fish spawning and settlement sites) for a variety of aquatic and birds species and coordinate management of 280 acres of the open water portion of impoundments to increase foraging opportunities for water birds.

Discussion: Over 70 percent of the refuge is aquatic habitats, with the bulk represented in the Indian River Lagoon and with a smaller portion in the impoundments. Several federally listed species occur in or use the aquatic habitats of the refuge: Johnson's seagrass; bald eagle; wood stork; Atlantic salt marsh snake; Eastern indigo snake; American alligator; green, loggerhead, leatherback, hawksbill, and Kemp's ridley sea turtles; and West Indian manatee. Since the fish spawning and settlement sites found in the estuary on the refuge are so important to the future of certain fish species, it is imperative that they be protected (e.g., two of the three known sea trout spawning sites in the southern Indian River Lagoon are located in the refuge). Refuge staff will work with Indian River Mosquito Control District to actively manage and monitor the impoundments for multiple objectives, including wildlife feeding areas (e.g., for wood storks, shorebirds, neotropical migratory birds, and waterfowl), fisheries, salt marsh habitat, mangrove habitat, and mosquito control. With over a decade of the same management operations for the impoundments, no conflicts or impacts to federally listed species have been found. Managing the water levels in the impoundments has proven foraging benefits for wood storks. The refuge will continue to acquire all applicable permits related to management activities regarding aquatic habitats.

Strategies:

- Coordinate management, including enforcement, protection, and lease agreement modifications with appropriate agencies to sustain key fish spawning and settlement sites (e.g., spotted seatrout, black drum, and silver perch). Work with State of Florida to modify the lease agreement or develop a new approach to provide protection for these key sites. Management actions to limit negative wildlife and habitat impacts could include, but are not limited to the seasonal closure of specific areas to protect key fish spawning and settlement sites and the establishment of pole only zones in sensitive, shallow, seagrass areas. Work with appropriate public agencies to identify and evaluate the existing impacts to important fish habitat and reduce impacts to important fish habitat. Maintain the ban on mechanical harvesting of shellfish in the refuge.
- Determine existing boat traffic and associated impacts to aquatic habitats and associated species.
- Coordinate with the Service's South Florida Fisheries Resource Office and the Florida Fish and Wildlife Conservation Commission to conduct the State Creel Survey and other independent surveys to determine catch per unit effort and angler success on the refuge.
- Continue managing impoundments with Indian River Mosquito Control District (i.e., Bird's and Pete's impoundments) and modify management to maximize conditions for shorebirds. Monitor conditions to limit pesticide use, as appropriate.
- Determine species' needs for water levels, durations, and depths in refuge impoundments.
- Determine invertebrate fauna under present impoundment management. Investigate options to increase production and availability of food and habitat for migrating birds.
- Monitor shorebird use of the impoundments of the refuge. Implement a monitoring program for July, August, and September to include possible juvenile shorebirds making early migration. Address the need of these juvenile shorebirds for shoreline habitat. Implement the International Shorebird Survey protocol for shorebird surveys.

- Build observation platforms for surveys. Incorporate impoundment dike vegetation as habitat managed for neotropical migratory birds.
- Investigate the influence of nutrient dynamics of impounded mangrove wetlands and the role of Rotational Impoundment Management in black mangrove community domination.
- Investigate the habitat needs of the smalltooth sawfish (federally endangered). Adapt management of aquatic habitats as necessary to support this species.
- Investigate the needs of the habitat needs of the opossum pipefish (which is considered a candidate species). Adapt management of aquatic habitats as necessary to support this species.

Objective B.6: Migratory and Resident Bird Habitats

Throughout the 15-year life of the plan, manage the refuge's sub-tropical barrier island and lagoonal habitats to support the nesting, resting, and foraging of migratory and resident native birds of the Peninsular Florida Physiographic Region.

Discussion: A number of migratory neotropical birds utilize coastal hammocks as a migration stop-over site and for overwintering. Protecting, restoring, and managing suitable habitat is increasingly important as Florida develops and remaining hammocks and coastal woodlands are fragmented or decimated, leaving fewer and fewer sites for migratory birds. Table 5 outlines the land use/land cover classifications anticipated within the 15-year life of the comprehensive conservation plan. Outlined habitat restoration, creation, and management activities to support refuge wildlife, including migratory and resident bird species are varied and include restoring about 67 acres of upland forests to maintain approximately 73 acres on the refuge; maintaining 5.3 acres in an old field (i.e., refugia habitat for southeastern beach mouse also benefits migratory and resident birds); restoring, creating, and maintaining about 425 acres of maritime hammock; maintaining about 743 acres of mangrove swamps; and maintaining several wetlands, ponds, and marshes totaling about 140 acres. The refuge will continue to acquire all applicable permits related to management activities regarding migratory and resident birds.

Strategies:

- Allow areas associated with high topography within impoundments to be colonized by patches of low shrubs/brush and include thorny shrub species.
- Provide a mosaic of recently mowed dikes and medium-tall grass dike habitats to support anis, kingfishers, kingbirds, and shrikes.
- Enhance cordgrass/rush for nesting habitat in salt marshes for wrens. Provide sedge-dominated shallow marsh habitats with scattered shrubs (with little or no standing water) in winter.
- Enhance scrub thickets adjoining marshes for warblers. In winter and during migration, provide dikes with short grass and saline-tolerant cover. Provide patches of dense willows near water. Provide shade trees near impounded wetlands, freshwater ponds, and sloughs.
- Manage for a mix of coastal cordgrass/black needlerush/drop-seed/saltgrass/marsh elder habitats for sparrows.
- Manage large expanses of open grassland environments near impoundments year-round and during migration for blackbirds.
- Increase the availability of habitat for painted buntings on the refuge.
- Restore and manage habitats for wintering and breeding rails. (Increasing the amount of emergent wetlands available will benefit all four species of rails: clapper, king, yellow, and black.)

Continue working with the partners to protect and conserve the natural and cultural resources of the refuge and the Indian River Lagoon system.

Objective C.1: Inholdings
Seek to acquire or otherwise protect the remaining inholdings, totaling ±403 acres, within the refuge's existing acquisition boundary within the 15-year life of the plan.

Discussion: The protection of additional lands is subject to the contribution of those lands to the biological needs of the refuge and national funding priorities. Land acquisition is subject to its contribution to the overall habitat configuration, its contribution to the overall forest configuration, and its contribution to fish and wildlife populations and habitat objectives, as well as subject to whether or not landowners are interested in selling their lands. Land acquisition assists in overall efforts to establish and/or sustain source populations of migratory birds, endangered, threatened, and resident species.

Due to high development pressures experienced in this area, the Service has identified several priority tracts in the existing acquisition boundary for inclusion under refuge management. The highest priority tract that the Service wants to acquire is the Tor West Tract (±44.59 acres). Additional key inholdings of about 14.73 acres that are second priority acquisitions include lands that would join two refuges: the Paskor Tract (±4.49 acres) and the United Real Estate Venture Tract (±10.24 acres). The United Real Estate Venture Tract was formerly called the Wilcox and Mills tracts [i.e., Tracts 49 of the Pelican Island acquisition and Tract 376 of the Archie Carr acquisition (Wilcox Tract), 6.56 acres, and Tract 59 of the Pelican Island acquisition and Tract 377c of the Archie Carr acquisition (Mills Tract), 3.68 acres]. (Although the former Mills Tract includes a substantial residence, it is surrounded by refuge lands and this tract would help buffer those surrounding refuge lands). (Figure 14 delineates the priority land acquisitions.) Once these and other inholdings are acquired, refuge staff will develop restoration plans to mimic natural conditions and hydrology, based on the refuge's wildlife and habitat priorities.

Strategies:

- Focus acquisition efforts on the priority tracts.
- Prioritize remaining inholding tracts and seek to acquire or otherwise manage these tracts. Establish acquisition priorities based on greatest threats and habitat needs.
- Initiate and continue contact with all landowners within the acquisition boundary. Determine the status of willing sellers.
- Develop a coordinated approach with partners to appropriately locate areas of greatest conservation concern.
- Seek partnerships with conservation organizations and others to complete the refuge's acquisition boundary.

Objective C.2: Bureau of Land Management Withdrawal
Within 10 years and before 2019, seek to obtain fee title ownership or permanent management authority from the Bureau of Land Management (BLM) for BLM's 37.5-acre withdrawal within the refuge's existing acquisition boundary.

Figure 14. Land acquisition priorities (as of October 2003)

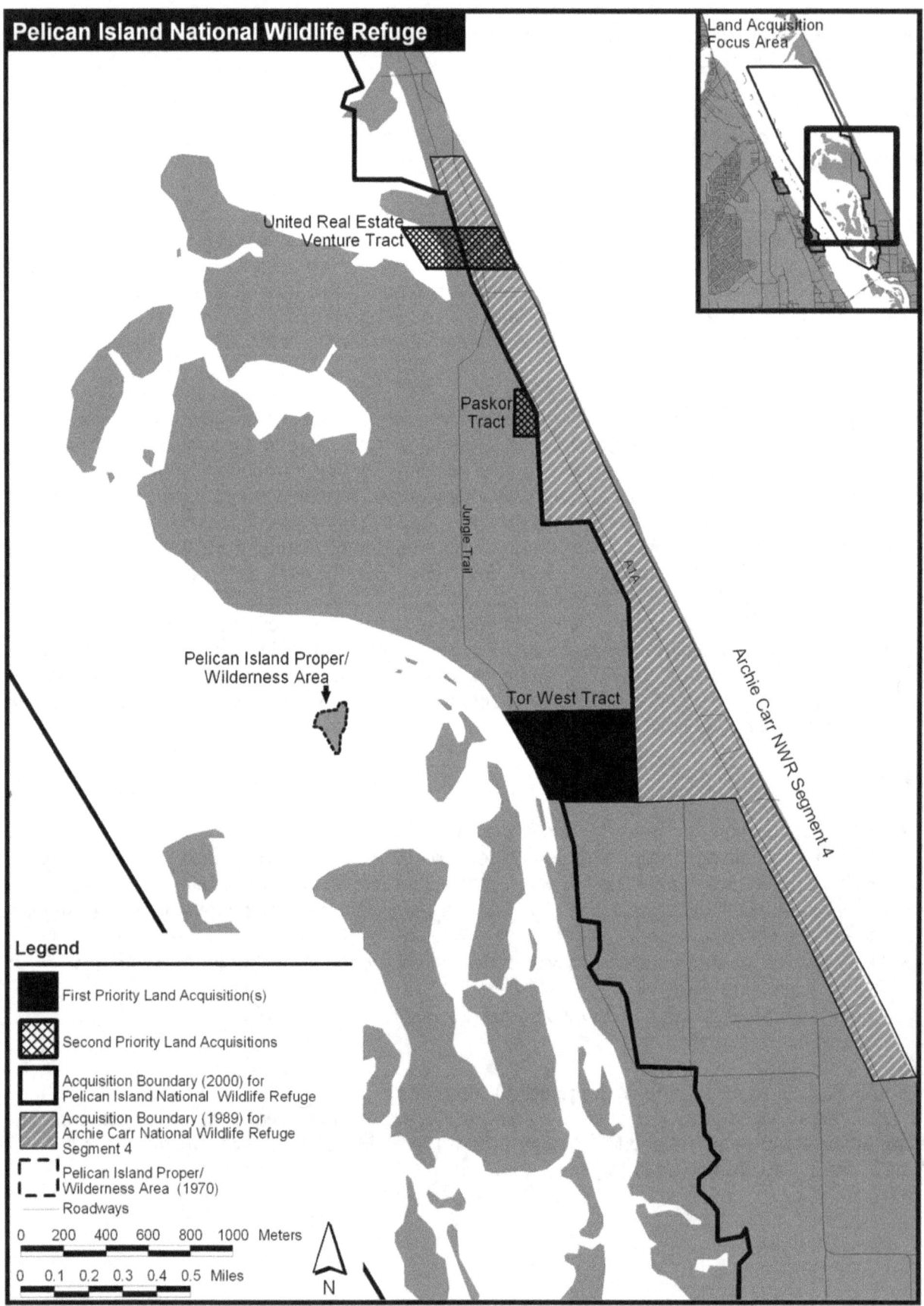

Pelican Island National Wildlife Refuge

Land Acquisition Focus Area

United Real Estate Venture Tract

Paskor Tract

Jungle Trail

A1A

Pelican Island Proper/ Wilderness Area

Tor West Tract

Archie Carr NWR Segment 4

Legend

◼ First Priority Land Acquisition(s)

▨ Second Priority Land Acquisitions

☐ Acquisition Boundary (2000) for Pelican Island National Wildlife Refuge

▨ Acquisition Boundary (1989) for Archie Carr National Wildlife Refuge Segment 4

⌐ ⌐ Pelican Island Proper/ Wilderness Area (1970)

— Roadways

0 200 400 600 800 1000 Meters

0 0.1 0.2 0.3 0.4 0.5 Miles

N

Discussion: Under a 40-year withdrawal from public domain, which expires in 2019, the Bureau of Land Management has title to 37.5 acres, which are currently managed by the Fish and Wildlife Service as part of the refuge.

Strategy:

- Coordinate the transfer of title of the Bureau of Land Management property.

Objective C.3: **Duck Point**
Within 10 years of plan approval, work with the partners to seek to protect fishes, wading birds, shorebirds, and other wildlife from disturbance within the refuge's existing acquisition boundary at a targeted 33 acres of the nearly 144-acre Duck Point site.

Discussion: Beyond the higher priority acquisitions outlined under objectives C.1 and C.2, the Service will also pursue management agreements for and acquisitions of the other inholdings (e.g., a management agreement for the targeted 33-acres of the Duck Point site).

Strategy:

- Develop a coordinated approach with partners to appropriately locate areas of greatest conservation concern.

Objective C.4: **Technical Assistance**
Throughout the 15-year life of the plan, provide technical assistance and, when appropriate, utilize private lands conservation programs to develop partnerships with landowners to achieve wildlife and habitat objectives to protect fishes, wading birds, shorebirds, and other wildlife characteristic of the southern Indian River Lagoon.

Discussion: The refuge will continue working with the partners and providing technical assistance for the conservation of natural resources on and off the refuge, including the 33-acre Duck Point site, the spoil islands off Duck Point, and area impoundments.

Management of the publicly owned 33-acre Duck Point site should include the installation of water control structures to reconnect the impoundments to the tidal estuary, mimicking the tidal regime, providing access for fisheries, and allowing for the natural development of shellfish nursery habitats. (The Duck Point site and adjacent lands are one of the options for the location of a visitor center for the refuge.)

Located between the main portion of the refuge and the proposed Duck Point management area, five spoil islands (totaling ±2 acres) are serving as important nesting and foraging areas for a variety of birds. They are adjacent to publicly owned and managed lands and waters (e.g., Service, State of Florida, and Florida Inland Navigation District). The refuge and the partners should coordinate management to protect these islands and the birds using them.

The Indian River Mosquito Control District manages impoundments along the Indian River Lagoon, off the refuge. The refuge will provide technical assistance to increase feeding opportunities for birds such as wood storks in many of these impoundments.

Strategies:

- Coordinate land conservation activities with private, local, state, and federal conservation land owners and managers.
- Conduct seminars for local land managers (private and public) on habitat management, current research and monitoring, and watershed issues.
- Communicate with adjacent and key landowners and other community organizations and participate in local Chamber of Commerce to promote outreach and cooperation in the management of the refuge and adjacent resources.
- Coordinate with the partners to enable better wildlife and habitat management of Duck Point and the adjacent spoil islands.

Objective C.5: **Kroegel Homestead Land Preservation**
Within the 15-year life of the plan, acquire and protect at least the core 15.71 acres of the Kroegel Homestead (which was the home of the first National Wildlife Refuge Manager) to provide future interpretation for visitors regarding the conservation pioneer, Paul Kroegel; the refuge; and the history of the National Wildlife Refuge System to increase awareness of the refuge, wildlife conservation, and the National Wildlife Refuge System.

Discussion: The Kroegel Homestead is an integral piece of the history of the National Wildlife Refuge System, Pelican Island Refuge, and the local community. Several options exist for management of the Kroegel Homestead site, including managing the existing structures and site as an interpretive site or developing a modest visitor center on the site. A Preliminary Project Proposal and Visitor Center Scoping Review in 2000 identified the Kroegel Homestead and adjacent parcels as the preferred site for a visitor center. (Other potential sites for a visitor center facility include Duck Point; the Environmental Learning Center on Wabasso Island, just south of the refuge; and a refuge site in the Jungle Trail area.) The establishment of a modest visitor center facility on the Kroegel Homestead is subject to negotiations with the Kroegel family and the partners. Negotiations are underway with the Kroegel family to acquire the Paul Kroegel parcel and the rest of the core tract. The Service, Indian River County, the State of Florida, and other partners are intent on purchasing this site with the Service acting as the lead manager. The entire Kroegel Homestead acquisition boundary is approximately 66 acres, while the core tract is 15.71 acres. (See Figure 15 for the Kroegel Homestead acquisition boundary and the 15.71-acre core tract. Also, please see Goal D, Education and Visitor Services, for a more complete discussion regarding the development of a visitor center for the refuge.)

Strategies:

- Continue working with the partners to acquire and manage the Kroegel Homestead.
- Continue pursuing funding options for acquisition of this site (e.g., through grants).
- After acquisition, submit the Kroegel Homestead for inclusion in the National Historic Register as a National Historic Landmark.

Objective C.6: **Lease Agreement**
Within five years of plan approval and before 2018, pursue the authority to enforce federal fish and wildlife regulations on all refuge-owned and managed lands and waters by working with the State of Florida and other partners to modify the existing state lease.

Figure 15. Core Kroegel homestead tract

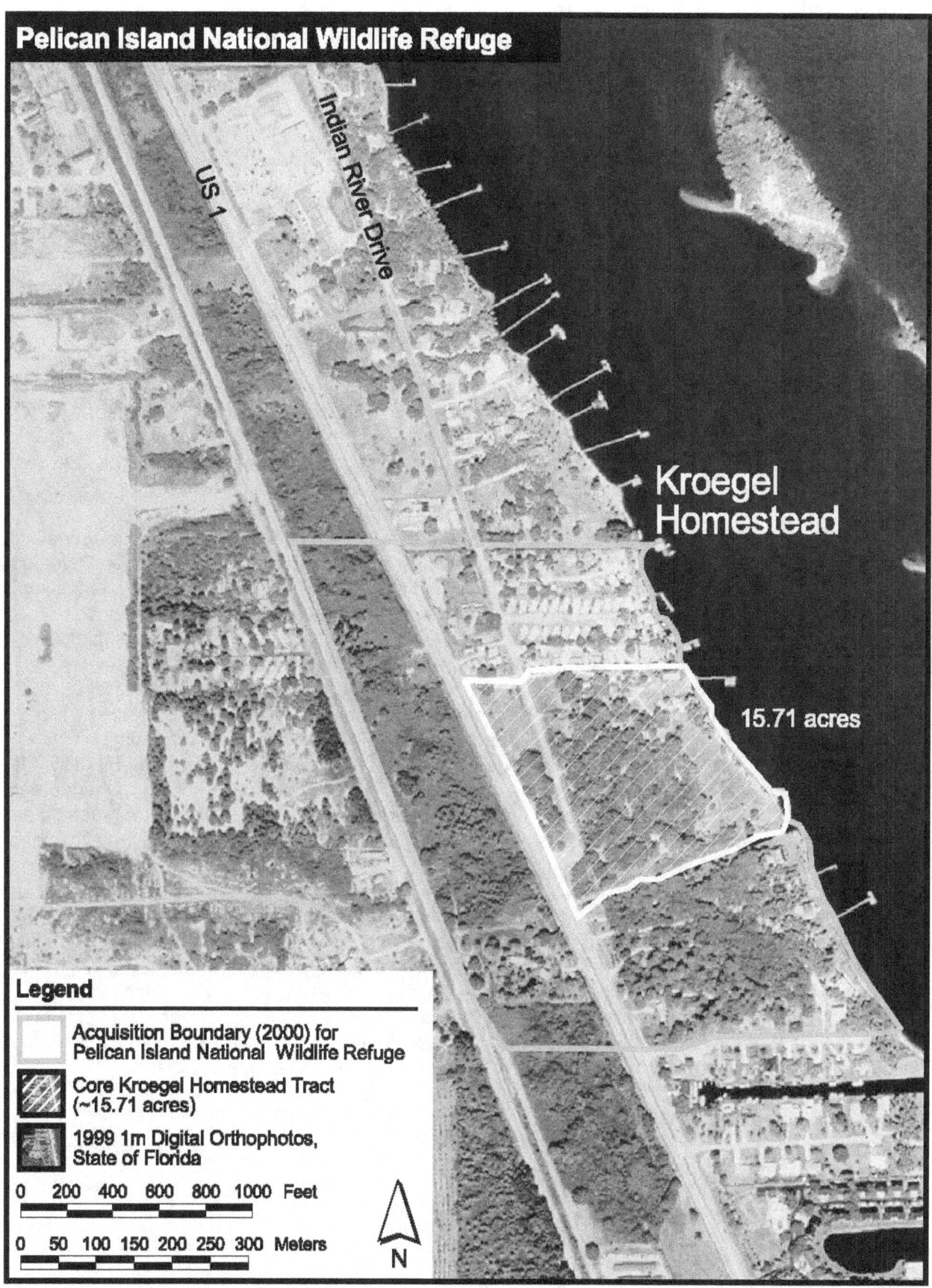

Pelican Island National Wildlife Refuge

US 1

Indian River Drive

Kroegel
Homestead

15.71 acres

Legend

Acquisition Boundary (2000) for
Pelican Island National Wildlife Refuge

Core Kroegel Homestead Tract
(~15.71 acres)

1999 1m Digital Orthophotos,
State of Florida

0   200   400   600   800   1000   Feet

0   50   100   150   200   250   300   Meters

N

Discussion: In cooperation since 1968, the Service has leased the bulk of the refuge from the State of Florida. To better understand the lease between the Service and the State of Florida, it is necessary to look at the ownership history of some of these lands and waters. In 1909, 6 years after establishing Pelican Island Refuge, President Roosevelt expanded the refuge by Executive Order, "embracing all small islands within sections 9 and 10, T.31S. R.39E.," later interpreted to include nearly 174 acres. In 1963, the Bureau of Land Management further expanded the refuge to 774 acres. In 1968 (with the official transfer in 1970), the State of Florida claimed the area of these two expansions under the Swamp and Overflow Act as state lands and waters. Then later in 1968, the State of Florida leased 4,640 acres of state lands and waters to the Service as part of Pelican Island Refuge. Today, this lease covers ±4,737.54 acres, which constitutes 88 percent of the lands and waters under current refuge management and 77 percent of the refuge's acquisition boundary. This lease was amended in 2000 and expires in 2018 with an option to renew for another 25 years.

Under the current lease agreement with the State of Florida, traditional uses are allowed within the leased area of the refuge.

> The right of the public to use the area for traditional navigation, boating, bathing, shell fishing, and commercial and sport fishing shall not be restricted, with the exception of a 410(-)foot buffer zone surrounding Pelican Island (Government Lot 3, Township 31 South, Range 39 East, Indian River County). This buffer zone is measured from the mean high water line of said Island and extending out into the Indian River.

The current lease agreement within the State of Florida does not specify control of using personal watercraft (like jet skis) and camping on spoil islands which are uncontrolled on the refuge. Camping on the spoil islands may be determined to be a traditional use under the lease agreement, but using personal watercraft is unlikely to qualify as traditional as of 1968 (the date of the original lease agreement). Using personal watercraft and camping negatively impact manatees, turtles, migratory birds, and other native species using the refuge. The refuge and the State of Florida must work together to limit negative wildlife and habitat impacts. Management actions to limit these negative impacts could include, but are not limited to, seasonal closures of specific areas to protect key fish spawning and settlement sites, closed areas around islands to protect nesting and foraging birds, elimination of bank fishing from all natural islands, slow speed and no wake zones, and pole only zones, as well as better management for multi-species benefits of the mosquito control management activities in Bird's and Pete's impoundments by Indian River Mosquito Control District. At such time as the lease is altered or it is otherwise feasible, all uses not considered compatible will be eliminated (e.g., using personal watercraft and camping).

As part of the comprehensive conservation planning effort, the Service and the Florida Fish and Wildlife Conservation Commission (FWC) worked together to develop revised language regarding the lease area and the implementation of FWC and Service regulations in the leased area. Fishing regulations and restrictions will be coordinated between the Service and the FWC, which exercises jurisdiction under the Florida Constitution with respect to marine life. FWC regulations will apply on the leased portion of the refuge, in support of refuge management of fishing as a priority public use. Other regulations implemented by the Service in furtherance of its overall management responsibilities will be coordinated with FWC as needed.

Strategies:

- Consider various options, including amending the present lease agreement with the State of Florida, using an inter-agency approach to apply refuge regulations to all refuge-managed areas, developing a Memorandum of Understanding with the State of Florida, and creating special management areas.
- If a lease amendment or other approach will not accomplish this objective, create special management areas within the lease for designated areas such as rookeries, roosts, foraging areas, and fish spawning sites. Some of these will be applied only during critical periods (e.g., for rookeries during nesting). These special management areas could be tested with short term (i.e., 5-year and 10-year) experimental management agreements. Post these sites with refuge signs and specific regulations, as appropriate.
- Apply current research to implement needed buffer zones (e.g., Rodgers and Schwikert 2000) under whatever lease or agreement is applicable to a particular site (e.g., bird rookery). Ensure that staff monitors the effectiveness of these buffer zones.
- Coordinate with the partners on law enforcement issues of the refuge (e.g., through a law enforcement team). (Since all the law enforcement partners are part of the National Estuary Program for the Indian River Lagoon, all have a stake in the law enforcement issues of the refuge.) Continue to work with the Florida Department of Environmental Protection's Coastal and Aquatic Managed Areas office to increase the presence of federal and state law enforcement on the refuge.
- Pursue the authority to protect the few known spawning sites in the Indian River Lagoon for spotted seatrout, black drum, and silver perch.
- Phase out camping and using personal watercraft within the refuge's boundary.

GOAL D: EDUCATION AND VISITOR SERVICES

Promote awareness and appreciation within the local community and amongst refuge visitors of the unique values of the wildlife and habitats of the refuge's sub-tropical and barrier island system and of the National Wildlife Refuge System.

Discussion: The National Wildlife Refuge System Administration Act of 1966, as amended by the National Wildlife Refuge System Improvement Act of 1997, states that national wildlife refuges must be protected from incompatible or harmful human activities to ensure that Americans can enjoy the Refuge System long into the future. Before activities or uses are allowed on a national wildlife refuge, the uses must be found to be compatible. A compatible use is one that will not materially interfere with or detract from the fulfillment of the mission of the Refuge System or the purposes of the refuge [§668ee(1) USC]. "Wildlife-dependent recreational uses may be authorized on a refuge when they are compatible and not inconsistent with public safety" [§668dd(d)(3)(A)(iii) USC,]. See Appendix V for the compatibility determinations.

In order to implement a comprehensive visitor services program, additional staff will be needed, including a Refuge Ranger. In order to provide wildlife viewing and environmental education and interpretation opportunities, new facilities will be developed. With additional staff and facilities, the Service is eager to welcome and orient visitors, develop key resource awareness, provide and manage priority public use opportunities, maintain cultural resources, and project a positive image of the Refuge System and of the Fish and Wildlife Service. Deficiencies in current Pelican Island recreation and environmental education activities have been evaluated and the outlined goal, objectives, and strategies support the purposes of the refuge and the mission of the Refuge System.

A Preliminary Project Proposal and Visitor Center Scoping Review in 2000 identified the Kroegel Homestead and adjacent parcels as the preferred site for a visitor center. (Other potential sites considered for a visitor center facility included Duck Point; the Environmental Learning Center on Wabasso Island; St. Sebastian River Buffer Preserve; and a site between the Kroegel Homestead and Duck Point.) Refuge land between A1A and Jungle Trail was not considered at that time because of political opposition. The establishment of a modest visitor center facility on the Kroegel Homestead is subject to negotiations with the Kroegel family and the partners. Recent attempts in 2004 to acquire the Kroegel Homestead failed. Thus, all other options should be reconsidered for constructing a modest visitor center, including Refuge land between A1A and Jungle Trail. A modest visitor center is generally defined as one that will not exceed 6,000 square feet.

Objective D.1: Bank Fishing
Within 10 years of plan approval, improve opportunities for high quality bank fishing and designate, map, and sign these sites within the Indian River Lagoon portion of the refuge.

Discussion: Under the existing lease agreement with the State of Florida, fishing and boating are not restricted by the refuge in the leased area. Current uses include those which are negatively impacting wildlife and habitats (e.g., using personal watercraft and camping on the spoil islands). Current fishing activities and boating are impacting key fish spawning sites (e.g., boat propellers can damage submerged aquatic vegetation and juvenile fish). To limit negative wildlife and habitat impacts, the refuge will provide opportunities for bank fishing in less sensitive areas, allowing this use to occur on the refuge in a compatible manner. Opportunities for less restrictive fishing will continue to exist in the Indian River Lagoon, outside of the refuge's boundary. Most shellfish leases within the refuge have been relocated to a centralized area (called the Aquaculture Use Zone) and transferred outside the refuge's lease boundary with the State of Florida. All remaining shellfish leases will need to be transferred or reviewed for compatibility.

Strategies:

- As appropriate, coordinate management with the State of Florida and seek to modify stipulations in the agreement impacting key resources.
- Develop maps and brochures identifying bank fishing sites and include regulatory and educational information. Locate these maps and brochures at all refuge kiosks and the visitor center, at the city of Sebastian's Riverview Park kiosk, and at Indian River County's Wabasso Causeway kiosk. Evaluate other boats ramps for distribution of maps and brochures.
- Conduct regular patrol and enforcement activities.
- Work with the partners and public to consider and implement any needed regulations, such as seasonal closures of specific areas to protect key fish spawning and settlement sites, closed areas around islands to protect nesting and foraging birds, and pole only zones. Eliminate bank fishing from all natural islands of the refuge.
- Coordinate with the state to transfer remaining shellfish leases outside of the refuge boundary.

Objective D.2: Wildlife Observation and Photography
Within five years of plan approval, develop and maintain refuge visitor facilities, including a wildlife drive and additional trails and boardwalks, in the Jungle Trail area to provide opportunities to view and photograph wildlife characteristic of the southern Indian River Lagoon.

Discussion: Figure 13 details the existing and proposed public use facilities in the Jungle Trail area, including the existing dike trails, the Centennial Trail boardwalk, the rookery observation tower, the proposed wildlife drive, additional trails, and boardwalks, as well as the parking and restroom facilities constructed and maintained by Indian River County. Several of the existing and proposed public use facilities are or will be handicapped accessible (e.g., Centennial Trail, observation tower, visitor center, and restroom facilities). Figure 16 outlines the existing and proposed visitor facilities for the entire refuge (i.e., the visitor facilities anticipated to be available during the 15-year life of this plan). The refuge will continue to acquire all applicable permits related to constructing visitor facilities.

The refuge will make all efforts possible and practicable to limit wildlife impacts related to increased visitation. Measures to limit wildlife impacts related to increased visitation include establishing and enforcing closed areas (e.g., for bird rookeries), controlling access (e.g., open only certain hours, open only certain seasons, and open to limited numbers of visitors), and conveying ethical wildlife viewing messages (e.g., through brochures, interpretive talks, and presentations).

Strategies:

- Maintain the existing dike trails, boardwalk, and observation tower.
- Seek funding within the Service and with the partners to develop and maintain the proposed wildlife drive, additional trails and boardwalks, and other visitor facilities.
- Develop interpretive signs and brochures for the trails, wildlife drive, boardwalks, and observation tower.
- Offer volunteer-led interpretive tours and programs.
- Provide wildlife checklists for the refuge at informational kiosks.
- Conduct regular patrol and enforcement activities

Objective D.3: **Environmental Education**
Within 10 years of plan approval, conduct environmental education and outdoor classroom programs, activities, and tours for local schools, groups, and organizations to increase awareness and understanding of the importance of the refuge's sub-tropical barrier island, lagoonal habitats and wildlife, and Wilderness Area, and the importance of the refuge to the Indian River Lagoon, the South Florida Ecosystem, and the National Wildlife Refuge System.

Discussion: Given the mass development of the landscape and the sensitivity of many of the resources, environmental education is one of the best ways to increase awareness and understanding to change behaviors to better protect these resources. During the public scoping process, environmental education was one of the top issues mentioned. With additional staff, the refuge will be able to coordinate with community-based environmental education partners to increase awareness and understanding of the refuge, the National Wildlife Refuge System, threatened and endangered species, and other resources (e.g., shorebirds, migratory birds, hydrologic cycle, coastal and estuary systems, and biological diversity) by annually conducting at least eight environmental education programs on-site or off-site and by annually conducting at least one outdoor classroom activity on-site or off-site. Off-site locations for environmental education activities will include local schools, the Environmental Learning Center, and key sites on nearby public conservation lands. On-site locations include the proposed visitor center and the public use facilities in the Jungle Trail area (Figure 16). Included in these education efforts and materials will be an ethical wildlife viewing message. Environmental education partners include Environmental Learning Center, Environthon, St. Johns River Water Management District, St. Sebastian River Buffer Preserve (Florida Department of Environmental Protection), Sebastian Inlet State Park (Florida Department of Environmental Protection), and the school district of Indian River County. Partnerships and resources are needed to conserve Wilderness by developing a program to foster knowledge and understanding of wilderness values. The refuge is increasingly becoming a place for study and research. The refuge will continue to acquire all applicable permits related to management activities regarding environmental education.

Figure 16. Existing and proposed refuge visitor and office facilities

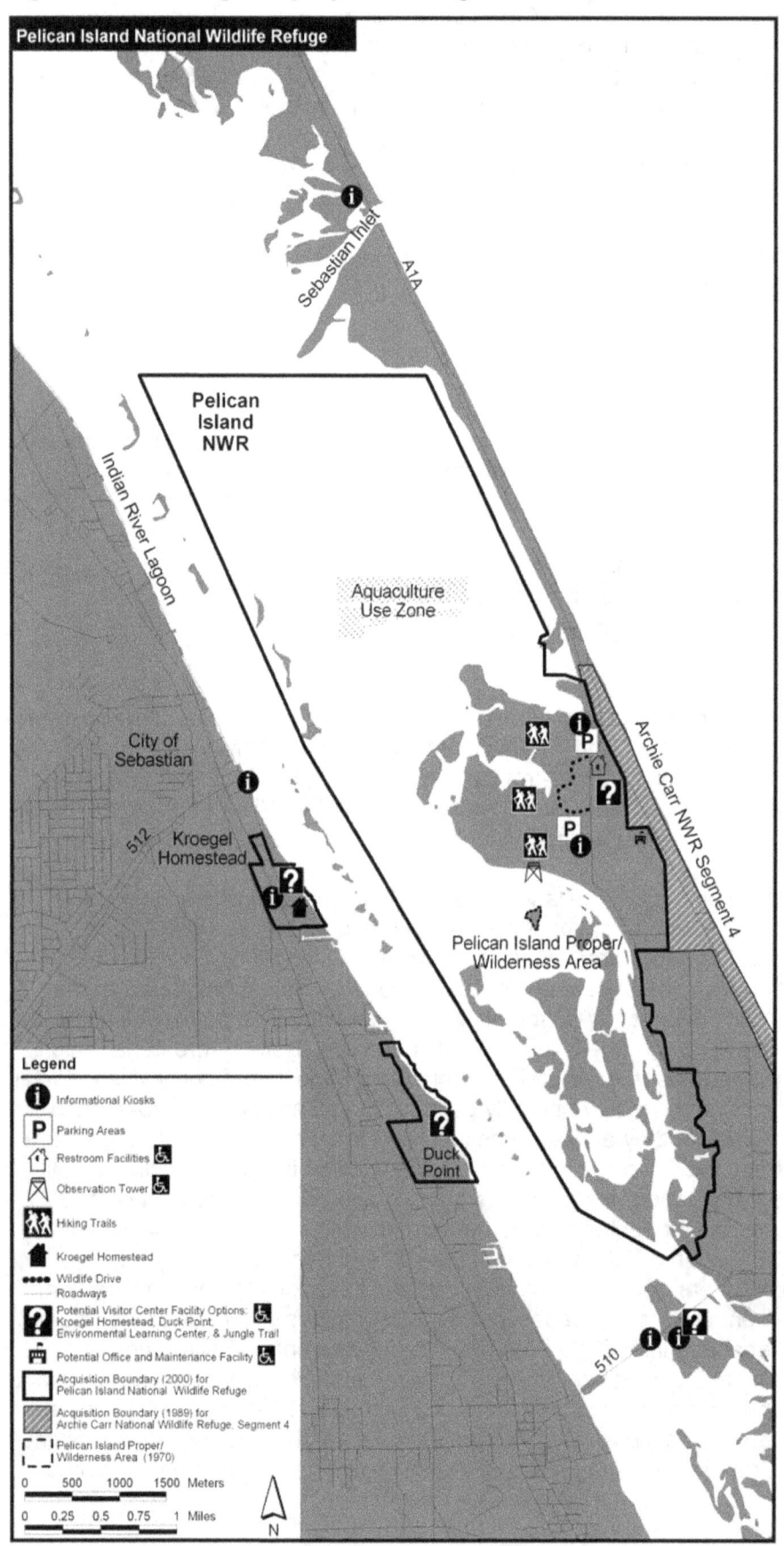

Strategies: (General)

- Develop a local working group of environmental education partners as a sub-group of the Pelican Island Working Group. This working group will coordinate existing education efforts and plan a cohesive and comprehensive environmental education program for the area.
- Engage Pelican Island Preservation Society heavily in producing and providing environmental education materials, facilities, and activities.
- Maintain facilities and manage programs to support environmental education activities.
- Construct a modest visitor center to support environmental education activities.
- Identify and engage new partners to further environmental education efforts in the area, including partners in the business community (e.g., The Disney Company through Disney's Vero Beach Resort).
- Coordinate with Sebastian River High School to help students fulfill community service requirements.
- Work with the partners (e.g., Environmental Learning Center and Brevard County Barrier Island Ecosystem Center) to increase awareness of the importance of healthy, functional coastal and estuarine habitats.
- Sample participants in environmental education and outdoor classroom programs, activities, and tours to measure the trend in the awareness and understanding of the importance of the refuge's sub-tropical barrier island and lagoonal habitats and wildlife and the importance of the refuge to the Indian River Lagoon, the South Florida Ecosystem, and the National Wildlife Refuge System.

Strategies: (Refuge Users)

- Provide educational talks to local user groups.
- Coordinate management with volunteers to educate refuge visitors (utilizing signs, brochures, and permit information) about how to reduce threats to wildlife.
- Work with the partners to develop stick-on console maps for watercraft, showing environmentally sensitive areas for waterborne recreationists (e.g., shallow seagrasses, rookeries/roosts, foraging areas, and closed areas).
- Educate the public on the need for buffers to limit wildlife disturbances and on the regulations for these areas. Work with partners to develop and disseminate brochures regarding disturbance effects on nesting, roosting, and foraging birds and the impacts of boating and personal watercraft.
- Educate people boating and fishing in and around the refuge about how monofilament fishing line, discarded nets, litter, and abandoned traps pose threats to fish and wildlife.

Strategies: (Wildlife and Habitats)

- Coordinate management with local sea turtle and educational groups (e.g., Friends of the Carr Refuge, Sea Turtle Preservation Society, Sea Turtle Survival League, Caribbean Conservation Corporation, Ocean Conservancy, and Environmental Learning Center) to continue and expand sea turtle information and education activities.
- Coordinate management with environmental education partners to increase public awareness and appreciation of wood storks (e.g., through talks, educational materials, and brochures).
- Educate the public about the importance of protecting fish spawning and settlement sites through outreach programs and information provided at informational kiosks.

- Determine the applicability of Shorebird Sister Schools and Sister Cities programs and adaptability of Shorebird Sister School materials for Pelican Island. (For more information on Shorebird Sister Schools, see http://sssp.fws.gov/index.cfm.)
- Determine the applicability of the Great Shorebird Trail initiative for the Pelican Island area.
- Implement a shorebird education program or component.
- Increase the understanding of how local habitat conditions affect shorebird abundance and use of the refuge.
- Implement a migratory bird education program or component. Provide educational materials on migratory birds at all informational kiosks and the visitor center.
- Increase awareness and appreciation of threatened and endangered species by providing education materials to schools, private landowners, policymakers, elected officials, and refuge visitors. Provide educational materials at informational kiosks and the visitor center.
- Increase public awareness about the southeastern beach mouse and about the value of the coastal dune ecosystem.
- Increase awareness of the Atlantic salt marsh snake.

Strategies: (Wilderness Stewardship)

- Include wilderness education materials and programs into refuge education efforts.
- Prepare a binder, including briefing statements, sample interpretive programs, digital photos, and a PowerPoint program on CD.
- Integrate wilderness themes into refuge interpretive services, including media development and the proposed visitor center.
- Develop a Pelican Island Wilderness fact sheet and newspaper article template.
- Contribute information, research findings, and data to Wilderness.net.
- Conduct training for refuge permanent and seasonal staff, volunteers, cooperating associations, researchers, and others on wilderness management policy and techniques as needed.
- Distribute wilderness management information to special task teams, volunteers, interns, researchers, and visitors where appropriate.
- Conduct education awareness workshops focused on wilderness stewardship management at Pelican Island Refuge as appropriate.

Objective D.4: Interpretation

Within five years of plan approval, provide interpretive opportunities to increase visitor awareness and understanding of the refuge's sub-tropical barrier island and lagoonal habitats and wildlife, especially the threatened and endangered species of the refuge and provide interpretive opportunities to increase visitor awareness and understanding of the history and importance of the refuge and the Refuge System.

Discussion: Interpretation plays a key role in a visitor's experience and environmental awareness. With increased staff, volunteers, and facilities, the refuge would be positioned to offer interpretive tours and programs. Interpretive panels at informational kiosks and along the boardwalks and trails will enhance the quality of experience and help increase environmental awareness. (See Figure 13 for the facilities in the Jungle Trail area, including the restroom and parking facilities being constructed and maintained by Indian River County.) The refuge should offer materials, facilities, and services to local businesses (e.g., at marinas and boat launch areas), schools, and residents to increase awareness and understanding of the purposes of refuge and the mission of Fish and Wildlife Service and to convey an ethical wildlife viewing message. The refuge will continue to acquire all applicable permits related to conducting interpretive programs and constructing any associated visitor facilities.

Strategies:

- Provide wildlife checklists for the refuge at all informational kiosks.
- Seek funding to develop and maintain the proposed wildlife drive and other facilities in the Jungle Trail area.
- Develop and maintain interpretive signs and brochures for the trails, wildlife drive, boardwalks, and observation tower.
- Maintain the Internet website with public notice of refuge events.
- Develop and maintain directional signs, brochures, and newsletters.
- Train volunteers and offer volunteer-led interpretive tours and programs.
- Construct a modest visitor center to support interpretive activities.
- Conduct regular patrol and enforcement activities.
- Create an entry for the refuge in the Great Florida Birding Trail Guide beyond the reference under the entry for Sebastian Inlet State Park. Provide Great Florida Birding Trail guides at informational kiosks throughout the refuge.
- Participate in other festivals and events in the area beyond the annual Pelican Island Wildlife Festival.
- Increase participation in local events and organizations and regularly provide refuge management updates.
- Provide outreach materials to local businesses and schools and at all informational kiosks.
- Work with the commercial operations and provide outreach and educational materials and training to the commercial operators and guides.
- Sample participants in interpretive programs and activities to measure the trend in the awareness and understanding of the refuge's sub-tropical barrier island and lagoonal habitats and wildlife, especially the threatened and endangered species of the refuge and the history and importance of the refuge and the Refuge System.

GOAL E. REFUGE ADMINISTRATION

Develop and implement a comprehensive refuge program, including providing sufficient staff, facilities, equipment, and volunteers to protect and manage the natural, cultural, and historical resources and features that define the birthplace of the National Wildlife Refuge System.

***Objective E.1:* Staff**
Within the 15-year life of the plan, provide a full complement of eleven permanent, full-time, well-trained staff to protect and manage the natural, cultural, and historical resources of the sub-tropical barrier island and lagoonal systems of the refuge.

Discussion: Figure 17 delineates the proposed organizational structure and staff for the refuge over the 15-year life of the plan.

Strategies:

- Staff the refuge with two permanent full-time refuge management positions (Refuge Manager and Assistant Refuge Manager), three permanent full-time biological program positions (Refuge Biologist and two Biological Science Technicians) and needed seasonal Biological Science Technicians, three permanent full-time public use program positions (two Refuge Rangers and a Refuge Officer), an Administrative Office Assistant, a Maintenance Worker (Heavy Equipment Operator), and a Supply Technician.

- Manage a comprehensive employee training program to ensure expertise in all program areas.

Objective E.2: **Volunteers**
Increase the participation of volunteers by 50 percent from 40 active volunteers to 60 within 10 years of plan approval to augment refuge staff, projects, and programs.

Discussion: The refuge currently has nearly 300 volunteers, with an active core of 40 dedicated volunteers who contribute time, money, and labor to a variety of refuge management activities from exotic plant control to public outreach. The refuge provides an orientation to all new volunteers, with special attention on federally listed species found on the refuge and on ethical wildlife viewing.

Figure 17. Proposed organizational structure

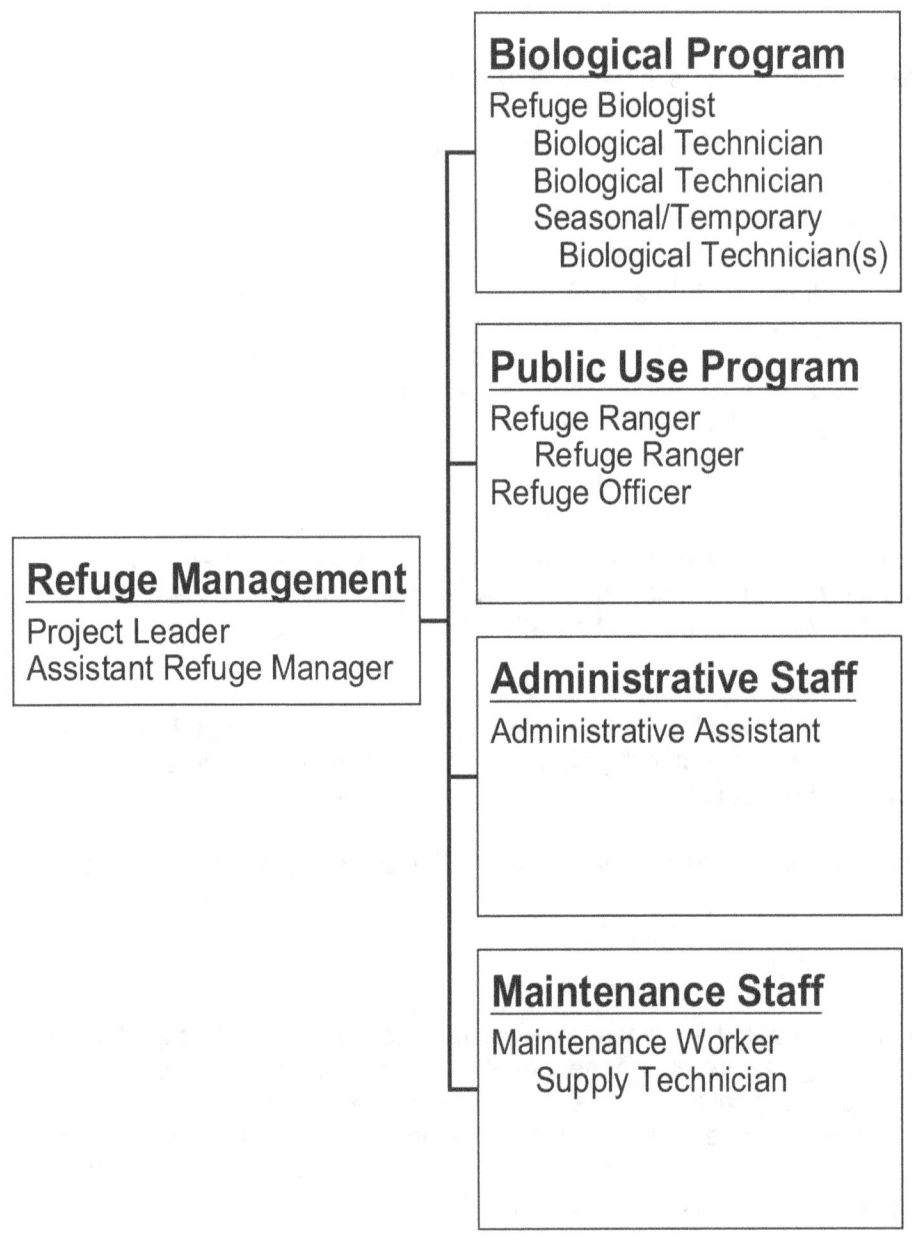

Biological Program
Refuge Biologist
   Biological Technician
   Biological Technician
   Seasonal/Temporary
      Biological Technician(s)

Public Use Program
Refuge Ranger
   Refuge Ranger
Refuge Officer

Refuge Management
Project Leader
Assistant Refuge Manager

Administrative Staff
Administrative Assistant

Maintenance Staff
Maintenance Worker
   Supply Technician

Strategies:

- Manage a comprehensive volunteer training program to ensure expertise in all program areas.
- Manage volunteer and student intern programs to compliment refuge staff and programs and to provide opportunities for interpretive activities and environmental education. Utilize volunteers to assist with refuge management activities, including the public use program (e.g., bird tours, annual wildlife festival, education and outreach efforts, trash cleanup, and boardwalk construction) and the biological program (e.g., bird surveys and exotic plant control).
- Coordinate with local groups (e.g., Pelican Island Preservation Society, Pelican Island Audubon Society, Friends of the Carr Refuge, Environmental Learning Center and Marine Resources Council) to conduct joint projects and to help recruit new volunteers for refuge projects.
- Contact Sebastian River High School about developing a volunteer program that will meet refuge needs and that will help fulfill the high school students' community volunteer requirements. Activities might include a refuge cleanup program, data collection to meet refuge data needs (e.g., bird surveys), and outreach programs (e.g., educate the high school students and then have them make informative presentations to area elementary, middle, and high school classes).
- Have volunteers and staff make informative and educational presentations about the refuge to local homeowners' associations and recruit new refuge volunteers from these groups.

Objective E.3: **Researchers**

Provide assistance and direct logistical support to qualified researchers to support ongoing cooperative investigations on the refuge and, within one year of plan approval, require a refuge special use permit for any and all research activities occurring on the refuge.

Discussion: The refuge provides orientation information to all researchers regarding all federally listed species found on the refuge. Requiring special use permits for all research activities, public and private, will help the refuge to track research activities on the refuge and will supply additional information to the refuge to better enable management decisions. Each special use permit will contain conditions necessary to ensure compatibility with the purposes of the refuge and other applicable missions, laws, and policies. Further, each special use permit will require the annual submission to the refuge of copies of annual or final reports or other data reporting mechanisms. The Refuge Manager will deny permits for any research activities that do not further the purposes and vision of the refuge or that otherwise violate existing policies, laws, or other rules. (As a result of this planning process, the refuge began issuing some special use permits in May 2002.) Further, all researchers are required to obtain all applicable permits before the commencement of research activities on the refuge.

Strategies:

- Require the application for and receipt of appropriate refuge permits for all research activities conducted within the lands and waters of the refuge.
- Coordinate all research activities conducted within the refuge through special use permits and provide technical oversight, assistance, and research support to individuals, agencies, and other institutions interested in conservation issue resolution on the refuge.
- Use special use permits to track research activities. Require annual updates and require the submission to the refuge of copies of all annual or final reports or other data reporting mechanisms.
- Market research needs to universities and public and non-profit research entities (e.g., Biological Resources Division, U.S. Geological Survey and Smithsonian Institute).

Objective E.4: **Visitor Center**

Throughout the 15-year life of the plan, pursue the development of a modest visitor center for Pelican Island National Wildlife Refuge to enable compatible, wildlife-dependent recreational use of the refuge, including fishing, observing and photographing wildlife, and participating in environmental education and interpretation; to tell the story of the refuge and the Refuge System; to increase recognition of the Fish and Wildlife Service; and to increase awareness of the threatened and endangered species, migratory birds, native wildlife, and native habitats of the sub-tropical lagoonal and barrier island system of the refuge.

Discussion: The preferred site for the proposed visitor center is at the Kroegel Homestead, the home of Paul Kroegel, the first Refuge Manager. The 1999 vision document identified the need to protect the Kroegel Homestead from development pressures being experienced in the area. The Service and its partners have been working together to purchase and manage the site (e.g., Indian River County purchased the Rodney Kroegel parcel, with the Service assisting in management of the site). A Preliminary Project Proposal in 1999 identified the Kroegel Homestead and adjacent properties as the preferred site for a visitor center and expanded the refuge's acquisition boundary to include the Homestead. And, a public use review in May 2001 identified the Kroegel Homestead as the most appropriate site for a visitor center. The Kroegel Homestead is located on the mainland, across the Intracoastal Waterway from Pelican Island proper and the rest of the refuge on the barrier island. Historic structures persist on the site. The history of the city of Sebastian is inextricably woven with the history of the refuge and the Kroegel Homestead, making this site key to interpreting the history and future of the refuge, the city, and the Refuge System. The annual Pelican Island Wildlife Festival is held just over 1/2-mile down the road from the Kroegel Homestead in the city of Sebastian's Riverview Park. Key issues involve negotiations with the Kroegel family for acquisition of the site and development of a modest visitor center that is in keeping with the historic character and nature of the site. Although all of these factors support the recommendation of siting a visitor center at the Homestead, key issues remain concerning the size of a visitor center and the level of public access. Kroegel family members, surrounding neighbors, and local partners wish to ensure that a visitor facility is in keeping with the historic character and nature of the site and that visitor access does not intrude on the privacy of the remaining family members and neighbors. These issues may prevent the Service from developing a visitor center on the Homestead in the foreseeable future.

Other options exist for the development of a visitor center for Pelican Island Refuge. In 1999, the Service identified a second site at Duck Point. However, most of this site is under public ownership through the Florida Inland Navigation District as a remediation and storage site for dredged material from the Intracoastal Waterway. The remainder of the Duck Point site is under private ownership which is proceeding with the development of condominiums. A third option for the location of a visitor center is on the barrier island portion of the refuge in the Jungle Trail area, near the public use facilities of the refuge. However, this option involves concerns with barrier island construction and increased visitation. A fourth option involves co-locating a visitor facility at the Environmental Learning Center on Wabasso Island just south of the refuge. This option includes concerns regarding ease of access, organizational identity, and site management. Regardless of the option selected, the refuge will acquire all applicable permits related to constructing a visitor center.

Strategies:

- Continue pursuing the location of a modest visitor center facility at the Kroegel Homestead.
- Pursue other options if the Kroegel Homestead location is not feasible.

Objective E.5: **Administrative/Maintenance Facilities**
Within 10 years, develop administrative/maintenance facilities sufficient to support refuge operations by providing office space in conjunction with the planned visitor center and/or by providing office space and a maintenance facility on a 5-acre site in the Jungle Trail area.

Discussion: The South Florida Ecological Services Field Office in Vero Beach currently provides office space to refuge personnel. All refuge staff are located in the Vero Beach office, which is about 30 minutes from the refuge. While the refuge does have a couple of pole sheds on the barrier island, other maintenance facilities are shared with the State of Florida at Sebastian Inlet State Park. The main office space is proposed to be co-located with the proposed visitor center. Another option is to build offices in conjunction with maintenance facilities on a 5-acre site in the Jungle Trail area, on the barrier island portion of the refuge, adjacent to the public use area (Figure 16). Regardless of the option selected, the refuge will acquire all applicable permits related to constructing administrative and maintenance facilities.

Strategies:

- Continue holding office space at the South Florida Ecological Services Field Office in Vero Beach until such time as sufficient facilities are constructed.
- Develop office facilities in conjunction with the planned visitor center.
- Develop maintenance and office facilities on a 5-acre site in the Jungle Trail area to be more accessible to the refuge and to the public facilities on the barrier island.

GOAL F. CULTURAL RESOURCES

Maintain and preserve, in perpetuity, the archaeological and historical resources of the refuge, especially Native American sites (e.g., Ais Indian sites) and the Kroegel Homestead (home of the first Refuge Manager).

Objective F.1: **Archaeological Resources**
Continue to coordinate with Indian River County, the State of Florida Historic Preservation Office, and other partners to list key archaeological sites in the State of Florida's Master Site File and to provide increased protection to these sites.

Discussion: The refuge includes several archaeological sites. Since these sites are fairly accessible to disruption, vandalism, and theft, additional protection is necessary.

Strategies:

- Consult with Native American tribes in Florida (i.e., Seminole and Miccosukee tribes) for input into management activities related to these sites.
- Conduct regular patrol and enforcement activities.
- Continue to work with the partners to list key sites in Florida's Master Site File.

Objective F.2: **Historical Resources**
Continue to coordinate with Indian River County, the State of Florida Historic Preservation Office, and other partners to manage the Kroegel Homestead and pursue the addition of this site to the National Historic Register as a National Historic Landmark.

Discussion: The refuge and the Kroegel Homestead are integral threads in the local community. The Kroegel Homestead is locally and nationally historically significant as the home of the first Refuge Manager. The Kroegel family is still involved in the local community and continues to live on the homestead. Beyond being an important historical element of the National Wildlife Refuge System, this site allows a visitor the opportunity to view the refuge and Pelican Island proper from the western shore of the Indian River Lagoon, much as Paul Kroegel did 100 years ago. (The Service and the partners continue to pursue acquisition of the Kroegel Homestead. This objective and these strategies are contingent upon this acquisition.)

Strategies:

- Develop some type of visitor facility on this site (e.g., kiosk, interpretive panels and viewing scopes, or a visitor center) in keeping with whatever agreements and/or conditions that are applied to the Homestead.
- Conduct regular patrol and enforcement activities.

V. Plan Implementation

BACKGROUND

As required by the National Wildlife Refuge System Improvement Act of 1997, the Service will manage all refuges in accordance with an approved comprehensive conservation plan, which, when implemented, will achieve refuge purposes; help fulfill the Refuge System mission; maintain and, where appropriate, restore the biological integrity, diversity, and environmental health of the refuge; help achieve the goals of the National Wilderness Preservation System; and meet other mandates.

FUNDING NEEDS

This plan recommends funding that is substantially above current budget allocations and subject to Congressional allocations on an annual basis. Capitol improvement projects, like the proposed visitor center, are generally funded based on local influences rather than on Refuge System or Service priorities. Pelican Island National Wildlife Refuge will effectively enhance interpretive and educational programs with a new visitor center and facilities to accommodate wildlife viewing in an undisturbed setting. The refuge also needs better scientific information on which to gauge the immediate and long-term impacts of recreational uses on wildlife and its habitat.

The recommended funding outlined is not a commitment from Congress or the Service for staff, operational, and maintenance increases, but represents a future management framework to meet the goals, objectives, and strategies identified in this plan. Other possible funding sources include grants, fee demonstration program, mitigation funds, and donations. See Table 6 for the current refuge staff and associated costs.

The Refuge System currently faces a backlog of maintenance and equipment needs. Under current conditions the needs of Pelican Island Refuge, which are recorded in the deferred Maintenance Management System (MMS), total $6.2 million. These needs will continue under this plan. See Table 7 for the currently unfunded MMS projects.

The currently unfunded Refuge Operating Needs (RONS) projects total $830,000 in first-year costs with $355,010 in annual recurring costs. These projects are in addition to the base operating budget of the refuge, which was $300,500 in fiscal year 2002. See Table 8 for the currently unfunded RONS projects. See Table 9 for the proposed staff and associated costs and Table 10 for the priority projects and estimated costs.

In addition to these projects, a variety of needed research projects exist today. These research projects cover a wide range of management issues, including threats and impacts to refuge wildlife and habitat; biology, life history, and habitat components of threatened and endangered species and other species of management concern (e.g., land crabs, woodrats, and green anoles); juvenile fish status; water quality; contaminants; wildlife disturbances; fibropapilloma disease; and the impacts of red tide events.

Table 6. Current staff and costs

Position	Estimated Annual Recurring Cost
Refuge Manager	$87,000
Refuge Biologist (funded 2001)	$86,000
Refuge Ranger (funded 2001)	$86,000
Biological Technician (funded 2001)	$53,000
Assistant Manager (funded 2003)	$80,000
Administrative Assistant (funded through 2004 rollover)	$53,000
Total	**$445,000**

Table 7. Current unfunded Maintenance Management System projects

Refuge Priority Rank	MMS Project Name (FY 2002)	Estimated Cost
1	Construct Administrative Office	$491,000
2	Construct Visitor Center Phase I	$899,000
3	Construct Visitor Center Phase II	$2,000,000
4	Construct Visitor Center Phase III	$1,357,000
5	Rehabilitate 2000 Pole Barn and Service Road	$56,000
6	Repair 1970 Pole Barn	$56,000
7	Replace Honda ATV	$6,000
8	Replace 1999 4x4 Dodge Ram 1500 Pickup	$23,000
9*	Construct Pelican Island Buffer Wildlife Drive	$632,000
10*	Construct public use facilities **	$425,000
None	Replace 2001 4x4 Dodge Ram 2500 Pickup	$25,000
None	Replace 2001 4x4 Chevrolet Tahoe	$32,000
None	Replace 2001 Ford Econoline Van	$24,000
None	Replace 2002 Dodge 3500 Van	$19,000
None	Replace 1992 Turner Gorilla Mower	$14,000

Refuge Priority Rank	MMS Project Name (FY 2002)	Estimated Cost
None	Replace 1992 John Deere Tractor	$19,000
None	Replace Bush Hog 2610L Flexwing Mower	$8,000
None	Replace New Holland 7610 Farm Tractor	$33,000
None	Replace Alamo FMM 2251 Tree Shredder	$27,000
None	Replace New Holland TV 140F-100 Bi-directional Tractor	$80,000
None	Replace Caterpillar 420 Backhoe/Loader	$72,000
None	Replace Caterpillar D5G LGP Dozer	$84,000
None	Replace Pathfinder 2400 Flats Boat	$37,000
None	Replace 2001 Forest River Travel Trailer	14,000
Total		**$6,433,000**

Notes:

* Not ranked in MMS
** Partially completed

Table 8. Current unfunded Refuge Operating Needs System projects

Refuge Priority Rank	RONS Project Name (FY 2002)	Estimated First Year Cost	Estimated Annual Recurring Cost
1	Provide management and planning for Pelican Island NWR - Project Leader	$152,000	$87,000
2	Administrative Assistant Position	$118,000	$53,000
3	Refuge Officer Position	$125,000	$60,000
4	Maintenance Worker Position (Heavy Equipment Operator)	$125,000	$60,000
5	Radio System	$25,000	$0
6	Exotic Plant Control	$60,000	$10,000
7	Property Management Position for SAMMS	$114,000	$49,000
8	Construct a Maintenance Facility for Pelican Island NWR	$111,000	$46,000
Total		**$830,000**	**$365,000**

Table 9. Proposed additional staff and costs

RONS/MMS Project Number	Objective Number(s)	Proposed Position	Estimated First Year Cost	Estimated Annual Recurring Cost
RONS 00007	A.1-7, B.1-6, C.1-4, D.1-4, E.1-5, F.1-2	Project Leader (to replace the current Refuge Manager position)	$152,000	$87,000
RONS 00006	A.1-7, B.1-6, C.1-4, D.1-4, E.1-5, F.1-2	Administrative Assistant (to fully fund this position)	$118,000	$53,000
	A.1-7, B.1-6, C.2, D.3, E.1-3	Biological Technician	$114,000	$49,000
	B.4-5, C.4, D.1-4, E.1-2, E.4-5, F.2	Refuge Ranger	$125,000	$60,000
RONS 99039	B.3-5, D.1-2, E.1-2, E.4, F.1	Refuge Officer	$125,000	$60,000
RONS 00005	B.1-2, B.4, B.6, E.1, E.5	Maintenance Worker/Heavy Equipment Operator	$125,000	$60,000
RONS 02002	E.1	Supply Technician	$110,000	$45,000
Total			**$869,000**	**$414,000**

Table 10. Prioritized project needs and costs

RONS/ MMS Project Number(s)	Goal/ Objective Number(s)	Project Description	Estimated First Year Cost	Estimated Recurring Annual Cost
N/A*	A.4-6, B.3	Pelican Island Proper Shoreline Stabilization, Phase III	$2,000,000	$0
RONS 93006** RONS 99033*** RONS 00005 (partial)	A.5, A.7-8, B.2, D.3	Pelican Island Buffer Habitat Restoration, Phase I	$1,000,000	$0
		Pelican Island Buffer Habitat Restoration, Phase II	$1,000,000	$0
MMS 03006	E.1-3, E.5	Construct New Administrative Office	$470,000	$0
MMS 99051 MMS 99052	C.3, D.3, D.4, E.2, E.4-5, F.2	Construct Visitor Center Facility, Phase I	$861,000	$0

RONS/ MMS Project Number(s)	Goal/ Objective Number(s)	Project Description	Estimated First Year Cost	Estimated Recurring Annual Cost
MMS 99053		Visitor Center Facility, Phase II	$2,000,000	$0
		Visitor Center Facility, Phase III	$1,300,000	$35,000
RONS00007	A.1-7, B.1-6, C.1-4, D.1-4, E.1-5, F.1-2	Provide Management and Planning with Project Leader	$152,000	$87,000
RONS 00006	A.1-7, B.1-6, C.1-4, D.1-4, E.1-5, F.1-2	Staff administrative office with Administrative Assistant	$118,000	$53,000
RONS 99039	Goals A-F	Resource Protection with Refuge Officer	$125,000	$60,000
RONS 00005	A.7-8, E.1	Habitat Restoration and Maintenance Worker/Heavy Equipment Operator	$125,000	$60,000
RONS 99040	Goal E	Communication System	$25,000	$0
RONS 01003	A.6, A.8, B.4, B.5, B.6	Exotic Plant Control on Natural and Spoil Islands	$60,000	$10,000
RONS 03001	E.5	Construct Maintenance Facility	$170,000	$10,000
MMS 02002	E.5	Rehabilitate Pole Barn and Service Road	$54,000	$0
MMS 03000	E.5	Repair 1970 Pole Barn	$54,000	$0
MMS 02NNN	D.2, D.4	Jungle Trail Wildlife Drive	$764,000	$35,000
RONS 00004***	D.1-4, E.4-5, F.1-2	Jungle Trail Public Use Facilities, Signs, and Kiosks	$729,000	$35,000
N/A****	B.5	Impoundment Management with Biological Science Technician	$114,000	$49,000
N/A****	B.4, C.2, D.3-4	Public Outreach Projects with Refuge Ranger	$125,000	$60,000
RONS 99013***	C.3, D.4, F.2	Kroegel Homestead - protection and interpretation	$705,000	$10,000
N/A****	A.8, B.2, B.6	Purchase Dump Truck	$50,000	$0
N/A****	B.1-2, B.6	Purchase Fuel Tanks	$20,000	$0
N/A****	A.8, B.1, B.6	Purchase Fire Engine	$50,000	$0

RONS/ MMS Project Number(s)	Goal/ Objective Number(s)	Project Description	Estimated First Year Cost	Estimated Recurring Annual Cost
N/A****	A.8, B.1, B.6	Purchase Fire Plow	$20,000	$0
N/A****	A.8, B.1-2, B.6	Purchase Equipment Trailer	$30,000	$0
N/A****	A.6	Regional Shorebird Plan - portable pump	$40,000	$0
N/A****	A.6	Regional Shorebird Plan - 3-4 water control structures	$15,000	$0
N/A****	A.6, B.4, C.2	Shorebird Habitat Restoration	$50,000	$5,000
N/A****	A.6, B.4, C.2	Shoreline Stabilization for Natural and Spoil Islands	$50,000	$5,000
N/A****	A.5, B.2, B.6	Migratory Birds - habitat restoration and maintenance	$50,000	$5,000
N/A****	B.1	Refugia Habitat - restoration and maintenance	$50,000	$5,000
N/A****	A.1	Sea Turtles - surveys	$30,000	$15,000
N/A****	A.4	Wood Storks - surveys	$30,000	$5,000
N/A****	A.2	West Indian Manatee - habitat surveys	$30,000	$0
N/A****	A.3	Eastern Indigo Snake and Atlantic Salt Marsh Snake Surveys	$30,000	$0
N/A****	A.7-8, B.2, B.4	Exotic, Invasive, and Nuisance Species - survey and control	$30,000	$5,000
N/A****	A.6, B.4-5	Shorebirds - surveys	$30,000	$0
N/A****	A.7	Woodrat - surveys	$30,000	$0
N/A****	A.7	Diamondback Terrapin - surveys	$30,000	$0
N/A****	A.7	Land Crab - surveys	$30,000	$0
N/A****	A.7	Bobcat - surveys	$30,000	$0
N/A****	A.7	Small mammal - surveys	$30,000	$0
N/A****	B.5, C.2, D.1	Fisheries - surveying, monitoring, and protecting	$30,000	$5,000
N/A****	D.3	Environmental Education Projects and Teacher Materials	$30,000	$5,000

RONS/ MMS Project Number(s)	Goal/ Objective Number(s)	Project Description	Estimated First Year Cost	Estimated Recurring Annual Cost
N/A****	D.1-4	Public Use Maps/Brochures/Information	$20,000	$5,000
MMS 02001	A.8, B.1-2, B.6, E.1, E.5	Replace Honda ATV	$6,000	$0
MMS 02014	A.8, B.1-2, B.6, E.1, E.5	Replace Caterpillar 420 Backhoe/Loader	$69,000	$0
MMS 02019	A.8, B.1-2, B.6, D.2-4, E.1, E.5	Replace Bush Hog Mower	$8,000	$0
MMS 02017	A.8, B.1-2, B.6, E.1, E.5	Replace Alamo Shredder	$26,000	$0
MMS 02016	A.8, B.1-2, B.6, E.1, E.5	Replace New Holland Bi- directional Tractor	$77,000	$0
MMS 02015	A.8, B.1-2, B.6, E.1, E.5	Replace New Holland Farm Tractor	$32,000	$0
MMS 02010	E.1, E.5	Replace Dodge Pickup (1999)	$22,000	$0
MMS 02009	D.2-4, E.1, E.5	Replace Ford Van	$23,000	$0
MMS 02008	E.1, E.5	Replace Dodge Pickup (2001)	$24,000	$0
MMS 02007	E.1, E.5	Replace Chevrolet Tahoe	$31,000	$0
MMS 02005	E.1, E.5	Replace Pathfinder Boat	$35,000	$0
MMS 03002	A.8, B.1-2, B.6, E.1, E.5	Replace Caterpillar D5 LGP	$80,000	$0
MMS 03001	D.2-4, E.1, E.5	Replace Dodge Van (2002)	$18,000	$0
MMS 03003	A.8, B.1-2, B.6, E.1, E.5	Replace John Deere Tractor	$18,000	$0
MMS 03004	A.8, B.1-2, B.6, D.2-4, E.1, E.5	Replace Turner Mower	$13,000	$0
MMS 03005	E.1, E.5	Replace Travel Trailer	$13,000	$0
N/A****	Goals A-F	15-year CCP Update	$152,000	$0
Total			**$13,433,000**	**$564,000**

Notes:

*   Project funded through partnership with US Army Corps of Engineers and Florida Inland Navigation District under §1135
**   Project marked for deletion in RONS (funded through a partnership with Florida Department of Environmental Protection and Indian River County under Federal Aid program)
***   Project formerly in RONS
**** Project to be added to RONS (new project)

STEP-DOWN MANAGEMENT PLANS

The Service will prepare step-down management plans to provide strategies and implementation schedules for meeting goals and objectives identified in this comprehensive conservation plan. At present, Pelican Island National Wildlife Refuge has five step-down plans. All of these plans will be updated during the 15-year life of this plan. The existing management plans are:

- Fishing Plan, 1985;
- Wilderness Management Plan, 1986;
- Management Plan for Indian River Impoundment #2 (Bird's Impoundment), 1992;
- Management Plan for Indian River Impoundment #3 (Pete's Impoundment), 1992; and
- Fire Management Plan, 2001 (during this planning process).

Additional step-down plans will be developed. A single, integrated step-down plan will be developed addressing population management, habitat management, integrated pest management, and exotic species, based on the strategies defined in this comprehensive conservation plan and the direct relationship between program areas. A single, integrated step-down plan will be developed addressing priority wildlife-dependent recreation including fishing, wildlife observation, wildlife photography, and environmental education and interpretation. Table 11 lists the needed step-down management plans and their anticipated completion dates.

Table 11. New step-down management plans

New Step-down Management Plan	Anticipated Completion Date

Fish and Wildlife Populations and Habitat Management
    Population management
    Habitat management
    Integrated pest management
    Exotic species
    Hazard analysis and critical control point
	2007

Education and Visitor Service Management	2007
Cultural Resources Management	2008
Law Enforcement	2008

Special Area Management
    Western Hemisphere Shorebird Reserve
    Ramsar Convention on Wetlands
	2009

Fisheries Resources Management	2011

PARTNERSHIPS

The refuge will continue an aggressive approach to work with others to conserve, protect, and enhance fish and wildlife and their habitats. The Service is fully committed to maintaining and expanding joint endeavors and cooperates with educational institutions, researchers, local governments, state government, and other federal agencies, as well as organizations, schools, volunteers, and conservation organizations. To this end, the refuge will maintain and enhance existing partnerships, which include those listed partners, as well as the residents and business owners of the area.

- Abercrombie and Kent Global Foundation
- Anheuser-Busch
- Audubon of Florida
- Brad Smith Associates
- Caterpillar Corporation
- The City of Sebastian
- ConocoPhilips
- The Conservation Fund
- The Disney Company
- Eagle Optics
- East Coast Florida Aquatic Preserves Office, Florida Department Environmental Protection (FDEP), State of Florida
- Environmental Learning Center (ELC)
- Florida Department of Environmental Protection (FDEP), State of Florida
- Florida Fish and Wildlife Conservation Commission (FWC), State of Florida
- Florida Inland Navigation District (FIND)
- Florida Institute of Technology (FIT)
- Florida Power and Light
- Friends of the St. Sebastian River
- Hubbs-Sea World Research Institute
- Indian River Audubon Society
- Indian River County Board of Commissioners
- Indian River County Chamber of Commerce
- Indian River County Historical Society
- Indian River County School District
- Indian River Mall
- Indian River Mosquito Control District
- Indian River Lagoon Scenic Highway
- Kayaks Etc.
- Lewis Environmental Services
- Marine Resources Council (MRC)
- National Audubon Society
- National Fish and Wildlife Foundation
- National Park Service (NPS)
- National Wildlife Refuge Association (NWRA)
- Natural Resources Conservation Service (NRCS)
- North Beach Civic Association
- Pelican Island Audubon Society (PIAS)
- Pelican Island Elementary School
- Pelican Island Preservation Society (PIPS)
- Sebastian Area Chamber of Commerce
- Sebastian Inlet State Park, FDEP, State of Florida
- Sebastian River Area Historical Society
- Sebastian River Boat Tours

- Sembler & Sembler, Inc.
- Sierra Club
- St. Johns River Water Management District (SJRWMD), FDEP, State of Florida
- Theodore Roosevelt Society
- Trust for Public Land (TPL)
- University of Central Florida
- U.S. Army Corps of Engineers (USACE)
- U.S. Environmental Protection Agency (EPA), National Estuary Program
- U.S. Postal Service
- Wild Birds Unlimited

Potential new partnerships for the refuge include local business owners; commercial tour boat operations; additional local elementary, middle, and high schools; new residents; additional research centers and universities; National Marine Fisheries Service; and National Oceanic and Atmospheric Administration.

PLAN REVIEW AND REVISIONS

Monitoring the Service's performance while implementing this plan is critical to its successful implementation. Monitoring and evaluation allows the Service, other government agencies, the public, and the partners to measure and evaluate progress. The Service will monitor, evaluate, and determine whether or not progress is being made towards achieving the refuge's purposes, vision, and goals. Monitoring will address habitat or population objectives and the effects of management activities. Through adaptive management, evaluation of monitoring and research results may indicate the need to modify refuge objectives or strategies.

The Service will review this plan annually to decide if it requires any revisions. The plan will be modified along with associated management activities whenever this review or other monitoring and evaluation determine that changes are needed to achieve planning unit purpose(s), vision, and goals. The Service will revise this plan when significant new information becomes available, ecological conditions change, major refuge expansion occurs, or when the need to do so is identified during plan review. At a minimum, plan revision will occur every 15 years. All plan revisions will follow the procedures outlined in current policy and will require compliance with the National Environmental Policy Act. The Service will conduct ongoing public involvement and continue informing and involving the public regarding management of this refuge.

I. Glossary

adaptive management – responding to changing ecological conditions so as to not exceed productivity limits of a specific place.

alternative – a reasonable way to address the identified problem or satisfy the stated need (40 CFR 1500.2).

anadromous – fish that spend a large proportion of their life cycle in the ocean and return to fresh water to breed.

aquatic – growing in, living in, or dependent upon water.

biological integrity – biotic composition, structure, and function at the genetic, organism, and community levels consistent with natural conditions, and the biological processes that shape genomes, organisms, and communities.

biota – the plants and animals of an area.

categorical exclusion – a category of actions that do not individually or cumulatively have a significant effect on the human environment and have been found to have no such effect in procedures adopted by a Federal agency pursuant to the National Environmental Policy Act (40 CFR 1508.4).

CFR – Code of Federal Regulations.

compatibility determination – the process required before any public use is allowed to occur on a refuge. A compatible use is one which, in the sound professional judgment of the Refuge Manager, will not materially interfere with or detract from fulfillment of the Refuge System Mission or refuge purpose(s). The 1997 National Wildlife Refuge System Improvement Act requires that a compatibility determination be made by the Fish and Wildlife Service before any use may be allowed on a refuge.

compatible use – an allowed use that will not materially interfere with, or detract from, the purposes for which the unit was established (Service Manual 602 FW 1.4). A compatible use is one that has been determined to be so through the compatibility determination process.

comprehensive conservation plan – a document that describes the desired future conditions of a refuge or planning unit and provides long-range guidance and management direction to achieve the purposes of the refuge, help fulfill the mission of the System, maintain and, where appropriate, restore the biological integrity, diversity, and environmental health of each refuge and the System, and meet other mandates.

conservation – the management of natural resources to prevent loss or waste. Management actions may include preservation, restoration, and enhancement.

conservation easement – a legal agreement between a landowner and a land trust (a private, nonprofit conservation organization) or government agency that permanently limits a property's uses in order to protect its conservation values.

cooperative agreement – the legal instrument used when the principal purpose of the transaction is the transfer of money, property, services or anything of value to a recipient in order to accomplish a public purpose authorized by Federal statute and substantial involvement between the Service and the recipient is anticipated.

cultural resource – evidence of historic or prehistoric human activity, such as buildings, artifacts, archaeological sites, documents, or oral or written history. Cultural resources include historically, archaeologically, and/or architecturally significant resources.

database – a collection of data arranged for ease and speed of analysis and retrieval, usually computerized.

easement – an agreement by which a landowner gives up or sells one of the rights on his/her property. For example, a landowner may donate a right-of-way across his/her property to allow access.

ecology – the branch of science that studies the distribution and abundance of organisms and the relationship between organisms and their environment.

ecosystem – a biological community together with its environment, functioning as a unit. For administrative purposes, the Service has designated 53 ecosystems covering the United States and its possessions. These ecosystems generally correspond with watershed boundaries and vary in their sizes and ecological complexity.

endangered species – any species which is in danger of extinction throughout all or a significant portion of its range.

Endangered Species Act – adopted in 1973 to provide protection for species in danger of becoming extinct.
§4 - outlines procedures and criteria for (1) identifying and listing threatened and endangered species; (2) identifying, designating, and revising critical habitat; (3) developing and revising recovery plans; and (4) monitoring species removed from the list of threatened and endangered species.
§7 - outlines procedures for interagency cooperation to conserve federally listed species and designated habitat.
§9 - prohibits the taking of endangered species of fish and wildlife, as well as most threatened species of fish and wildlife.
§10 - provides exceptions to the §9 prohibitions, with the most relevant exceptions being scientific take permits (to enable scientific research or to enhance propagation or survival of a listed species) and incidental permits (as part of an otherwise legal activity).

endemic – native to and restricted to a particular geographical region.

environment – the complex of climatic, geologic, hydrologic, soils, and biotic factors acting upon organisms.

Environmental Assessment – A concise public document, prepared in compliance with the National Environmental Policy Act, that briefly discusses the purpose and need for an action, alternatives to such action, and provides sufficient evidence and analysis of impacts to determine whether to prepare an environmental impact statement or finding of no significant impact (40 CFR 1508.9).

environmental education – education aimed at producing a citizenry that is knowledgeable concerning the biophysical environment and its associated problems, aware of how to help solve these problems, and motivated to work toward their solution (Stapp et al. 1969).

environmental health – Abiotic composition, structure, and functioning of the environment consistent with natural conditions, including the natural abiotic processes that shape the environment.

Environmental Impact Statement – A detailed written statement required by section 102(2)(C) of the National Environmental Policy Act, analyzing the environmental impacts of a proposed action, adverse effects of the project that cannot be avoided, alternative courses of action, short-tern uses of the environment versus the maintenance and enhancement of long-term productivity, and any irreversible and irretrievable commitment of resources (40 CFR 1508.11).

estuaries – deepwater tidal habitats and adjacent tidal wetlands that are usually semi-enclosed by land but have open, partly obstructed, or sporadic access to the open ocean, and in which ocean water is at least occasionally diluted by freshwater runoff from the land.

extirpated – no longer occurring in a given geographic area; the removal, elimination, or disappearance of a species or subspecies from a part of its range.

fauna – the collection of wildlife in a particular region.

federally listed species – a species listed under the federal Endangered Species Act of 1973, as amended, either as endangered, threatened or species at risk (formerly candidate species).

federally threatened species – any species which is likely to become an endangered species within the foreseeable future throughout all or a significant portion of its range.

Finding of No Significant Impact – A document prepared in compliance with the National Environmental Policy Act, supported by an environmental assessment, that briefly presents why a federal action will have no significant effect on the human environment and for which an environmental impact statement, therefore, will not be prepared (40 CFR 1508.13).

flora – the collection of plants in a particular region.

goal – descriptive, open-ended, and often broad statement of desired future conditions that conveys a purpose but does not define measurable units.

habitat – the place where a particular type of plant or animal lives. An organism's habitat must provide all of the basic requirements/components for life and should be free of harmful contaminants.

Florida Natural Areas Inventory (FNAI) Global Rank – a ranking of a species, natural community, bird rookery, spring, sinkhole, cave, or other ecological feature based on the world-wide status of that element.

•	critically imperiled globally because of extreme rarity (5 or fewer occurrences or less than 1,000 individuals) or because of extreme vulnerability to extinction due to some natural or man-made factor
G2	imperiled globally because of rarity (6-20 occurrences or less than 3,000 individuals) or because of vulnerability to extinction due to some natural or man-made factor
G3	either very rare and local throughout its range (21-100 occurrences or less than 10,000 individuals) or found locally in restricted range or vulnerable to extinction from other factors
G4	apparently secure globally (may be rare in parts of range)
G5	demonstrably secure globally
T1	G1 equivalent for subspecies or varieties
T2	G2 equivalent for subspecies or varieties
T3	G3 equivalent for subspecies or varieties
T4	G4 equivalent for subspecies or varieties
T5	G5 equivalent for subspecies or varieties

Florida Natural Areas Inventory (FNAI) State Rank - a ranking of a species, natural community, bird rookery, spring, sinkhole, cave, or other ecological feature based on the status of that element in Florida.

	critically imperiled in Florida because of extreme rarity (5 or fewer occurrences or less than 1,000 individuals) or because of extreme vulnerability to extinction due to some natural or man-made factor
S2	imperiled in Florida because of rarity (6-20 occurrences or less than 3,000 individuals) or because of vulnerability to extinction due to some natural or man-made factor
S3	either very rare and local throughout its range (21-100 occurrences or less than 10,000 individuals) or found locally in restricted range or vulnerable to extinction from other factors
S4	apparently secure in Florida (may be rare in parts of range)
S5	demonstrably secure in Florida
SU	due to lack of information, no rank or range can yet be assigned

Habitat Analysis and Critical Control Point (HACCP) Plan – a management tool that provides a structured method to identify risks and focus procedures in natural resource pathway activities. Understanding pathways and developing plans to reduce invasive species and prevent biological contamination is necessary to avoid unintended spread of species.

hydrology – the scientific studies of the properties, distribution, and effects of water in the atmosphere, on the earth's surface, and in soil and rocks.

Integrated Pest Management – sustainable approach to managing pests by combining biological, cultural, physical, and chemical tools in a way that minimizes economic, health, and environmental risks.

interjurisdictional fish – populations of fish that are managed by two or more states or national or tribal governments because of the scope of their geographic distributions or migrations.

issue – any unsettled matter that requires a management decision; e.g., a Service initiative, an opportunity, a management problem, a threat to the resources of the unit, a conflict in uses, a public concerns, or the presence of an undesirable resource condition. Issues should be documented, described, and analyzed in the CCP even if resolution cannot be accomplished during the planning process (Service Manual 602 FW 1.4).

land use/land cover – an assessment of the use of land (e.g., for agricultural purposes) or the vegetative cover [e.g., temperate/tropical hardwood (maritime hammock)].

management plan – a plan that guides future land management practices on a tract of land. In the context of this environmental impact statement, management plans would be designed to produce additional wildlife habitat along with the primary products, such as timber or agricultural crops.

mitigation – actions taken to compensate for the negative effects of a particular project or action. Wetland mitigation usually takes the form of restoration or enhancement of a previously damaged wetland or creation of a new wetland.

MMS – Maintenance Management System, Fish and Wildlife Service.

mosaic – a variety of different habitats intermixed in a relatively small area; several successional stages intermixed within a vegetation type.

National Environmental Policy Act of 1969 – requires all agencies, including the Service, to examine the environmental impacts of their actions, incorporate environmental information, and use public participation in the planning and implementation of all actions. Federal agencies must integrate NEPA with other planning requirements, and prepare appropriate NEPA documents to facilitate better environmental decision making (from 40 CFR 1500).

National Wildlife Refuge System – all lands, waters, and interests therein administered by the US Fish and Wildlife Service as wildlife refuges, wildlife ranges, wildlife management areas, waterfowl production areas, and other areas for the protection and conservation of fish, wildlife, and plant resources.

natural conditions – conditions thought to exists from the end of the Medieval Warm Period to the advent of the industrial era (approximately 950 AD to 1800 AD), based upon scientific study and sound professional judgment.

objective – a concise statement of what we want to achieve, how much we want to achieve, when and where we want to achieve it, and who is responsible for the work. Objectives derive from goals and provide the basis for determining strategies, monitoring refuge accomplishments, and evaluating the success of strategies. Objectives are attainable, time-specific, and measurable.

old field – an area that was formerly cultivated or grazed and where woody vegetation has begun to invade. If left undisturbed, it will eventually succeed into a forest.

partnership – a contract or agreement entered into by two or more individuals, groups of individuals, organizations or agencies in which each agrees to furnish a part of the capital or some in–kind service, i.e., labor, for a mutually beneficial enterprise.

priority public uses – hunting, fishing, participating in environmental education, participating in environmental interpretation, observing wildlife, and photographing wildlife. These six priority public uses are outlined in the 1997 National Wildlife Refuge System Improvement Act.

private land – land that is owned by a private individual, group of individuals, or non– governmental organization.

private landowner – any individual, group of individuals or non–governmental organization that owns land.

protection – mechanisms such as fee title acquisition, conservation easements or binding agreements with landowners that ensure land use and land management practices will remain compatible with maintenance of the species population at the site.

public involvement – a process that offers impacted and interested individuals and organizations an opportunity to become informed about, and to express their opinions on Service actions and policies. In the process, these views are studied thoroughly and thoughtful consideration of public views is given in shaping decisions for refuge management.

public land – land that is owned or otherwise managed as public land by the local, state, or federal government.

recovery – improvement in the status of listed species to the point at which listing is no longer appropriate under the criteria set out in §4(a)(1) of the Endangered Species Act; the process by which species' ecosystems are restored so they can support self-sustaining and self-regulating populations of the listed species as persistent members of native biotic communities.

refuge goals – descriptive, open-ended and often broad statements of desired future conditions that convey a purpose but do not define measurable units (Writing Refuge Management Goals and Objectives: A Handbook).

refuge purposes – the purposes specified in or derived from the law, proclamation, executive order, agreement, public land order, donation document, or administrative memorandum establishing, authorizing, or expanding a refuge, a refuge unit, or refuge subunit, and any subsequent modification of the original establishing authority for additional conservation purposes (Service Manual 602 FW 1.4).

Refuge Operating Needs System (RONS) – the Refuge Operating Needs System is a national database which contains the unfunded operational needs of each refuge. We include projects required to implement approved plans, and meet goals, objectives, and legal mandates.

reintroduction – the process of relocating a plant or animal species to a location where it historically occurred.

restoration – management actions that return a vegetative community or ecosystem to its original, natural condition or to something close to its natural state.

RONS – Refuge Operating Needs System, FWS.

runoff – water from rain, melted snow, or agricultural or landscape irrigation that flows over the land surface into a water body.

scoping – a process utilized to determine the scope of issues to be addressed.

species – a distinctive kind of plant or animal having distinguishable characteristics that can interbreed and produce viable young; a category of biological classification.

species of management concern – species present in the watershed for which the Refuge has a special management interest. A list of such species would include a mix of federally listed threatened and endangered species; migratory bird, especially declining species, neotropical migrants, colonial waterbirds, shorebirds, and waterfowl; marine mammals; sea turtles; interjurisdictional fish; state-listed threatened, endangered, special concern, and commercially exploited species; Audubon WatchList species for Florida; species on the Florida Natural Areas Inventory list; species listed by the Florida Committee on Rare and Endangered Plants and Animals; and key indicator species.

state land – public land owned by a state such as state parks or state wildlife management areas.

step-down management plans – step-down management plans describe management strategies and implementation schedules. Step-down management plans are a series of plans dealing with specific management subjects (e.g., croplands, wilderness, and fire) (Service Manual 602 FW 1.4).

strategy – a specific action, tool, technique, or combination of actions, tools, and techniques used to meet unit objectives.

succession – a natural sequence of changes in plant species and community structure over time, leading to a hypothesized stable climax community.

trust resource – one that through law or administrative act is held in trust for the people by the government. A federal trust resource is one for which trust responsibility is given in part to the federal government through federal legislation or administrative act. Generally, federal trust resources are those considered to be of national or international importance no matter where they occur, such as endangered species and species such as migratory birds and fish that regularly move across state lines. In addition to species, trust resources include cultural resources protected through federal historic preservation laws, nationally important and threatened habitats, notably wetlands, navigable waters, and public lands such as state parks and national wildlife refuges.

upland – dry ground; other than wetlands.

vegetation – plants in general or the sum total of the plant life in an area.

viable population – a population that will continue to occur in the area for the foreseeable future. In population modeling, minimum viable population (MVP) is the smallest number of individuals that are needed to maintain a species population in the long term.

visitor center – a permanently staffed building offering exhibits and interpretive information to the visiting public. Some visitor centers are co-located with refuge offices, others include additional facilities such as classrooms or wildlife viewing areas.

visitor contact station – compared to a visitor center, a contact station is a smaller facility which may not be permanently staffed.

watershed – the geographic area within which water drains into a particular river, stream or body of water. A watershed includes both the land and the body of water into which the land drains.

wetlands – The Fish and Wildlife Service's definition of wetlands states that "Wetlands are lands transitional between terrestrial and aquatic systems where the water table is usually at or near the surface or the land is covered by shallow water" (Cowardin, Carter, Golet, and LaRoe 1979).

wildlife – the mix of living organisms; includes plants and animals.

wildlife-dependent recreational use – "A use of a refuge involving hunting, fishing, wildlife observation and photography, or environmental education and interpretation." These are the six priority public uses of the System as established in the National Wildlife Refuge System Administration Act, as amended. Wildlife-dependent recreational uses, other than the six priority public uses, are those that depend on the presence of wildlife. We also will consider these other uses in the preparation of refuge comprehensive conservation plans, however, the six priority public uses always will take precedence.

wildlife management – the practice of manipulating wildlife populations, either directly through regulating the numbers, ages, and sex ratios harvested, or indirectly by providing favorable habitat conditions and alleviating limiting factors.

II. References

Apogee Research, Inc. 1996. Economic Assessment and Analysis of the Indian River Lagoon. Apogee Research, Inc. Bethesda, Maryland.

Barile, DD, W. Rathjen, P. Barile, and J. Steward. 1986. An Analysis of the Impact of a Ten-Year Storm Event on the Population of the Clam Mercenaria mercenaria in the Indian River. Florida Scientist. Vol. 49, Suppl. 1.

Brownall, L. W. (Nyack-on-Hudson, N.Y.) 1899. A Visit to Pelican Island, on Indian River, Florida. Pp.70-71. The Osprey.

Campbell, Paul, R. 1996. Population Projections for States - by Age, Sex, Race, and Hispanic Origin: 1995 to 2025. PPL-47. U.S. Bureau of the Census, Population Division. Washington, D.C. 105 pp.

Chapman, Frank M. 1914. Editorial. Pp. 124-125. Bird--Lore. Vol. XVI. No. 2. April 1, 1914.

Chapman, Frank M. 1901. Pelican Island Revisited. Pp. 3-8. Bird-Lore. Vol. III, No. 1. January-February 1901.

Cowardin, Lewis M, Virginia Carter, Francis C. Golet, and Edward T. LaRoe. 1979. Classification of Wetlands and Deepwater Habitats of the United States. U.S. Fish and Wildlife Service. Washington, D.C. 30 pp.

Cox, James A., and Randy S. Kautz. 2000. Habitat Conservation Needs of Rare and Imperiled Wildlife in Florida. Office of Environmental Services, Florida Fish and Wildlife Commission, Tallahassee, Florida. 156pp.

Deyrup, Mark and Richard Franz, eds. 1994. Rare and Endangered Biota of Florida - Volume IV: Invertebrates. Series editor - Ray E. Ashton, Jr. University Press of Florida. Gainesville, Florida. 798 pp.

Eck, C., K. Webster, and S.P. Lewis. 1998a. Archaeological Resource Assessment Survey of the Kennedy East and West Tracts. Pelican Island National Wildlife Refuge. Orchid Island, Indian River County, Florida.

Ehrhart, L. M., W. E. Redfoot, and D. A. Bagley. 1996. A Study of the Population Ecology of In-Water Marine Turtle Populations on the East-Central Florida Coast From 1982-96. Final Report to NOAA National Marine Fisheries Service, Miami, Florida. 164pp.

Eisler, R. 1993. Zinc Hazards to Fish, Wildlife, and Invertebrates: A Synoptic Review. U.S. Fish and Wildlife Service. Biological Report 10. Washington, D.C. 106 pp.

Eljera, Bert. 2001b. "Census Data Finds a New Wrinkle." Vero Beach Press Journal. May 23, 2001. Vero Beach, Florida.

Florida Audubon Society. 1918. A Defense of the Pelican. By the Florida Audubon Society. 1-10 pp.

Florida Department of Environmental Protection. 1999b. Sebastian Inlet State Park Information. http://www.dep.state.fl.us/parks/District_3/SebastianInlet/ . Tallahassee, Florida.

Florida Department of Labor and Employment Security. 2000. Florida Labor Market Trends, December 2000. Tallahassee, Florida. 6 pp.

Florida Department of Transportation. 1998. Archaeological Resource Assessment Survey of the Surman Tract Pelican Island National Wildlife Refuge Orchid Island, Indian River County, Florida.

Florida Fish and Wildlife Conservation Commission. 2004a. 2003 Boating Accident Statistical Report. http://myfwc.com/law/boating/2003stats/2003StatBook1.pdf/ . Tallahassee, FL. 78 pp.

Florida Fish and Wildlife Conservation Commission. 2004b. Manatee Mortality Statistics. http://floridamarine.org/ . Tallahassee, FL.

Florida Fish and Wildlife Conservation Commission. 2000. Birding Economics. http://floridabirdingtrail.com/fwc/viewing/gfbt/economics.htm . Tallahassee, Florida.

Florida Natural Areas Inventory. 1998. Tracking Florida's Biodiversity. http://www.fnai.org/ . Florida Department of Environmental Protection, The Nature Conservancy, and National Heritage Program Network. Tallahassee, Florida.

Frakes, Bob. 2001. Personal communications on June 13 and August 29, 2001 between Pelican Island National Wildlife Refuge's Refuge Biologist, Mark Graham, and Bob Frakes, Supervisory Contaminant Ecologist, Ecological Services, U.S. Fish and Wildlife Service. Vero Beach, Florida.

Gardner, Tom. 1990. Indian River Lagoon: Spoil Island Management Plan. Prepared by Bureau of Submerged Lands and Preserves, Division of State Lands. 170 pp.

Gibbs, Morris. 1891. A Trip to Pelican Island. Pp 124-125. The Oologist. Vol. IIX.

Gilmore, R. Grant Jr., Christopher J. Donohoe, Douglas W. Cooke, and David J. Herrema. 1981. Fishes of the Indian River Lagoon and Adjacent Waters, Florida. Harbor Branch Foundation, Inc. Technical Report No. 41. Ft. Pierce, Florida.

Graham, Frank Jr. 1990. The Audubon Ark. Alfred A Knopp, N.Y. 41-47 pp.

Hornaday, W.T. 1894. "The Pelicans". Indian River Advocate. April, 13, 1894.

Hunter, Chuck, Jaime Collazo, Bob Noffsinger, Brad Winn, David Allen, Brad Harrington, Marc Epstein, and Jorge Saliva. 2000. U.S. Shorebird Conservation Plan: Southeastern Coastal Plains-Caribbean Regional Shorebird Plan. Atlanta, Georgia. 53 pp.

Indian River Lagoon National Estuary Program. 1996. The Indian River Lagoon Comprehensive Conservation and Management Plan. Palatka, Florida. 357 pp.

Indian River Mosquito Control District. 1992b. Management Plan for Indian River Impoundment #3 (Pete's). Vero Beach, Florida. 48 pp.

Job, Herbert K. 1903. The City of the Pelicans. Pp. 367-375.

Johnson, Ann F., James W. Muller, and Kelly A. Bettinger. 1993b. An Assessment of Florida's Remaining Coastal Upland Natural Communities: Southeast Florida. Florida Natural Areas Inventory. Tallahassee, Florida.

Kanaski, R.S. 2000. Archaeological Survey of a Proposed Wetland Restoration Project. Pelican Island National Wildlife Refuge. Indian River County, Florida. U.S. Fish and Wildlife Service. Atlanta, Georgia. 18 pp.

Keystone Center. 1991. Final Consensus Report of the Keystone Policy Dialogue on Biological Diversity on Federal Lands. Keystone, Colorado. 96pp.

Lenze, David G. 2002. Florida: Long-term Economic Forecast 2002, Volume 2 – State and Counties. Bureau of Economic and Business Research, University of Florida. Gainesville, Florida. 503 pp.

Lewis Environmental Services, Inc. 2000. Installation of a Breakwater and Spartina Planting, the Phase I Shoreline Restoration Project, Pelican Island National Wildlife Refuge, Florida. A summary report of U.S. Fish and Wildlife Service's Merritt Island National Wildlife Refuge, Titusville, Florida. 13 pp.

Lewis, R. R. and F. M. Dunstan. 1975a. Possible Role of Spartina alterniflora Loisel in Establishment of Mangroves in Florida. Pp. 82-100 in R.R. Lewis (ed.) Proceedings of the Second Annual Conference on Restoration of Coastal Vegetation in Florida. 203 pp.

Lewis, Roy R. III. 1999. Time Zero Report for the Cross Bayou Mangrove Restoration Site, Pinellas County, Florida. Lewis Environmental Services, Inc. Tampa, Florida. 32 pp.

Lewis, Roy R. III. 1982b. Mangrove Forests. Ch. 8, pp. 154-171 in R.R. Lewis (ed.) Creation and Restoration of Coastal Plant Communities. CRC Press, Boca Raton, Florida. 219 pp.

McCulloch, Steve. 2002. Personal communication on February 12, 2002 between Pelican Island National Wildlife Refuge's Refuge Manager, Paul Tritaik, and Steve McCulloch, Research Scientist, Harbor Branch Oceanographic Institute, Ft. Pierce, Florida.

Moler, Paul E., ed. 1992. Rare and Endangered Biota of Florida - Volume III: Amphibians and Reptiles. Series editor - Ray E. Ashton, Jr. University Press of Florida. Gainesville, Florida. 291 pp.

Myers, Ronald J. and John J. Ewel, ed.s. 1990. Ecosystems of Florida. University of Central Florida Press. Orlando, Florida. 632 pp.

O'Bryan, P. and D. Carlson. 1993. Aerial Bird Surveys at Bird's (IRC #2) and Pete's (IRC #3) Impoundments - Year 3, Final Report.

Ogden, John C. Unknown Date. Habitat Management Guidelines for the Wood Stork in the Southeast Region. U.S. Fish and Wildlife Service. 9pp.

Parkinson, Randall W., and Colleen Dunlevey. 1999a. Action Plan: Shoreline Stabilization of Pelican Island. Final Report to U.S. Fish and Wildlife Service, Pelican Island National Wildlife Refuge, Sebastian, Florida.

Partners in Flight Bird Prioritization Technical Committee. 1998. PIF Priority Score Website. http://www.cbobirds.org/pif/index.html . Version 98.1. Colorado Bird Observatory. Brighton, Colorado.

Rodgers, J.A. Jr., A.S. Wenner, and S.T. Schwikert. 1988. The Use and Function of Green Nest Material by Wood storks. Pp. 411-423. Wilson Bull., Vol. 100, No. 2.

Rodgers, James A. Jr. and Stephen T. Schwikert. 2000. Buffer Zone Distances to Protect Foraging and Loafing Waterbirds from Disturbance by Personal Watercraft and Outboard-powered Boats. Bureau of Wildlife Diversity Conservation, Florida Fish and Wildlife Conservation Commission. Gainesville, Florida.

Rudolph, T.P. and C.O. Braley. 1981. Cultural Resources Survey, Pelican Island National Wildlife Refuge, Florida. Contract A-51309(81). Archaeological Services Division, National Park Service. 75 pp.

Smith, Brad and Robin Lewis. 2001. Environmental Resource Permit Application to St. Johns River Water Management District for the U.S. Fish and Wildlife Service at Pelican Island National Wildlife Refuge. Brad Smith Associates, Inc. and Lewis Environmental Services, Inc.

Snyder, J.R., A. Herndon, and W.B. Robertson, Jr. 1990. Pp. 230-279 in Ecosystems of Florida (R.L. Myers and J.J. Ewel, eds.). University of Central Florida Press. Orlando, FL.

South Atlantic Fishery Management Council. 2001. Magnuson-Stevens Act/NEPA Scoping Document: Using Marine Protected Areas in the South Atlantic. Charleston, South Carolina. 23 pp.

Spence, Donald J. 1998. Composition and Change of Maritime Hammock Flora in East-Central Florida After 20 Years. A thesis submitted Graduate School of College of Arts and Sciences, University of Central Florida. Orlando, Florida. 82 pp.

St. Johns River Water Management District. 1999. Seagrass Change Poster. /sjr/irl/arcview/proj/poster_sg_change2.apr. 2/8/1999. SJRWMD. Palatka, FL.

St. Johns River Water Management District. 2005. District Water Management Plan. SJRWMD. Palatka, FL. 70 pp.

Stapp, William B., D. Bennet, W. Bryan, J. Fulton, J. MacGregor, P. Nowak,. J. Wan, R. Wall, and S. Havlick. 1969. The Concept of Environmental Education. Journal of Environmental Education. 1(1): 30-31.

U.S. Census Bureau. 2000a. 1997 Economic Census, Volume 1, MAICS Report Series. http://www.census.gov/epcd/www/econ97.html . Washington, D.C.

U.S. Census Bureau. 2000c. County Population Estimates for July 1, 1999 and Population Change for July 1, 1998 to July 1, 1999. CO-99-1. U.S. Bureau of the Census, Population Division. Washington, D.C.

U.S. Census Bureau. 2000e. U.S. Census 2000 Redistricting Data (Public Law 94-171). http://www.census.gov and http://factfinder.census.gov .

U.S. Census Bureau. 1998. Population Profile of the U.S.: 1997. Current Population Reports, Series P23-194. Washington, D.C. 61 pp.

U.S. Department of Agriculture-Soil Conservation Service. 1993. Indian River Lagoon Agricultural Land Use Inventory and Discharge Study. Gainesville, Florida.

U.S. Department of Energy. 1999. Carbon Sequestration Research and Development. Washington, D.C.

U.S. Environmental Protection Agency. 2000a. Atlas of America's Polluted Waters. EPA 840-B-00-002. Office of Water (4503F), U.S. Environmental Protection Agency. Washington, D.C. 58 pp.

U.S. Fish and Wildlife Service. 2000. Southeastern Coastal Plains-Caribbean Region Report: U.S. Shorebird Conservation Plan. Atlanta, Georgia. 45 pp.

U.S. Fish and Wildlife Service. 1999b. Pelican Island: Honoring a Legacy. Washington, D.C. 14 pp.

U.S. Fish and Wildlife Service. 1999d. 50 CFR Part 17, Endangered and Threatened Wildlife and Plants; Review of Plant and Animal Taxa That Are Candidates or Proposed for Listing as Endangered or Threatened. Vol. 64, No. 205.

U.S. Fish and Wildlife Service. 1998. South Florida Ecosystem Plan. Atlanta, Georgia. 60 pp.

U.S. Fish and Wildlife Service. 1982. Florida Atlas of Breeding Sites for Herons and their Allies: 1976-78. Biological Services Program. 2 pp.

U.S. North American Bird Conservation Initiative Committee. 2000a. The North American Bird Conservation Initiative in the United States: A Vision of American Bird Conservation. 21 pp.

Unknown. 1894. "Protect Pelican Island". Indian River Advocate. April, 27 1894.

West, Carol T and David G Lenze. 2000. Florida: Long-term Economic Forecast 2000, Volume 2 - State and Counties. Bureau of Economic and Business Research, University of Florida. Gainesville, Florida. 5 pp.

III. Relevant Legal Mandates

Several procedural and substantive requirements of federal and applicable state and local laws and regulations affect refuges. The key laws, treatises, conventions, and executive orders are listed.

- Lacey Act (1900), as amended
- Antiquities Act (1906)
- Weeks-McLean Law (1913)
- Canadian United States Migratory Bird Treaty (Convention between the United States and Great Britain for Canada for the Protection of Migratory Birds) (1916)
- Migratory Bird Treaty Act (1918 and 1978)
- Migratory Bird Conservation Act (1929), as amended
- Migratory Bird Hunting and Conservation Stamp Act (1934)
- Fish and Wildlife Coordination Act (1934), as amended
- Historic Sites Act (1935)
- Refuge Revenue Sharing Act (1935), as amended
- Convention between the United States of America and the Mexican States for the Protection of Migratory Birds and Game Animals (1936)
- Federal Aid in Wildlife Restoration Act, as amended (1937)
- Bald and Golden Eagle Protection Act (1940), as amended
- Convention of Nature Protection and Wildlife Preservation in the Western Hemisphere (1940)
- Convention on International Trade in Endangered Species of Wild Fauna and Flora (1943)
- Flood Control Act (1944), as amended
- Transfer of Certain Real Property for Wildlife Conservation Purposes Act (1948)
- Refuge Trespass Act (1948)
- Federal Property and Administrative Services Act (1949), as amended
- Federal Aid in Fish Restoration Act (1950)
- Fish and Wildlife Act (1956), as amended
- Waterfowl Depredations Prevention Act, as amended (1956)
- Fish and Wildlife Coordination Act (1958)
- Cooperative Research and Training Units Act (1960)
- Wetlands Loan Act (1961)
- Refuge Recreation Act (1962), as amended
- Water Resources Planning Act (1962), as amended
- Refuge Revenue Sharing Act (1964), as amended
- Wilderness Act (1964)
- Land and Water Conservation Fund Act (1965), as amended
- National Wildlife Refuge System Administrative Act (1966)
- National Historic Preservation Act (1966)
- Freedom of Information Act (1967)
- Architectural Barriers Act (1968)
- National Trails System Act (1968)
- Wild and Scenic Rivers Act (1968)
- National Environmental Policy Act (1969)
- Executive Order 11514 - Protection and Enhancement of Environmental Quality (1970)
- Executive Order 11593 - Protection and Enhancement of the Cultural Environment (1971)
- Clean Water Act (1972)

- Convention on Wetlands of International Importance (1972)
- Executive Order 11644 - Use of Off-road Vehicles on Public Lands (1972), as amended (Executive Order 11989, 1977)
- Federal Environmental Pesticide Control Act (1972), as amended
- Federal Water Pollution Control Act Amendments (1972), as amended
- Endangered Species Act (1973), as amended
- Rehabilitation Act (1973)
- Archaeological and Historic Preservation Act (1974)
- Environmental Education Act (1975)
- Federal Land Policy Management Act (1976)
- Clean Air Act (1977), as amended
- Clean Water Act (1977)
- Executive Order 11988 - Floodplain Management and Wetlands Preservation (1977)
- Executive Order 11989 - Use of Off-road Vehicles on Public Lands (1977)
- Executive Order 11990 - Protection of Wetlands (1977)
- Fish and Wildlife Improvement Act (1978)
- American Indian Religious Freedom Act (1978)
- Archaeological Resources Protection Act (1979)
- Administrative Procedures Act (1979)
- Fish and Wildlife Conservation Act (1980)
- Executive Order 12372 - Intergovernmental Review of Federal Programs (1982)
- The Food Security Act (1985)
- Emergency Wetlands Resources Act (1986)
- North American Wetlands Conservation Act (1989)
- Federal Noxious Weed Act (1990)
- Native American Graves Protection and Repatriation Act (1990)
- Americans with Disabilities Act (1992)
- Wild Bird Conservation Act (1992)
- Executive Order 12898 - Environmental Justice in Minority Populations and Low-income Populations (1994)
- Secretarial Order 3127 (602 DM 2) - Contaminants and Hazardous Waste Determination (1995)
- Executive Order 12996 - Management and General Public Use of the National Wildlife Refuge System (1996)
- Executive Order 13007 - Indian Sacred Sites (1996)
- National Refuge System Improvement Act (1997) (and subsequent policies)
- Executive Order 13084 - Consultation and Coordination with Indian Tribal Governments (1998)

IV. Biota

Species on various lists found at Pelican Island National Wildlife Refuge (85)

Common Name	Scientific Name	Federal Status (14)	State Status (45)	FCREPA Status (54)*	FNAI Status (54)**	WatchList Status (11)
Mammals (2)						
West Indian manatee	*Trichechus manatus latirostris*	Endangered	Endangered	Endangered	G2? S2?	
Southeastern beach mouse	*Peromyscus polionotus niveiventris*	Threatened	Threatened	Threatened	G5T1, S1	
Fishes (12)						
Smalltooth Sawfish	*Pristis pectinata*	Endangered				
Atlantic Sturgeon	*Acipenser oxyrinchus*		Species of Special Concern	Threatened		
Opossum Pipefish	*Microphis brachyurus lineatus*	Candidate		Threatened	G5, S2	
American Eel	*Anguilla rostrata*	Candidate				
Bigmouth Sleeper	*Gobiomorus dormitor*			Threatened	G5, S2	
River Goby	*Awaous tajasica*			Threatened	G5, S1S2	
Slashcheek Goby	*Ctenogobius pseudofasciatus*			Threatened	G3G5, S1	
Mountain Mullet	*Agonostomus monticola*			Rare	G5, S3	

Species on various lists found at Pelican Island National Wildlife Refuge (85)

Common Name	Scientific Name	Federal Status (14)	State Status (45)	FCREPA Status (54)*	FNAI Status (54)**	WatchList Status (11)
Mangrove Rivulus	*Kryptolebias marmoratus*		Species of Special Concern	Species of Special Concern	G5, S3	
Striped Croaker	*Bairdiella sanctaeluciae*			Species of Special Concern	G5, S2	
Spottail Goby	*Ctenogobius stigmaturus*			Species of Special Concern		
Common Snook	*Centropomus undecimalis*		Species of Special Concern			
Amphibians and Reptiles (9)						
Green Sea Turtle	*Chelonia mydas*	Endangered	Endangered	Endangered	G3, S2	
Hawksbill Sea Turtle	*Eretmochelys imbricata*	Endangered	Endangered	Endangered		
Kemp's Ridley Sea Turtle	*Lepidochelys kempii*	Endangered	Endangered	Endangered		
Atlantic Salt Marsh Snake	*Nerodia clarkii taeniata*	Threatened	Threatened	Endangered		
Gopher Tortoise	*Gopherus polyphemus*		Species of Special Concern	Threatened	G3, S3	
Loggerhead Sea Turtle	*Caretta caretta*	Threatened	Threatened	Threatened	G3, S3	

Species on various lists found at Pelican Island National Wildlife Refuge (85)

Common Name	Scientific Name	Federal Status (14)	State Status (45)	FCREPA Status (54)*	FNAI Status (54)**	WatchList Status (11)
Eastern Indigo Snake	*Drymarchon corais couperi*	Threatened	Threatened	Species of Special Concern	G4T3, S3	
Leatherback Sea Turtle	*Dermochelys coriacea*	Endangered	Endangered	Rare	G3, S2	
American Alligator	*Alligator mississippiensis*	Threatened	Species of Special Concern		G5, S4	
Invertebrate (1)						
Mangrove Crab	*Aratus pisonii*			Threatened		
Birds (43)						
Wood Stork	*Mycteria americana*	Endangered	Endangered	Endangered	G4, S2	
Piping Plover	*Charadrius melodus*	Threatened	Threatened	Endangered	G3, S2	Global
Eastern Brown Pelican	*Pelecanus occidentalis carolinensis*		Species of Special Concern	Threatened	G4, S3	
Magnificent Frigatebird	*Fregata magnificens*			Threatened	G5, S1	
Osprey	*Pandion haliaetus*			Threatened	G5, S3S4	
Southern Bald Eagle	*Haliaeetus leucocephalus leucocephalus*	Threatened	Threatened	Threatened	G4, S3	
Southeastern American Kestrel	*Falco sparverius paulus*		Threatened	Threatened	G5T3T4, S3?	

Species on various lists found at Pelican Island National Wildlife Refuge (85)

Common Name	Scientific Name	Federal Status (14)	State Status (45)	FCREPA Status (54)*	FNAI Status (54)**	WatchList Status (11)
American Oystercatcher	*Haematopus palliatus*		Species of Special Concern	Threatened	G5, S3	National
Least Tern	*Sterna antillarum*		Threatened	Threatened	G4, S3	
Reddish Egret	*Egretta rufescens*		Species of Special Concern	Rare	G4, S2	National
Roseate Spoonbill	*Ajaia ajaja*		Species of Special Concern	Rare	G5, S2S3	
Swallow-tailed Kite	*Elanoides forficatus*			Threatened	G4, S2S3	
Short-tailed Hawk	*Buteo brachyurus*			Rare	G4?, S3	
Mangrove Cuckoo	*Coccyzus minor*			Rare		
Black-whiskered Vireo	*Vireo altiloqus*			Rare	G5, S3	
Louisiana Waterthrush	*Seiurus motacilla*			Rare		
American Redstart	*Setophaga ruticilla*			Rare		
Great White Heron	*Ardea herodias occidentalis*			Species of Special Concern	G5T2, S2	
Great Egret	*Ardea alba*			Species of Special Concern	G5, S4	
Little Blue Heron	*Egretta Caerulea*		Species of Special Concern	Species of Special Concern	G5, S4	

Species on various lists found at Pelican Island National Wildlife Refuge (85)

Common Name	Scientific Name	Federal Status (14)	State Status (45)	FCREPA Status (54)*	FNAI Status (54)**	WatchList Status (11)
Snowy Egret	Egretta thula		Species of Special Concern	Species of Special Concern	G5, S4	
Tricolored heron	Egretta tricolor		Species of Special Concern	Species of Special Concern	G5, S4	
Black-crowned Night Heron	Nycticorax nycticorax			Species of Special Concern	G5, S3?	
Yellow-crowned Night Heron	Nyctanassa violacea			Species of Special Concern	G5, S3?	
White Ibis	Eudocimus albus		Species of Special Concern	Species of Special Concern	G5, S4	
Glossy Ibis	Plegadis falcinellus			Species of Special Concern	G5, S2	
Cooper's Hawk	Accipiter cooperii			Species of Special Concern	G4, S3?	
Wilson's Plover	Charadrius wilsonia			Species of Special Concern		National
Royal Tern	Sterna maxima			Species of Special Concern	G5, S3	

Species on various lists found at Pelican Island National Wildlife Refuge (85)

Common Name	Scientific Name	Federal Status (14)	State Status (45)	FCREPA Status (54)*	FNAI Status (54)**	WatchList Status (11)
Sandwich Tern	Sterna sandvicensis			Species of Special Concern	G5, S2	
Caspian Tern	Sterna caspia			Species of Special Concern	G5, S2?	
Black Skimmer	Rynchops niger		Species of Special Concern	Species of Special Concern	G5, S3	
Hairy Woodpecker	Picoides villosus			Species of Special Concern	G5, S3?	
Merlin	Falco columbarius			Status Undetermined	G5, SU	
Florida Prairie Warbler	Dendroica discolor paludicola			Status Undetermined	G5T3, S3	National
Painted Bunting	Passerina ciris			Status Undetermined		National
Bachman's Sparrow	Aimophila aestivalis				G3, S3	Global
Snowy Plover	Charadrius alexandrinus					Global
Short-billed Dowitcher	Limnodromus griseus					National
Whimbrel	Numenius phaeopus					National

Species on various lists found at Pelican Island National Wildlife Refuge (85)

Common Name	Scientific Name	Federal Status (14)	State Status (45)	FCREPA Status (54)*	FNAI Status (54)**	WatchList Status (11)
Florida Clapper Rail	*Rallus longirostrus scottii*				G5T3?, S3?	
Mottled Duck	*Anus fulvigula*					National
Peregrine Falcon	*Falco peregrinus*		Endangered	Endangered	G4, S2	
Plants (18)						
Giant Leather Fern	*Acrostichum danaeifolium*		Commercially Exploited			
Curtiss' (Sandhill) Milkweed	*Asclepias curtissii*		Endangered		G3, S3	
Hand Fern	*Cheiroglossa palmata*				G4, S2	
Christmas Berry	*Crossopetalum ilicifolium*		Endangered			
Butterfly Orchid	*Encyclia tampensis*		Commercially Exploited			
Beach Creeper	*Ernodea littoralis*		Threatened			
Johnson's Seagrass	*Halophila johnsonii*	Threatened			G2, S2	
Crested Coralroot	*Hexalectris spicata*		Endangered			
Pineland Lantana	*Lantana depressa*		Endangered			
Simpson Stopper	*Myrcianthes fragrans (=Eugenia simpsonii)*		Threatened			
Shell Mound Prickly Pear Cactus	*Opuntia stricta*		Threatened			

Species on various lists found at Pelican Island National Wildlife Refuge (85)

Common Name	Scientific Name	Federal Status (14)	State Status (45)	FCREPA Status (54)*	FNAI Status (54)**	WatchList Status (11)
Cinnamon Fern	*Osmunda cinnamomea*		Commercially Exploited			
Pepper (Unnamed)	*Peperomia humilis*		Endangered			
Inkberry	*Scaevola plumieri*		Threatened			
Inflated (Reflexed) Wild Pine	*Tillandsia balbisiana*		Threatened			
Giant Wild Pine; Giant Air Plant	*Tillandsia utriculata*		Endangered			
Coastal Vervain	*Verbena maritima*		Endangered		G3, S3	
Tampa Vervain	*Verbena tampensis*		Endangered		G1, S1	
Communities and Sites (5)						
Coastal Strand Community					G3?, S2	
Maritime Hammock Community					G4, S2	
Shell Mound Community					G3, S2	
Bird Rookery					confirmed occurrence	
Manatee Aggregation Site					confirmed occurrence	

* Although the FCREPA list includes 54 species found at Pelican Island NWR, an additional 3 species have an undetermined status.
** The FNAI list includes 54 species, 3 communities, and 2 sites.
Notes:
FCREPA = Florida Committee on Rare and Endangered Plants and Animals
FNAI = Florida Natural Areas Inventory
WatchList = Audubon WatchList for Florida
Summary:
2 mammals, 10 fishes, 9 amphibians and reptiles, 1 invertebrate, 43 birds, 18 plants, 3 communities, and 2 sites

V. Compatibility Determinations

Introduction:

The Fish and Wildlife Service reviewed several uses for compatibility during the process of developing the Comprehensive Conservation Plan for Pelican Island National Wildlife Refuge. Descriptions and anticipated impacts of each of these uses are addressed separately. However, the Uses through the Other Applicable Laws, Regulations, and Policies sections, the Literature Cited section, and the Approval of Compatibility Determinations section apply to each use. If one of these uses is considered outside of the Comprehensive Conservation Plan for Pelican Island National Wildlife Refuge, then those sections become part of that compatibility determination.

Uses:

Several uses were evaluated to determine their compatibility with the mission of the Refuge System and the purposes of the refuge: 1) fishing; 2) participating in environmental education; 3) participating in interpretation activities; 4) observing wildlife; 5) photographing wildlife; 6) participating in research activities; 7) controlling mosquitoes; 8) managing citrus groves; and 9) participating in commercial ecotour operations.

Refuge Name:

Pelican Island National Wildlife Refuge

Establishing and Acquisition Authorities:

Established by an unnumbered Executive Order on March 14, 1903
Executive Order 1014, January 26, 1909
16 USC §1534 Endangered Species Act
16 USC §742(f) Fish and Wildlife Act
16 USC §668dd National Wildlife Refuge System Administration Act

Refuge Purposes:

Pelican Island National Wildlife Refuge was established in 1903 "as a preserve and breeding ground for native birds" through an unnumbered Executive Order and expanded in 1909 by Executive Order 1014. Pelican Island National Wildlife Refuge "shall be administered by him (the Secretary of the Interior) directly or in accordance with cooperative agreements and in accordance with such rules and regulations for the conservation, maintenance, and management of wildlife, resources thereof, and its habitat thereon" [16 USC §664 (Fish and Wildlife Coordination Act)]. The refuge shall "conserve fish, wildlife, and plants, including those which are listed as endangered species or threatened species" [16 USC §1534 (Endangered Species Act)]. Further, the refuge serves "...the development, advancement, management, conservation, and protection of fish and wildlife resources... [16 USC §742(f)(a)(4) (Fish and Wildlife Act)] ...for the benefit of the United States Fish and Wildlife Service, in performing its activities and services...." [16 USC §742(f)(b)(1) (Fish and Wildlife Act)]. Later, the Refuge Recreation Act was also applied to the Refuge "...for (1) incidental fish and wildlife-oriented recreational development, (2) the protection of natural resources, (3) the conservation of endangered species or threatened species..." [16 USC §460k-1 (Refuge Recreation Act)]. The existence of the refuge serves the "...conservation, management, and restoration of the fish, wildlife, and plant resources and their habitats for the benefit of present and future generations of Americans..." [16 USC §668dd(a)(2) (National Wildlife Refuge System Administration Act)]. Finally, the Pelican Island Wilderness Area "...shall be administered for the use and enjoyment of the American people in such manner as will leave them (wilderness areas) unimpaired for future use and enjoyment as wilderness, and so as to provide for the protection of these areas, the preservation of their wilderness character, and for the gathering and dissemination of information regarding their use and enjoyment as wilderness...." [16 USC 1 1 21 (note) (Wilderness Act)].

National Wildlife Refuge System Mission:
As outlined in the 1997 National Wildlife Refuge System Improvement Act, the mission of the National Wildlife Refuge System is to administer a national network of lands and waters for the conservation, management, and where appropriate, restoration of the fish, wildlife, and plant resources and their habitats within the United States for the benefit of present and future generations of Americans.

Description of Use:

Fishing
Fishing is a common public use within and around the refuge. Fishing within the refuge includes commercial and recreational fishing and shell fishing within the Indian River Lagoon. Several methods of fishing are employed, including boat fishing, wade fishing, and bank fishing. Bank fishing currently occurs from the spoil islands and is proposed for selected sites in the upland areas of the refuge (these sites will be identified on refuge maps). Bank fishing is prohibited from Pelican Island proper. No boat launch facilities are located on the refuge, therefore, all boat launch activities must occur off the refuge (e.g., parking and loading and unloading boats). The refuge will prepare, provide, and update brochures and maps detailing the designated locations for these and other public uses.

Since the Indian River Lagoon portion of the refuge is managed by the refuge through an agreement with the State of Florida, this use is also governed by this management agreement that allows for traditional uses, as listed.

> The right of the public to use the area for traditional navigation, boating, bathing, shell fishing, and commercial and sport fishing shall not be restricted with the exception of a 410(-)foot buffer zone surrounding Pelican Island (Government Lot 3, Township 31 South, Range 39 East, Indian River County). This buffer zone is measured from the mean high water line of said island and extending out into the Indian River.

As part of the comprehensive conservation planning effort, the Service and the Florida Fish and Wildlife Conservation Commission (FWC) worked together to develop revised language regarding the lease area and the implementation of FWC and Service regulations in the leased area. Fishing regulations and restrictions will be coordinated between the Service and the FWC, which exercises jurisdiction under the Florida Constitution with respect to marine life. FWC regulations will apply on the leased portion of the refuge, in support of refuge management of fishing as a priority public use. Other regulations implemented by the Service in furtherance of its overall management responsibilities will be coordinated with FWC as needed.

Availability of Resources: The primary refuge resources required for this use involve the associated law enforcement needs. However, since this area is under management agreement with the State of Florida and since that agreement spells out the right of the public to use the area for commercial and sport fishing, the State of Florida also shares this law enforcement responsibility.

Anticipated Impacts of Use: Fishing activities are anticipated to have minimal impact on the resources of the refuge. The potential exists for wildlife to become entangled in monofilament fishing line (e.g., birds and juvenile sea turtles). The potential also exists for illegal take of fish (e.g., defined by species, size, and sex), accidental collision with wildlife (e.g., boat collisions with manatees, sea turtles, and dolphins), disturbance of wildlife (e.g., fish spawning areas and bird rookeries), and unintentional damage to seagrass beds (e.g., prop scarring), however, these incidents and impacts are anticipated to be minimal. Further, minor trampling of vegetation may occur as anglers access areas to bank fish; however, this impact is expected to be minor and short lived. And, unfortunately, littering is always possible. Recreational clammers may impact seagrass beds either by trampling, or by raking the bottom for clams. Restrictions on the use will help ensure minimal impacts. Further, as impacts become evident, additional measures will be taken to limit or eliminate these impacts (e.g., the creation of closed area buffers around key bird rookeries and fish spawning areas). Educational activities will be provided to encourage proper use and disposal of monofilament line.

Public Review and Comment: During the public scoping process for the Pelican Island National Wildlife Refuge Draft Comprehensive Conservation Plan and Environmental Assessment, five public meetings were conducted (during May and June 2000). Verbal and written comments were recorded regarding a variety of subjects, including uses of the refuge. Further, during the public comment and review period for the draft plan and environmental assessment, opportunity was provided to the public to submit comments during a 60-day review period (July 27, 2005 to September 26, 2005).

Determination (check one below):

	Use is Not Compatible
X	Use is Compatible, with the Listed Stipulations

Stipulations Necessary to Ensure Compatibility: The refuge will prepare, provide, and update brochures and maps designating these and other public uses and areas, along with associated restrictions. (Contact the Refuge Manager for details on these designated areas and any associated restrictions.)

Fishing regulations and restrictions will be coordinated with the Refuge Manager, Refuge Biologist, the Fish and Wildlife Service's Southeast Regional Office, and the State of Florida. State of Florida game species, bag limits, seasons, and fishing methods apply on the refuge.

Bank fishing from spoil islands shall be permitted only during daylight hours. Bank fishing is prohibited from all other areas except from the north dike of Bird's Impoundment and from Paul's Island. Once Paul's Island is restored for use by wildlife, bank fishing will then be prohibited from Paul's Island. Bank fishing shall be banned from Pelican Island proper.

Shellfish harvesting is restricted in those areas delineated by state regulations (generally south of Spratt's Point and Paul's Island, east of the Intracoastal Waterway, and north of Wabasso Island). This area, designated as Conditionally Restricted, is only open to permit holders who are authorized to relay and purify shellfish and is only open when environmental conditions allow. Shellfish harvesting is permitted in the area designated as Conditionally Approved (north of Spratt's Point and Paul's Island, south of Coconut Point at Sebastian Inlet, and east of the Intracoastal Waterway) when environmental conditions allow. Harvesting clams by rakes in any seagrass bed is prohibited. It is unlawful to harvest shellfish from the commercial shellfish lease areas. (Contact the Refuge Manager for more information and details on the locations of these clamming areas.)

Commercial shellfish leases are not considered appropriate for the refuge. However, the lease with the State of Florida currently removes these areas from refuge management and restrictions. If at any time these areas are included under refuge management, all commercial shellfish leases will be terminated.

All fishing tackle must be attended at all times.

Law enforcement activities will help ensure compliance with applicable laws and regulations and will help protect the resources of the refuge.

Vessel use by anglers will be restricted in accordance with the lease with the State of Florida in key areas to prevent damage to sensitive resources of the refuge (e.g., vessel use must occur outside of the designated buffer of Pelican Island proper to limit disturbance to the rookery).

If the Refuge Manager determines that resources of the refuge are experiencing disturbance or damage or that the fishery resource is being damaged, the Refuge Manager will work with the State of Florida to enact necessary measures of protection (e.g., implement buffers of key areas and seasonally close key areas).

Justification: Fishing is a priority public use, as defined under the 1997 National Wildlife Refuge System Improvement Act. Further, fishing activities can enhance the public's understanding and appreciation of wildlife and wild places and should enhance refuge management and the mission of the National Wildlife Refuge System. Further, commercial fishing and sport fishing are specifically spelled out as public uses of the Indian River Lagoon portion of the refuge in the management agreement between the refuge and the State of Florida.

NEPA Compliance for Refuge Use Description: *Place an X in appropriate space.*

_____Categorical Exclusion without Environmental Action Statement
_____Categorical Exclusion and Environmental Action Statement
__X__Environmental Assessment and Finding of No Significant Impact
_____Environmental Impact Statement and Record of Decision

Mandatory 15-Year Re-evaluation Date: <u>July 13, 2021</u>

Description of Uses:

Environmental Education, Environmental Interpretation, Wildlife Observation, and Wildlife Photography
Each of these uses is a priority public use of the National Wildlife Refuge System.

Environmental education activities seek to increase public knowledge and understanding of the importance of wildlife, habitats, ecosystem functions, habitat protection, habitat management, and refuge management. Typical activities are expected to include field trips guided by refuge staff and/or a teacher/professor, offsite classroom programs (e.g., at the school and at the Environmental Learning Center), nature study at designated locations (e.g., in the public use areas around Jungle Trail), and programs at the proposed visitor center facility.

Interpretation includes those activities and supporting infrastructure that translate refuge management activities, natural resources, and cultural history for the refuge visitor. Supporting infrastructure for interpretive programs includes the planned visitor facility, informational kiosks throughout and near the refuge, interpretive signs throughout the refuge, trails in the Jungle Trail area, boardwalks in the Jungle Trail area, the observation tower overlooking Pelican Island proper in the Jungle Trail area, and the wildlife drive in the Jungle Trail area. Showcasing the birthplace of the National Wildlife Refuge System and honoring Paul Kroegel, proposed interpretive programs include habitat management, restoration activities, environmental processes, biodiversity, the water cycle, threatened and endangered species, and the history of Pelican Island National Wildlife Refuge and the National Wildlife Refuge System. The preferred site for the planned visitor center facility is at the Kroegel Homestead, while other potential sites include a refuge site on the barrier island in the Jungle Trail area; the Environmental Learning Center, just south of the refuge on Wabasso Island; and a site in the Duck Point area.

People visit national wildlife refuges to observe wildlife in their natural environments. Visitors to the refuge hope to see wildlife by driving and bicycling down Jungle Trail, driving along the wildlife drive in the Jungle Trail area (with no bicycling on the wildlife drive), boating in the Indian River Lagoon, walking on the designated trails and boardwalks in the Jungle Trail area, looking out from the observation tower in the Jungle Trail area, and visiting the Kroegel Homestead on the mainland for a view of Pelican Island proper and the Indian River Lagoon.

Wildlife photography is an outgrowth of wildlife observation. Photographers hope to see wildlife by driving and bicycling down Jungle Trail, driving along the wildlife drive in the Jungle Trail area (with no bicycling on the wildlife drive), boating in the Indian River Lagoon, walking on the designated trails and boardwalks in the Jungle Trail area, looking out from the observation tower in the Jungle Trail area, and visiting the Kroegel Homestead on the mainland for a view of Pelican Island proper and the Indian River Lagoon.

The associated visitor center, parking areas, restroom facility, wildlife drive, boardwalk, observation tower, trails, and other facilities outlined in the Comprehensive Conservation Plan for the refuge support these wildlife-dependent, priority public use activities. The plan outlines a proposed visitor center facility to support these activities. The preferred site for this facility is at the Kroegel Homestead on the mainland, across the Indian River Lagoon from Pelican Island proper. The proposed wildlife drive is a ½-mile-long drive providing viewing opportunities of wildlife in different habitats. This wildlife drive is planned to be located just west of Jungle Trail. Further, an observation tower will provide wildlife viewing opportunities of Pelican Island proper. A 170-meter-long boardwalk slowly rises to the tower. This boardwalk and tower are located southwest of the wildlife drive in the Jungle Trail area. The restroom facility and parking areas at the northern and southern ends of the wildlife drive in the Jungle Trail area will support these public uses. Additional trails and trail connectors around the wildlife drive, east and west of Jungle Trail, are planned to further support these public use activities. The refuge will prepare, provide, and update brochures and maps detailing the designated locations for these and other public uses of the refuge.

Availability of Resources: The refuge and Indian River County are partnering to provide visitor facilities at the refuge. Indian River County constructed and maintains the two parking areas and the restroom facility in the Jungle Trail area. Indian River County is also pursuing the purchase of the Kroegel Homestead, while the Fish and Wildlife Service has committed to managing the Kroegel Homestead. The refuge is responsible for funding, constructing, and managing a visitor center facility, the wildlife drive, trails, boardwalks, the observation tower, signs, interpretive lands, informational kiosks, and other visitor support facilities. However, the majority of the facilities are currently unfunded. The refuge and its partners are pursuing various avenues for this funding, including agency funds, cost-sharing, and grants. Further, the refuge is increasing membership in the friends' group, Pelican Island Preservation Society, to help with outreach activities, environmental education programs, and guided tours (e.g., special bird tours), as well as to raise funds and provide volunteer staff for refuge programs.

Anticipated Impacts of the Uses: Construction of facilities (e.g., trails, parking areas, restroom facility, wildlife drive, boardwalks, and observation tower) is anticipated to alter the habitats at those particular sites under construction. However, the existing habitat is primarily abandoned citrus groves and the alteration is minor, discrete, and limited to a particular location. Properly locating these facilities and properly implementing environmental protection measures during construction will limit any negative environmental impacts. Long-term impacts from proposed construction activities are not anticipated to be significant. Further, most of the proposed facilities are to be located in disturbed habitats that are undergoing restoration (e.g., citrus groves are being restored to maritime hammock). The preferred location of the proposed visitor center facility is on the mainland, in the developed landscape around the city of Sebastian, at the Kroegel Homestead. No negative impacts are expected from siting the proposed visitor center facility at the Kroegel Homestead, while the historic features and structures of the Homestead will be protected along with its historic character and centuries-old vegetation.

As a result of increased visitation and public use, some illegal activities have the potential to increase (e.g., littering and taking wildlife, including plants). Further, other uses not allowed on the refuge or not allowed in some areas of the refuge may also occur and have negative impacts (e.g., bicycling on the impoundment trails may cause wildlife disturbances and may potentially cause increased erosion). Minor temporary wildlife disturbances may result from the occurrence of the approved public use activities (e.g., temporary wildlife disturbances may result from an outdoor classroom activity and minor trampling of vegetation may occur during group bird watching tours) and minor loss of wildlife may occur as a result of collisions with vehicles on Jungle Trail or on the wildlife drive, but these impacts are not anticipated to be significant.

If impacts are determined to be sufficient, then refuge management will further restrict or eliminate the associated use(s).

Public Review and Comment: During the public scoping process for the Pelican Island National Wildlife Refuge Draft Comprehensive Conservation Plan and Environmental Assessment, five public meetings were conducted (during May and June 2000). Verbal and written comments were recorded regarding a variety of subjects, including uses of the refuge. Further, during the public comment and review period for the draft plan and environmental assessment, opportunity was provided to the public to submit comments during a 60-day review period (July 27, 2005 to September 26, 2005).

Determination (check one below):

	Use is Not Compatible
X	Use is Compatible, with the Listed Stipulations

Stipulations Necessary to Ensure Compatibility: These uses are limited to daylight hours. Public access is limited to only those so designated areas. The refuge will develop, provide, and update brochures and maps designating these and other public uses and areas, along with associated restrictions. (Contact the Refuge Manager for details on these designated areas and any associated restrictions.) Bicycling is limited to only Jungle Trail (bicycling is not allowed on the wildlife drive, on any of the trails, on the impoundment dikes, off-road or off-trail, or anywhere else on the refuge). Adaptive management will address any negative impacts to wildlife and habitats from these uses to limit or eliminate these negative impacts. If human impacts are determined to be detrimental to resources of the refuge, the Refuge Manager may implement measures to limit or eliminate these impacts, including the closure of an area either completely or limited by season, time of day, type of access (e.g., by foot and by vehicle), or other factor. This includes all areas associated with these uses, such as the wildlife drive, observation tower, trails, boardwalks, and spoil and lagoonal islands. Further, to ensure public safety, the Refuge Manager will close access to the wildlife drive and other areas during incidents of high water (e.g., during flooding events and hurricanes) or for other safety reasons. Prior to all construction activities, the refuge will obtain all necessary permits. Law enforcement and education are key components to ensure continued compatibility of these uses. Refuge staff will monitor and document any negative impacts of these uses, taking corrective measures as necessary to limit or eliminate impacts to the resources of the refuge.

Justification: Environmental education, environmental interpretation, wildlife observation, and wildlife photography are priority public uses, under the 1997 National Wildlife Refuge System Improvement Act. Not only do these uses enhance the public's understanding and appreciation of wildlife and wild places, but these uses also further the purposes of the refuge and the mission of the National Wildlife Refuge System.

NEPA Compliance for Refuge Use Description: *Place an X in appropriate space.*

_____Categorical Exclusion without Environmental Action Statement
_____Categorical Exclusion and Environmental Action Statement
__X__Environmental Assessment and Finding of No Significant Impact
_____Environmental Impact Statement and Record of Decision

Mandatory 15-Year Re-evaluation Date: <u>July 13, 2021</u>

Description of Use:

Research
Research is the planned, organized, and systematic gathering of data to discover or verify facts. In principle, research conducted on the refuge by universities, co-op units, non-profit organizations, and other research entities furthers refuge management and serves the purposes and vision of the refuge. All research activities, whether conducted by public agencies, public research entities, universities, private research groups, or any other entity, shall be required to obtain special use permits from the refuge. All research activities will be overseen by the Refuge Biologist and Refuge Manager.

Availability of Resources: Other than the administration of associated special use permits, no refuge resources are required for this use.

Anticipated Impacts of the Use: Generally, impacts from research are minimal. Occasionally, slight or temporary wildlife or habitat disturbances may occur (e.g., minor trampling of vegetation may occur when researchers access monitoring plots). However, these impacts are not significant, nor are they permanent. Also, a small number of individuals might be collected for further scientific study, but these collections are anticipated to have minimal impact on the populations from which they came.

Public Review and Comment: During the public scoping process for the Pelican Island National Wildlife Refuge Draft Comprehensive Conservation Plan and Environmental Assessment, five public meetings were conducted (during May and June 2000). Verbal and written comments were recorded regarding a variety of subjects, including uses of the refuge. Further, during the public comment and review period for the draft plan and environmental assessment, opportunity was provided to the public to submit comments during a 60-day review period (July 27, 2005 to September 26, 2005).

Determination (check one below):

	Use is Not Compatible
X	Use is Compatible, with the Listed Stipulations

Stipulations Necessary to Ensure Compatibility: All research conducted on the refuge must further the purposes of the refuge and the mission of the National Wildlife Refuge System. To ensure that research activities are compatible, the refuge requires that a special use permit be obtained before any research activity may occur. Research proposals must be submitted for special use permits in advance of the activity to allow for review by refuge staff to ensure minimal impacts to the resources of the refuge. Each special use permit may contain conditions under which the research will be conducted. Each special use permit holder will submit annual reports to the refuge updating the refuge on research activities, progress, findings, and other information. Further, each special use permit holder will provide copies of findings, final reports, and/or other documentation at the end of each project. The refuge will deny permits for research proposals that are determined to not serve the purposes of the refuge and the mission of the National Wildlife Refuge System. The refuge will also deny permits for research proposals that are determined to negatively impact resources or that materially interfere with or detract from the purposes of the refuge. All research activities are subject to the conditions of their permits.

Justification: Research activities provide important benefits to the refuge and to the natural resources supported by the refuge. Supporting management, research conducted on the refuge can lead to new discoveries, new facts, verified information, and better management decisions. Research has the potential to further the purposes of the refuge and the mission of the National Wildlife Refuge System.

NEPA Compliance for Refuge Use Description: *Place an X in appropriate space.*

_____Categorical Exclusion without Environmental Action Statement
_____Categorical Exclusion and Environmental Action Statement
__X__Environmental Assessment and Finding of No Significant Impact
_____Environmental Impact Statement and Record of Decision

Mandatory 10-Year Re-evaluation Date: July 13, 2016

Description of Use:

Mosquito Control
The Indian River Mosquito Control District conducts mosquito control activities on the refuge and in Bird's and Pete's impoundments based on Rotational Impoundment Management and Integrated Pest Management in pursuit of four management objectives:

- enhancement of fish and wildlife resources through marsh integration to the Indian River Lagoon;
- enhancement of water quality in the impoundments and the Indian River Lagoon;
- enhancement of wading bird feeding opportunities; and
- reduction of the sources of mosquitoes, minimizing the need for pesticide applications.

Basically, the emphasis of mosquito control management is on source reduction (i.e., to prevent or limit mosquito breeding). These mosquito control activities include monitoring and modifying water levels in the impoundments (through water control structures and pumping activities), maintaining these water control structures and pumps, and maintaining the dikes. As needed, integrated pest management activities include seasonal flooding, larviciding, open marsh water management, and ground ultra low volume adulticiding. Larviciding mosquito control activities are conducted 10-15 times per year. Adulticiding mosquito control activities are generally not conducted, unless unusual circumstances occur (e.g., extremely large hatches or documented human health threats). The mosquito control trucks and all-terrain vehicles access the impoundments through an unpaved road and the impoundment dikes. Additional activities include periodic/occasional water quality monitoring, vegetation monitoring, and wildlife monitoring. Various flooding strategies have been explored and implemented during the winter to maximize production of wading bird foraging sources.

Availability of Resources: The Indian River Mosquito Control District funds and implements these mosquito control activities. Thus, no refuge resources are required to administer this use, other than reviewing management plans and being aware of operations and pesticides to be used.

Anticipated Impacts of the Use: Mosquito control activities have the potential for a variety of impacts. Potential impacts of chemicals on non-target organisms are a concern and are considered prior to mosquito control operations. Potential negative impacts to invertebrates from chemical applications may result in decreases in density and diversity of insects, arachnids, and/or crustaceans, thus negatively impacting food sources for various birds. Mosquito control activities also have the potential to decrease functionality of the impoundment for shorebirds, depending on the flooding and drawing down of the impoundment. The potential also exists to flood out ground nests during rotational impoundment management. Further, temporary wildlife or habitat disturbances may occur during actual operations (e.g., wildlife disturbance and temporary trampling of vegetation during pesticide application by all-terrain vehicle).

Public Review and Comment: During the public scoping process for the Pelican Island National Wildlife Refuge Draft Comprehensive Conservation Plan and Environmental Assessment, five public meetings were conducted (during May and June 2000). Verbal and written comments were recorded regarding a variety of subjects, including uses of the refuge. Further, during the public comment and review period for the draft plan and environmental assessment, opportunity was provided to the public to submit comments during a 60-day review period (July 27, 2005 to September 26, 2005).

Determination (check one below):

	Use is Not Compatible
X	Use is Compatible, with the Listed Stipulations

Stipulations Necessary to Ensure Compatibility: Mosquito control management plans were developed for all impoundments of the refuge. These management plans provide conditions under which mosquito control operations are approved. Additional stipulations to ensure compatibility of this use are listed.

- A Refuge Special Use Permit is required and must be renewed annually.
- Larval control may only be conducted when breeding is widespread, as documented by sampling conducted by the Indian River Mosquito Control District.

- Priority for treatments will be given to those chemicals with the least effect on non-target organisms (e.g., BTI).
- The Refuge Manager has final approval for all pesticide treatments.
- Indian River Mosquito Control District shall submit to the refuge a final report at the end of each year.
- No flights shall be conducted over the Wilderness Area (i.e., Pelican Island proper), nor over the closed area buffer around the Island.
- Indian River Mosquito Control District shall notify the Refuge Manager by phone of all pesticide applications, including areas and acreages to be treated, pesticide to be applied, date and time of planned treatment, method of application, and data supporting the need for treatment.
- In developing approaches to specific treatments, consideration will be given to avoiding or minimizing impacts to the resources of the refuge.
- Refuge staff shall be allowed to inspect operations at any time.
- All pesticides used must be included in the refuge's Pesticide Use and Disposal Management Plan. If a pesticide proposed for use is not included in this step-down plan, the Refuge Manager must review and approve its use before any application occurs.
- The Indian River Mosquito Control District shall immediately notify the Refuge Manager of any chemical spills, threats to human safety on the refuge, human disturbance, or wildlife disturbance that may occur as a consequence of its mosquito control operations.

Justification: Under the right environmental conditions, the impoundments of the refuge are productive habitats for population explosions of saltmarsh mosquitoes. The abandoned citrus groves are also potential breeding sites for freshwater-inhabiting mosquitoes. The refuge exists in a developed human landscape, where mosquitoes represent a potential disease threat to public health (e.g., West Nile Virus), as well as to wildlife. Mosquito control activities address health safety issues for the refuge and the community. Further, these mosquito control management activities support wildlife and habitat management activities by providing key foraging sources and areas for wading birds. The use, with the listed stipulations, does not materially interfere with the purposes of the refuge.

NEPA Compliance for Refuge Use Description: *Place an X in appropriate space.*

_____Categorical Exclusion without Environmental Action Statement
_____Categorical Exclusion and Environmental Action Statement
__X__Environmental Assessment and Finding of No Significant Impact
_____Environmental Impact Statement and Record of Decision

Mandatory 10-Year Re-evaluation Date: July 13, 2016

Description of Use:

Managing Interim Citrus Groves
Portions of the refuge, especially new acquisitions, include citrus groves. Until restoration activities are underway, these groves continue to be managed and harvested under a special use permit. Management activities by the grove operator include controlling exotics in the groves, benefiting adjacent native habitats of the refuge. If these groves were left fallow and un-managed, exotics would easily invade these disturbed agricultural areas, creating footholds and spreading into native habitats. The grove operator continues to manage the citrus grove, using irrigation and approved pesticides. Citrus is harvested by handpicking during the months of November through January.

This saves the refuge from leaving these lands fallow and from the burden of trying to manage these agricultural lands until funds are available for restoration to native habitats. As these groves are scheduled for restoration by the refuge, exotics and citrus are removed from the site.

Availability of Resources: Other than the management of special use permits and agreements, no refuge resources are required to administer this use.

Anticipated Impacts of the Use: Active grove operations have the potential to spread exotic plants (e.g., guinea grass) and to contribute nutrient and pesticide laden runoff to the Indian River Lagoon and adjacent native habitats. However, under specific conditions imposed under a special use permit, these negative impacts will be minimized. Without management of these lands by grove operators and before restoration by the refuge, these lands would have a greater potential for negative impacts on refuge habitats and wildlife through increased exotics (plants and animals) and the spread of these exotics into native habitats. This use is a short term, interim use in anticipation of future native habitat restoration activities.

Public Review and Comment: During the public scoping process for the Pelican Island National Wildlife Refuge Draft Comprehensive Conservation Plan and Environmental Assessment, five public meetings were conducted (during May and June 2000). Verbal and written comments were recorded regarding a variety of subjects, including uses of the refuge. Further, during the public comment and review period for the draft plan and environmental assessment, opportunity was provided to the public to submit comments during a 60-day review period (July 27, 2005 to September 26, 2005).

Determination (check one below):

	Use is Not Compatible
X	Use is Compatible, with the Listed Stipulations

Stipulations Necessary to Ensure Compatibility: Special use permits for citrus cultivation shall only be for temporary management or demonstration purposes. These permits may contain additional restrictions or conditions under which the permit holder must operate. Citrus cultivation shall use best management practices. Further, only those pesticides approved by the refuge shall be used on these groves. Grove operators shall control exotic plants in the groves. All irrigation systems shall be retained on the site after the close of the permit. As these groves are scheduled for restoration, the permit holder shall remove all citrus trees at the close of the permit. The refuge will charge the permit holder a nominal fee if the value of the services provided by the permit holder is not commensurate with the value of the harvest.

Justification: This use does not detract from or materially interfere with the purposes of the refuge. Further, this interim use serves refuge management goals. Without some type of management, these groves would end up serving as a source of exotics for the native habitats of the refuge. This interim management activity controls these exotics until restoration activities begin.

NEPA Compliance for Refuge Use Description: *Place an X in appropriate space.*

_____Categorical Exclusion without Environmental Action Statement
_____Categorical Exclusion and Environmental Action Statement
__X__Environmental Assessment and Finding of No Significant Impact
_____Environmental Impact Statement and Record of Decision

Mandatory 10-Year Re-evaluation Date: **July 13, 2016**

Description of Use:
Commercial Ecotour Operations
Ecologically based commercial boat and kayak tours currently operate in the Indian River Lagoon, offering wildlife viewing opportunities, especially of Pelican Island proper. These tours provide a service to refuge visitors by providing opportunities for wildlife observation, photography, and limited interpretation. Currently, three tour boats and two kayak companies operate year-round in the refuge. The tour boat operations generally run 7 days a week during the busy season (i.e., winter) and 5 days a week during the off season. Each of the tour boats can carry about 40 passengers, however, trips average about 15 passengers. Generally, each trip runs about 1.5 hours. The kayak tours generally run once a week during the busy season and very seldom during the off season. The tours generally include between 5 and 15 people. Each trip runs about 2 to 3 hours.

Since the Indian River Lagoon portion of the refuge is managed through an agreement with the State of Florida, this use is also governed by this management agreement that allows for traditional uses, as listed.

> The right of the public to use the area for traditional navigation, boating, bathing, shell fishing, and commercial and sport fishing shall not be restricted with the exception of a 410(-)foot buffer zone surrounding Pelican Island (Government Lot 3, Township 31 South, Range 39 East, Indian River County). This buffer zone is measured from the mean high water line of said island and extending out into the Indian River.

However, since this use is not one of these traditional uses outlined in the lease agreement with the State of Florida and since this use is not a use that was customarily being pursued within this leased area on or before May 23, 1968, it is subject to refuge regulations and restrictions by the Fish and Wildlife Service. (May 23, 1968 is the date of the original lease between the Service and the State of Florida.)

Land-based tours on fee title lands currently are limited to local educational groups. However, the potential for commercial bus tours requires that they be included for review under Commercial Ecotour Operations.

Availability of Resources: Other than the administration of associated special use permits and the possibility of intervention by law enforcement, no Refuge resources are required for this use.

Anticipated Impacts of the Use: Under certain restrictions, this use is anticipated to have minimal impacts. Occasionally, slight or temporary wildlife or habitat disturbances may occur. Tour boats sometimes can have negative impacts to seagrasses from prop scarring and anchoring. They can also disturb birds on the Pelican Island rookery or on other islands by approaching too fast or too near to an island. Measures should be implemented to limit or eliminate these impacts, including establishing mooring buoys in deeper waters to prevent damage to seagrasses and extending the closed area around Pelican Island or other key islands to provide a better buffer zone for wildlife on an island. The possibility exists for a collision between a tour boat and aquatic wildlife (e.g., West Indian manatee); however, education of tour boat operators and specific restrictions will help limit this possibility.

Public Review and Comment: During the public scoping process for the Pelican Island National Wildlife Refuge Draft Comprehensive Conservation Plan and Environmental Assessment, five public meetings were conducted (during May and June 2000). Verbal and written comments were recorded regarding a variety of subjects, including uses of the refuge. Further, during the public comment and review period for the draft plan and environmental assessment, opportunity was provided to the public to submit comments during a 60-day review period (July 27, 2005 to September 26, 2005).

Determination (check one below):

	Use is Not Compatible
X	Use is Compatible, with the Listed Stipulations

Stipulations Necessary to Ensure Compatibility: To ensure that commercial activities on the refuge are compatible, a special use permit will be required before any commercial activity subject to regulation by the Fish and Wildlife Service may occur. Each special use permit may contain conditions under which that particular activity will be conducted. All tour boat operators must be oriented by refuge staff (e.g., to provide these operators with background information on the refuge and information about key needs of some wildlife, such as nesting birds), with an annual refresher to be conducted by refuge staff. Further, the refuge shall supply educational and informational materials to the tour boat operators for distribution to participants. Refuge staff will spot check operations to monitor any impacts. One condition of the special use permit will address the requirement that the tour boat operators cover key points during their presentations (e.g., wildlife disturbance). Special use permits will also address a variety of other topics, such as areas of operation for these activities, areas to be avoided by these activities, speed limits (if necessary), water depths approved for these operations, and noise level limitations (e.g., from speakers or other amplifying devices).

Generally, all ecotour operations must avoid wildlife collisions, operate at or below posted speed limits, provide educational information, and stay outside the posted closed areas of Pelican Island proper or any other posted closed areas. Any violation of these or other applicable federal, state, or local regulations may lead to additional restrictions on the permit holder or revocation of the special use permit. The Refuge Manager may revise, amend, or revoke the permit of a commercial operation if that operation is in violation of the permit conditions (e.g., if the commercial operation is negatively impacting refuge wildlife and habitats or if the commercial operation is in violation of applicable state or federal laws). As needed, the Refuge Manager may limit the size, type, or number of commercial vehicles involved in ecotour operations. All ecotour operations will maintain a minimum level of liability insurance with notification of the Refuge Manager by the insurance company before or upon cancellation of the policy. All guides must possess all applicable current, valid state and federal licenses. Tour operators should not have serious criminal histories or histories of repeated state or federal game violations.

Justification: Ecotour operations, under the right conditions, can help further the mission of the National Wildlife Refuge System and can enhance public appreciation and understanding of the refuge and the resources it protects. Further, ecotour operations can provide educational materials to the participants, further enhancing the understanding, appreciation, and experience of the ecotour operators and the participants.

NEPA Compliance for Refuge Use Description: *Place an X in appropriate space.*

_____Categorical Exclusion without Environmental Action Statement
_____Categorical Exclusion and Environmental Action Statement
__X__Environmental Assessment and Finding of No Significant Impact
_____Environmental Impact Statement and Record of Decision

Mandatory 10-Year Re-evaluation Date: July 13, 2016

Literature Cited:

Indian River Mosquito Control District. 1992a. Management Plan for Indian River Impoundment #2 (Birds). Vero Beach, FL. 35 pp.

Indian River Mosquito Control District. 1992b. Management Plan for Indian River Impoundment #3 (Pete's). Vero Beach, FL. 48 pp.

U.S. Fish and Wildlife Service. 1999. Pelican Island: Honoring a Legacy. Washington, DC. 14 pp.

Approval of Compatibility Determinations:

The signature of approval covers all the compatibility determinations considered within the Comprehensive Conservation Plan for Pelican Island National Wildlife Refuge. If one of the descriptive uses is considered for compatibility outside of the plan, the approval signature becomes part of that determination.

Signature: _Signed_   4/10/06
     Refuge Manager   Date

Review: _Signed_   8/10/06
     Regional Compatibility Coordinator   Date

Review: _Signed_   8/18/06
     Refuge Supervisor   Date

Concurrence: _Signed_   8-21-06
     Regional Chief   Date
     National Wildlife Refuge System
     Southeast Region

VI. Avoidance and Minimization of Impacts to Federally Listed Species

The implementation of all goals, objectives, and strategies outlined in the comprehensive conservation plan will follow the refuge's best management practices and will pursue avoidance and minimization of impacts to federally threatened and endangered species, to the extent possible and practicable. Whenever and wherever prudent, the avoidance and minimization measures outlined in Appendix VI will be incorporated into the implementation of the comprehensive conservation plan to minimize the effect to federally threatened or endangered species.

ACTIONS TO MINIMIZE IMPACTS ON ALL FEDERALLY THREATENED AND ENDANGERED SPECIES ON THE REFUGE
Earthmoving Activities All earthmoving activities on the refuge will obtain all applicable permits before commencement. During the application for permits, conditions may be imposed to minimize any impacts that may be anticipated from proposed earthmoving activities. The refuge provides orientation information regarding federally threatened and endangered species found on the refuge to all new employees, volunteers, and contractors involved in earthmoving activities. The refuge will make all efforts possible and practicable to limit long-term wildlife impacts of earthmoving activities. For example, during the shoreline stabilization activities already conducted for the Pelican Island proper rookery, several measures were taken to limit impacts to the birds using the Island, including scheduling work around nesting season and other periods of increased wildlife activity. Similar measures are proposed for future shoreline stabilization projects. During earthmoving activities associated with exotic plant control, measures to limit wildlife impacts include preliminary assessments by qualified individuals to avoid burrows, nests, and other obvious signs of wildlife activity. During earthmoving activities associated with habitat restoration, measures to limit wildlife impacts include preliminary assessments by qualified individuals to avoid burrows, nests, and other obvious signs of wildlife activity.
Fire Management Activities Fire management is a tool employed for the benefit of wildlife, including improving habitat, controlling wildfires, and controlling or removing exotic plants. The refuge will make all efforts possible and practicable to limit long-term wildlife impacts of management activities. Measures employed to limit wildlife impacts related to fire management activities include scheduling fire prep and burns around nesting seasons and other periods of increased wildlife activity.

ACTIONS TO MINIMIZE IMPACTS ON ALL FEDERALLY THREATENED AND ENDANGERED SPECIES ON THE REFUGE
Exotic Plant Control and Removal Activities Refuges regularly and commonly use Garlon to control exotic plants with no measurable effects on federally listed threatened and endangered species. The refuge provides orientation information regarding federally threatened and endangered species found on the refuge to all new employees, volunteers, and contractors involved in controlling and removing exotic plants. All pesticides and herbicides are applied in accordance with label directions. The refuge will make all efforts possible and practicable to limit long-term wildlife impacts from management activities. Measures to limit wildlife impacts during the control and removal of exotic plants include preliminary assessments by qualified individuals to avoid burrows, nests, and other obvious signs of wildlife activity.
Research Activities All researchers on the refuge must obtain all applicable permits, including a refuge special use permit before the commencement of research activities on the refuge. During the application for permits, conditions may be imposed to eliminate or minimize any impacts that may be anticipated from a research proposal. The refuge provides orientation information regarding federally threatened and endangered species found on the refuge to all researchers.
Increased Visitation The refuge will make all efforts possible and practicable to limit wildlife impacts related to increased visitation. Measures to limit wildlife impacts related to increased visitation include establishing and enforcing closed areas (e.g., for bird rookeries), controlling access (e.g., open only certain hours, open only certain seasons, and open to limited numbers of visitors), conveying ethical wildlife viewing messages (e.g., through brochures, interpretive talks, and presentations), and controlling or eliminating inappropriate and incompatible uses.
Construction Activities All construction activities on the refuge will obtain all applicable permits before commencement. During the application for permits, conditions may be imposed to eliminate or minimize any impacts that may be anticipated from proposed construction. Future construction activities will be expected to require future consultations, once specific sites and structure footprints have been identified (e.g., another §7 will be required for the siting and building of a visitor center). The refuge will make all efforts possible and practicable to limit long-term wildlife impacts of management activities.
Impoundment Management With over a decade of the same management operations for the impoundments, no conflicts or impacts to federally threatened and endangered species have been identified. In fact, managing the water levels has proven to have foraging benefits for wood storks. The refuge will make all efforts possible and practicable to limit long-term wildlife impacts of management activities.

VII. Service's Response to Public Comments

The public review and comment period for the Draft Comprehensive Conservation Plan and Environmental Assessment for Pelican Island Refuge opened on July 27, 2005, and closed on September 26, 2005. Written comments were submitted by six members of the general public, one organization, one local government agency, one state government agency, and one Native American tribe and comments were submitted through the state clearinghouse, representing seven state governmental agencies. No comments were submitted by other federal agencies. The Citizen's for Florida's Waterways group is the only identified organization that submitted comments. The agencies submitting comments included: Indian River Mosquito Control District, Treasure Coast Regional Planning Council, St. Johns River Water Management District, State Historic Preservation Office, Florida Department of Transportation, Florida Department of Agriculture and Consumer Services, Florida Department of Environmental Protection, and Florida Fish and Wildlife Conservation Commission. The proposed activity was determined by the State of Florida to be consistent with the Florida Coastal Management Program. Further, the State Historic Preservation Office (in the Division of Historical Resources, Bureau of Historic Preservation, Florida Department of State) made no comments, but concurred with the draft plan and environmental assessment. And, the Miccosukee Tribe of Indians of Florida concurred with the selection of Alternative C as the proposed alternative.

Under NEPA, the Service must respond to substantive comments. For purposes of this comprehensive conservation plan, a substantive comment is one that was submitted during the public review and comment period which is within the scope of the proposed action (and the other alternatives outlined in the environmental assessment), is specific to the proposed action, has a direct relationship to the proposed action, and includes reasons for the Service to consider it. (For example, a substantive comment might be that the document referenced 500 individuals of a particular species, but that current research found 600. In such a case, the Service would likely update the plan to reflect the 600, citing the current research. While a comment that would not be considered substantive would be: "We love the refuge.")

The comments submitted during the public review and comment period were evaluated, summarized, and grouped into several categories: Fish, Wildlife, and Plant Populations; Habitats; Land Protection and Conservation; Education and Visitor Services; Refuge Administration; Alternatives; and References. The Service's responses to the comments are provided, by category.

FISH, WILDLIFE, AND PLANT POPULATIONS

Comment – Feral And Free Roaming Animals
One comment posed a question regarding the kinds of feral and free roaming animals recorded on the refuge (see page 15).

Service's Response
Page 15 was clarified in parentheses to include "…feral animals and free foaming pets (including feral and domestic cats and dogs)…"

Comment – Correction To Number Of Reptile And Amphibians On The Refuge
One comment submitted corrections to the number of reptile and amphibian species on the refuge: make corrections on page 17 to include nine snakes, seven lizards, and nine frogs and toads.

Service's Response

Comment noted. The refuge will continue to document all findings of fish and wildlife species on the refuge. As additional species are documented or verified on the refuge, the Service will amend the list of species for the refuge. The commenter did not provide the names of the reptile and amphibian species thought to occur on the refuge, nor did the commenter provide a citation for those species being documented on the refuge. The refuge would consider updating the list of species found on the refuge with additional information.

Comment – A1a Wildlife Underpass

One comment felt that installing a wildlife underpass under A1A is very important and should be included in the CCP.

Service's Response

The strategies under objectives A.7 and B.1 were modified to include working with the partners to evaluate the needs, costs, and benefits of installing wildlife underpasses. Objective B.1 does provide for a habitat connection between the beach and dune habitats and those habitats west of A1A to benefit southeastern beach mouse. To provide such a connection, the Service will evaluate the feasibility of a variety of measures, including underpasses. And, underpasses will be evaluated if warranted by the survey information resulting from Objective A.7, which recommends the development of baseline data for resident wildlife.

Comment – Least Terns

One comment outlined that no mention is made of providing a much-needed nesting area for least terns. An example was submitted in this comment regarding an artificial island of crushed rock was constructed at Bill Baggs (Cape Florida) State Park on Key Biscayne, which was utilized.

Service's Response

Comment noted. This comment is addressed under objectives B.4 and A.6.

HABITATS

Comment – Seagrass Loss

One comment outlined that the figures referenced for seagrass loss were not current and that the most recent figures indicate that the Indian River Lagoon system has lost very little seagrass from 1943 to date.

Service's Response

Comment noted. The cite included in the draft plan on page 36 is from the St. Johns River Water Management District (SJRWMD), which monitors seagrasses within the Indian River Lagoon system. Based on those data, the refuge has a mix of stable, increasing, and decreasing seagrass beds, while Indian River County experienced an overall 61 percent gain and southern Brevard County experienced an overall 73 percent loss from 1943 to 1992 (St. Johns River Water Management District 1999). Further, in its 2005 District Water Management Plan, the SJRWMD outlines that, overall, the Indian River Lagoon has lost about 18 percent of its seagrasses (St. Johns River Water Management District 2005).

Comment – Identify Bird's Impoundment And Paul's Island On A Map

One comment noted that Bird's Impoundment and Paul's Island are mentioned in the text, but are not identified on a map.

Service's Response
Figure 1 was updated to identify Bird's, Pete's, and the Deerfield impoundments and Paul's Island.

Comment – Erosion Impacts To Pelican Island Proper
One comment requested clarification on the erosion impacts to Pelican Island proper.

Service's Response
The last paragraph under Ecological Threats and Problems in Chapter I was updated to reflect that primary impacts to the erosion of Pelican Island were found to be from boat wakes, but that the potential for secondary impacts exists from dredging a deeper channel near the refuge.

Comment – Impoundments
One comment suggested that the goal for the impoundments should be full restoration of the salt marshes and mangroves by removing the dikes. The comment continued that under current conditions, land crabs are prevented from burrowing and have less area available to them. Further, it stated that diamondback terrapins require salt marsh, not impoundments. The comment also stated that eliminating mosquito larvae reduces prey for birds and that few shorebirds use the impoundments due to the artificial water levels in them.

Service's Response
Comment noted. This comment is addressed under Appendix V under the compatibility determination for mosquito control activities on the refuge. The Service has management agreements in place with Indian River County and Indian River Mosquito Control District to coordinate management of the impoundments to benefit wading birds and shorebirds, as well as to protect public health and safety through mosquito control activities. The agreements preclude the Service from fully restoring these impoundments, however, the Service coordinates with the Indian River Mosquito Control District to manage them under a Rotational Impoundment Management scheme to enhance fish and wildlife benefits. The refuge is committed to enabling future research to address life history needs of species such as diamondback terrapins and land crabs on the refuge (this is addressed under Objective A.7).

Comment – Restore The Deerfield Impoundment
One comment noted that on page 101, the breached Deerfield impoundment is referenced and that this impoundment is a candidate for restoration with removal of the dike.

Service's Response
Comment noted. Along with St. Johns River Water Management District (SJRWMD) (co-grantee) and Indian River Mosquito Control District (IRMCD) (co-grantee), the refuge manages the Deerfield Impoundments as a co-grantee under a Conservation Easement with Orchid Island Properties, Inc. (grantor). In improving the habitat conditions at the Deerfield Impoundments, the refuge will evaluate several options in coordination with the landowner, Orchid Island Properties, Inc., and the partners, SJRWMD and IRMCD. Any habitat enhancement, including dike removal, will require coordination under the stipulations of the Conservation Easement and the prior written approval of the grantor and other grantees.

Comment – Impoundment Management Plans
One comment stated that the management plan for Bird's impoundment was written in 1992 and should be rewritten.

Service's Response
Comment noted. The Service manages Bird's impoundment under agreement with Indian River

County and Indian River Mosquito Control District. The existing impoundment management plan will be updated when the refuge develops a habitat management step-down plan as outlined in the CCP.

Comment – Mosquito Control
Two opposing comments were submitted regarding mosquito control: one in opposition and one in support of mosquito control activities on the refuge.

One comment opposed mosquito control activities on the refuge: since so few homes are in the area, mosquito control is unnecessary and mosquito control, as it is now practiced, in not compatible with the recovery of declining wildlife dependent on the habitat that was destroyed to create the impoundments.

The Indian River Mosquito Control District (IRMCD) supports mosquito control activities on the refuge. Beyond the impoundments, the comment submitted by IRMCD was that it was appropriate to include most of the islands within the refuge in the mosquito control program, since these islands and the salt marshes of the refuge can be prolific mosquito producers (producing *Ochlerotatus taeniorhynchus* and *Ochlerotatus sollicitans*). Further, it was submitted that other areas of the refuge produce *Culex nigripalpus*, the local vector of St. Louis Encephalitis and West Nile Virus, making it extremely important for control of these mosquitoes to protect the comfort and health of refuge visitors, nearby residents, and wildlife.

Service's Response
Comments noted. These comments are addressed under Appendix V under the compatibility determination for mosquito control activities on the refuge. The Service has management agreements in place with Indian River County and Indian River Mosquito Control District to coordinate management of the impoundments to benefit wading birds and shorebirds, as well as to protect public health and safety through mosquito control activities in the impoundments and on several refuge islands.

Comment – Salt Marsh And Tidal Marsh Restoration
One comment noted that on page 49, the plan identifies 356 acres of salt marsh and a tidal marsh that will be restored. The comment requested clarification as to whether this was within or outside of the present impoundments.

Service's Response
Comment noted. This comment is addressed under Objective B.2, which proposes to restore 356 acres of salt marsh, mangrove swamp, and maritime hammock outside of the existing impoundments. The salt marsh and mangrove swamp restoration is proposed along the Indian River Lagoon shoreline. The maritime hammock restoration is proposed to occur in the Jungle Trail area.

Comment – 410-Foot Buffer For Pelican Island Proper Rookery
One comment was submitted in support of maintaining a 410-foot buffer around the Island, while it was stated that more could be done to keep disturbances by boat wakes to a minimum. Further, the comment requested that the buffer area be made a no motor zone.

Service's Response
Comment noted. This comment is addressed under Objective B.3, which proposes a 410-foot closed area buffer around this sensitive rookery island (reflecting current research). The closed area buffer is a no entry zone that limits wildlife disturbance from people getting too close to the nesting, feeding, and resting birds.

Comment – Buffer Shoal/Seagrass Preserve By Sebastian Inlet District Commission
One comment noted that the CCP makes no mention of the buffer shoal/seagrass preserve proposal by the Sebastian Inlet District Commission on the northwest side of the refuge. Further, the comment suggested that the Service designate the buffer shoal/seagrass preserve as a no motor zone to limit disturbances, but to allow access for wade fishing.

Service's Response
Comment noted. This comment is covered under Objective B.3. The partners needed to accomplish Objective B.3 have increased, with the Sebastian Inlet Tax District joining the effort as a newer partner. Future use of the buffer shoal/seagrass preserve will be evaluated and is anticipated to be part of the permit process, while also ensuring sustained integrity of the buffer shoal.

Comment – Treating Exotics
The comment requested the conduction of simple treatments on small areas of exotics, instead of severe mechanical habitat alteration as in the past. It stated that in the past, disturbed soil sprouted exotics, dirt piles smothered the *Cardisoma guanhumi* (land crab) colonies, and the perfect understory foraging area for neotropical migratory birds was eliminated.

Service's Response
Comment noted. Exotics are addressed under objectives A.8 and A.9. The Service is committed to restoring native habitats over the long term for the refuge. While it is recognized that restoration efforts inherently cause short-term disturbances, the long-term wildlife and habitat benefits of habitat restoration are the refuge's goal. Due to limited resources, the refuge is currently using volunteers to conduct smaller exotic control activities. As opportunities present themselves to conduct larger projects, the Service will work with the involved parties to further the habitat restoration goals and objectives of the refuge over the long term, while minimizing the scope of disturbance, as much as practicable, in the short term.

Comment – Citrus Groves
Two comments focused on not restoring the citrus groves.

One comment requested retaining a portion of the old citrus groves as preferred migrating and wintering habitat for buntings, grosbeaks, and other bird species. The comment stated that since the refuge does not have the manpower or budget to do a complete restoration of the maritime hardwood hammock, the refuge should not restore the citrus groves. It further stated that those groves that have been partially restored are overgrown disasters and were better off in a pre-restoration condition. And, it continued that until and unless a large grassy (old field) area is maintained with seed heads and tangled brush, the current plan to eradicate the groves will eliminate buntings, grosbeaks, and other migratory songbirds from the refuge. The comment suggested that the refuge retain the citrus groves until the needed habitat is replaced elsewhere on the refuge.

The other citrus comment outlined that the citrus groves will naturally change over time, which is preferable to the Service going in, digging them up, and causing environmental chaos.

Service's Response
Comments noted. The Service is actively working with the partners and seeking additional funds to continue restoration of the citrus groves to natural communities on the refuge. The Service is adapting restoration and management activities as new information becomes available and as new information is learned from previous restoration activities. As future habitat restoration activities are planned, the Service will work to minimize impacts and to meet the habitat needs for neotropical migratory birds using the refuge, including providing appropriate habitat nearby to the restoration

areas. (See Objective B.6 for additional information.) However, restoration inherently involves some level of disturbance. It is the intent that all citrus groves on the refuge will be restored to native habitat on the refuge within the 15-year time frame of the CCP. Managing citrus groves is a costly activity, using intensive management with irrigation, fertilizers, herbicides, and pesticides, contrary to refuge management goals. When the citrus groves were originally developed, the hydrology of the site was altered and ditches were excavated to help drain the site. These alterations of the landscape preclude the unaided change of citrus groves back to native habitat and require more active restoration activities. Without active management, citrus groves have been shown to provide conditions suitable for exotic, invasive, and nuisance species, instead of for native plants.

Comment – Prescribed Burning
One comment stated that no prescribed burning should be practiced. It further stated that fine particulate matter from such burning travels thousands of miles, settling in human lungs and causing pneumonia, heart attacks, strokes, lung cancer, and asthma. The comment stated that we need to protect the American people and provide clean air, not dirty air because this is an easy way for an area to be cleaned out: don't kill Americans because of this laziness.

Service's Response
Comment noted. Under the Service's biological integrity policy (see 601 FW 3), refuges are charged with maintaining and restoring biological integrity, diversity, and environmental health. And under fire policies (see 621 FW 1 and 621 FW 3), refuges are to employ prescribed fire whenever it is an appropriate tool for managing resources. Many of the habitats in Florida evolved with the natural and regular occurrence of fire, requiring fire to maintain these natural communities. However, due to a variety of factors, naturally occurring fire has been excluded from many areas (increasing the threat to public health and safety from wildfires). Prescribed fire is one of the management tools that helps fulfill the purposes of Pelican Island Refuge and the mission of the National Wildlife Refuge System, including helping restore and maintain biological integrity of refuge habitats and helping manage for threatened and endangered species and wildlife diversity. Prescribed fire offers two primary benefits: providing for habitat management and reducing threats to public health and safety from wildfires. Helping to protect public health and safety, prescribe fire maintains healthy levels of fuel loads, limits the occurrence of catastrophic fire, and provides for the direction of smoke (e.g., away from population centers). The refuge coordinates with local emergency management services and fire departments on all prescribed fires and wildfires. Further, the refuge notifies the public when prescribed burns are planned to allow neighbors to take any needed precautions. And, all prescribed fire is conducted using sound professional judgment under Service and Department of Interior policy and specified conditions, including under an approved plan, which minimizes smoke impacts, helping to protect public health and safety. Currently, the prescribed fire activities conducted and anticipated to be conducted on the refuge are generally small and infrequent.

Comment – Habitat Terms
One comment requested clarification between upland forest and maritime hammock.

Service's Response
Comment noted. As used in the CCP, the term upland forest includes all upland forested habitat types on the refuge, including maritime hammock (i.e., maritime hammock is a subset of upland forest).

LAND PROTECTION AND CONSERVATION

Comment – United Real Estate Venture Tract
One comment stated that it is very important to purchase the United Real Estate Venture Tract, since they have completely destroyed southeastern beach mouse dunes and wetland habitat.

Service's Response
Comment noted. This comment is addressed under Objective C.1, which prioritizes this tract for acquisition or other protection measure. The Torwest Tract, including the wetland fringe, is the highest priority for refuge acquisition due to its contributions to the refuge and provision of buffer areas for the Pelican Island proper rookery island. Although still a high priority, the United Real Estate Venture Tract is a second priority.

Comment – Kroegel Homestead And Visitor Center
One comment stated that the Service should acquire a portion of the Kroegel Homestead for a visitor center, if possible.

Service's Response
Comment noted. This comment is addressed under objectives C.5 and E.4, which address the acquisition of the Kroegel Homestead and the use of the site for some level of visitor use and interpretation. The Kroegel Homestead is the Service's preferred site for a visitor center.

EDUCATION AND VISITOR SERVICES

Comment – Volunteers
One comment noted that several volunteers should be on duty whenever the refuge is open to the public, including one at the observation tower and one along the marked trails and roads.

Service's Response
Comment noted. This comment is addressed in Objective E.2 in the CCP, which calls for an increase in the number of volunteers to augment refuge staff, projects, and programs, including providing for roving interpretive volunteers. As roving interpretive volunteers are available, they are placed at the observation tower and along the marked trails. As facilities to support volunteers are developed on the refuge and as the volunteer program grows, additional roving interpretive volunteers will be available to the public.

Comment – Web Cams
One comment suggested that the Service install several "Pelican Cams" on the refuge to allow for remote viewing of wildlife.

Service's Response
Comment noted. The refuge currently does not have the resources and facilities to accommodate "Pelican Cams." But, this idea will be considered in the future.

Comment – Bicycling
One comment objected to the complete prohibition of bicycles. It further suggested that the refuge create bicycle paths instead of a wildlife drive.

Service's Response
Comments noted. This comment is addressed under Appendix V Compatibility Determinations, under Environmental Education, Interpretation, Wildlife Observation, and Photography. Consistent with the provisions outlined in the National Wildlife Refuge System Improvement Act, the Service facilitates quality, appropriate, and compatible wildlife-dependent recreation programs. At Pelican Island Refuge these include fishing, observing and photographing wildlife, and participating in environmental education and interpretation. These priority public uses provide the public with an opportunity to learn about, enjoy, and appreciate natural resources, but not at the expense of the

natural environment. Any allowed use of the refuge, including these priority public uses, must be determined to be compatible with the refuge's purposes and with the mission of the National Wildlife Refuge System (see Appendix V for the compatibility determinations). Fundamental and supreme to the provision of these uses is the provision of viable and diverse fish and wildlife populations and the habitats upon which they depend. Those uses that do not support the purposes of the refuge, that threaten or disturb fish and wildlife populations, or that are not compatible public uses will not be approved or will be phased out on the refuge.

The provisions of the CCP do not ban bicycling from the refuge. However, under compatibility requirements, bicycling is limited to Jungle Trail due to impacts associated with conflicts between different user groups and due to impacts associated with disturbing and flushing wildlife. As outlined in the compatibility determinations and due to anticipated impacts, bicycling is not allowed on the proposed wildlife drive, on any of the trails, on the impoundment dikes, off-road or off-trail, or elsewhere on the refuge other than on Jungle Trail. Appendix V provides more information regarding approved uses for the refuge. As new information regarding the impacts to wildlife becomes available, the Service will re-evaluate the appropriateness of bicycling activities.

By providing a wildlife drive opportunity, the refuge provides a more universally accessible way for a variety of users to experience the refuge and wildlife. The Service is committed to providing more universal access to those areas where appropriate, compatible, possible, and practicable. Bicycle paths instead of a wildlife drive would limit the access to specific users.

Comment – Wildlife Drive
Three comments objected to the development of a wildlife drive on the refuge. It was expressed that such a use would increase visitation, would increase wildlife disturbance, and would expend funds that would be better spent on wildlife and habitat management activities.

Service's Response
Comments noted. As provided in the National Wildlife Refuge System Improvement Act (1997), all uses of a national wildlife refuge must be determined to be compatible with the purposes of the refuge. The wildlife drive proposal was reviewed and was determined to be compatible (see Appendix V). If the refuge finds unacceptable impacts from use of the wildlife drive, it may be closed or access may be limited by season, time of day, type of access, or other factor. The refuge will continue to work with its partners to fund and maintain the proposed wildlife drive.

Comment – Visitor Center
Three comments were submitted objecting to the development of a visitor center for the refuge. Two of the three comments preferred to spend the funds on habitat management activities, while the third felt that environmental education (which would occur at the proposed visitor center) was already covered by the Environmental Learning Center, Lagoon House, Sebastian Inlet State Park, and Brevard County. Further, one of the comments detailed that any visitor center facility should not be placed on the barrier island.

Service's Response
Comments noted. As outlined in the CCP and under objectives C.5 and E.4, the Service considered various alternatives in evaluating a refuge visitor center, including no visitor center, co-location with a partner (e.g., Environmental Learning Center), Kroegel Homestead, Duck Point, and the Jungle Trail area. The Service identified the preferred site for the proposed, visitor center as the Kroegel Homestead on the mainland. The Service determined that a modest refuge visitor center will best convey the National Wildlife Refuge System's wildlife first message and serve the purposes of the refuge, as well as serve the local communities and the growing numbers of area residents and tourists.

Comment – Future Visitation

One comment noted that the action alternatives (B and C) propose to increase the staff and budget, but make no estimate of the number of anticipated visitors that will utilize the proposed facilities. The comment suggested that the estimate needs to be part of the plan.

Service's Response

Comment noted. The Service did not develop use estimates for the action alternatives due to a variety of factors (e.g., lack of funding to conduct the needed studies). Under the National Wildlife Refuge System Improvement Act (1997), refuges will facilitate appropriate and compatible public uses. The refuge will monitor use levels and impacts to ensure that all uses remain appropriate and compatible. Once the threshold has been passed to make a use not appropriate and not compatible, the refuge will take measures to ensure that the use is maintained below the threshold or the refuge will eliminate the use, as necessary.

Comment – Fishing

One comment stated that fishing is detrimental to wildlife, since the discarded lines, snagged hooks, lost hooks, and lost lines contribute to bird mortality. It further stated that since fishing is a consumptive use, increased fishing opportunities for humans mean less resources for the large wading birds.

Service's Response

Comment noted. This comment is addressed under Appendix V in the compatibility determinations. Under the 1997 National Wildlife Refuge System Improvement Act, Congress identified six priority public uses that are appropriate to be considered for refuges, including fishing. If impacts from fishing are determined to be unacceptable, the Service will work with the State of Florida (under the lease agreement), as well as with other partners to minimize those impacts to ensure compatibility of approved fishing activities. Current activities to help limit negative impacts to wildlife from fishing include working with a variety of partners to recycle monofilament line, conducting waterway cleanups, and increasing awareness and understanding.

Comment – Wade Fishing

One comment requested that the Service designate access for wade fishing to offset the closed area buffer around the Pelican Island rookery and the buffer shoal/seagrass preserve by Sebastian Inlet District Commission.

Service's Response

Comment noted. This comment is addressed in the compatibility determination for fishing in Appendix V, which provides for wade fishing. Following approval of the final CCP, the refuge will update brochures and maps accordingly.

Comment – Kayak/Canoe Launch

One comment requested that the Service provide the public an access opportunity by building a very simple low cost kayak/canoe launch area on the refuge.

Service's Response

Comment noted. The Service would consider the possibility for a canoe/kayak launch on the wetland fringe of the Torwest tract, if this tract is acquired or otherwise put under management of the refuge.

Comment – Hunting

One comment called for the ban of all hunting from the refuge.

Service's Response
Comment noted. Hunting is not an approved use for the refuge.

REFUGE ADMINISTRATION

Comment – Refuge Budget
Two comments were submitted that proposed to spend the refuge's budget on wildlife first and not on visitor services. One of those comments also objected to the expenditure of funds on cultural resource management.

Service's Response
Comments noted. Under the National Wildlife Refuge System Improvement Act and Service policies (including compatibility policy, 603 FW 2), refuges are to facilitate appropriate and compatible wildlife-oriented public use opportunities. Further, under a variety of laws, regulations, and policies, including the National Historic Preservation Act, the refuge is mandated to protect and manage cultural resources.

Comment – Application of Service Regulations
One comment supported the application of Service regulations on all refuge-managed lands.

Service's Response
Comment noted. The comment is addressed under Objective C.6, which proposes that the Service coordinate with the State of Florida and other partners to enable the enforcement of federal fish and wildlife regulations on all refuge-owned and managed lands and waters. The Service and the Florida Fish and Wildlife Conservation Commission (FWC) worked together to develop revised language regarding the lease area and the implementation of FWC and Service regulations in the leased area. The discussion under Objective C.6 was expanded to reflect this revised language.

Fishing regulations and restrictions will be coordinated between the Service and the FWC, which exercises jurisdiction under the Florida Constitution with respect to marine life. FWC regulations will apply on the leased portion of the refuge, in support of refuge management of fishing as a priority public use. Other regulations implemented by the Service in furtherance of its overall management responsibilities will be coordinated with FWC as needed.

Comment – Personal Watercraft
One comment called for the phasing out of personal watercraft from the refuge (i.e., no jet skis in the refuge).

Service's Response
Comment noted. This comment is addressed under Objective C.6, which proposes that the Service coordinate with the State of Florida and other partners to enable the enforcement of federal fish and wildlife regulations on all refuge-owned and managed lands and waters. Further, the strategies under this objective call for the phasing out of personal watercraft within the refuge's boundary.

Comment – Two-stroke Motors
One comment called for the ban of all two-stroke motors from the refuge.

Service's Response
Comment noted. Under the current lease agreement with the State of Florida, the refuge does not have the authority to ban two-stroke motors from the refuge. Further, at this point in time, it is not practical or practicable to ban two-stroke motors from the refuge.

Comment – New Roads
One comment called for the ban of all new roads from the refuge.

Service's Response
Comment noted. The CCP outlines the future development of a short wildlife drive in the Jungle Trail area (see Figure 16). This was evaluated in the compatibility determinations in Appendix V and was found to be appropriate and compatible, supporting several priority public uses. Development, use, and maintenance of this road will minimize impacts to wildlife and habitat. Further, as needed to support refuge management and maintenance activities, the refuge would create new roads.

Comment – Grazing, mining, drilling, and logging
One comment called for the ban of all grazing, mining, drilling, and logging from the refuge.

Service's Response
Comment noted. These activities do not currently occur on the refuge and are not proposed to occur in the CCP.

Comment – Staffing Levels
One comment supported increasing the number of staff to accomplish the goals outlined in the CCP.

Service's Response
Comment noted. This comment is addressed under Objective E.1, which provides for the addition of staff to the refuge.

Comment – Administrative Office
One comment suggested that the Service build an office near the maintenance shed on refuge property.

Service's Response
Comment noted. This comment is addressed under Objective E.5, which provides options for the location of future administrative and maintenance facilities. The Service considered locating an office adjacent to existing pole sheds, but the option of co-locating the office either with the proposed visitor center or with future maintenance facilities was determined to better consolidate facilities and staff.

Comment – Partners
One comment requested that the Service list the Sierra Club as a partner of the refuge.

Service's Response
Within the CCP, Chapter V, Plan Implementation, was modified under the Partnerships section to include the Sierra Club on the list of partners.

Comment – Aquaculture
The Florida Department of Agriculture and Consumer Services, Division of Aquaculture requested that the Service provide additional information and clarify the compatibility of aquaculture leases and refuge management and land acquisition activities. Further, the agency requested clarification between the shellfish lease and aquaculture lease. The agency also asked why commercial shellfish leases are not considered compatible with the purposes of the refuge. The agency also asked if the CCP would address the aquaculture lease area that was transferred out of the refuge.

Service's Response

The aquaculture leases are those areas that are part of the Aquaculture Use Zone identified on Figure 2 in the CCP. In the late 1990s, the Service and the State of Florida worked together to consolidate the aquaculture leases and transfer them out of the lease agreement for Pelican Island National Wildlife Refuge. These areas are not part of the management boundary of the refuge (Figure 2 of the CCP shows the Aquaculture Use Zone to be out of the refuge) and, as such, are not addressed in the CCP. Shellfish leases are those remaining inholding lease areas that were not removed to the Aquaculture Use Zone. This comment is addressed under Objective D.1 and Appendix V. In Appendix V, under the fishing compatibility determination, on page 169 of the Draft CCP and EA, the third to the last paragraph was updated to read: "Commercial shellfish leases are not considered appropriate for the refuge." Under the 1997 National Wildlife Refuge System Improvement Act, refuges will facilitate appropriate and compatible, wildlife-dependent public uses, specifically hunting, fishing, wildlife observation, photography, environmental education, and interpretation. The refuge is currently working with the State of Florida to transfer the remaining shellfish leases out of the refuge. If commercial shellfish leases are to exist on the refuge, then they would need to meet the Service's requirements of compatibility. If they were determined to be inappropriate, those leases would need to be transferred out of the refuge or terminated from the refuge.

The Service will continue to coordinate with the Florida Department of Agriculture and Consumer Services regarding the Aquaculture Use Zone and the inholding shellfish leases.

Comment – Future Permits

Two state agencies submitted comments regarding future permits. The St. Johns River Water Management District (SJRWMD) commented that although all are intended to benefit fish and wildlife, some of the improvements planned during the 15-year life of the plan will require permits from the SJRWMD and/or Florida Department of Environmental Protection. The Florida Department of Transportation also commented that any proposed changes to the access from State Road A1A to the refuge would require a permit.

Service's Response

Comments noted. The Service is committed to working with all the governmental partners and complying with all applicable permit requirements.

Comment – Aquatic Preserves

The Florida Department of Environmental Protection (FDEP) requested that the Service consult with FDEP's East Central Florida Aquatic Preserves Manager to reduce conflicts between the CCP and the Aquatic Preserve management plans within the boundaries of the Indian River – Malabar to Vero Beach Aquatic Preserve. FDEP notes that concerns with the designation of the use of islands could be raised within the Indian River Lagoon Spoil Island Management Working Group. Further, FDEP requests that the CCP include administration of restoration grants by FDEP's Coastal and Aquatic Managed Areas (CAMA) office on pages 4, 8, or 49 of the CCP, since CAMA and other FDEP staff have spent more than 40 hours a month administering up to $2 million dollars in grant funds for the refuge. Also on page 49 FDEP requests that the discussion include some of the partnership's progress to date on Phase I of the Pelican Island restoration project.

Service's Response

The Service is unaware of any conflicts between the CCP and the Aquatic Preserve Management Plan. The Service will continue to work with FDEP and the East Central Florida Aquatic Preserve Manager to ensure that management actions are coordinated. The Service will also continue to work with the Indian River Lagoon Spoil Island Management Working Group. Pages 4 and 8 of the Draft CCP and EA were modified to mention the very successful partnership effort between FDEP and the

Service to conduct needed habitat restoration activities on the refuge. The discussion under Objective B.2 on page 49 was expanded to better explain the invaluable roles FDEP and Indian River County have played in this restoration project and to provide a summary update on progress of this restoration project.

Comment – Law Enforcement Presence
FDEP requested that a goal be included in the CCP to address partner efforts between the Service and the FDEP CAMA office to request increased federal and state law enforcement presence.

Service's Response
The fourth strategy under Objective C.6 was expanded to include that the Service will continue to work with FDEP's CAMA office to increase the presence of federal and state law enforcement on the refuge.

Comment – Mitigation Opportunities
The Florida Department of Transportation (FDOT) noted that the projects proposed in the CCP offer the potential for seagrass or estuarine mitigation by FDOT, including related to restoration activities such as erosion prevention, shoaling problems, and habitat restoration. FDOT requests coordination with the Service on these mitigation opportunities.

Service's Response
Comment noted. The refuge appreciates FDOT's interest in the future of the refuge. However, under the Service's mitigation policy (see 501 FW 2), mitigation is generally not allowed, since the lands and waters of the refuge are already targeted for restoration and will be restored in the future. Although mitigation has been used on Refuge System lands in limited and exceptional circumstances, it is the policy of the Service to not allow for the establishment of mitigation banks on units of the National Wildlife Refuge System. When and if exceptional circumstances do arise, the Service would be interested in coordinating with FDOT.

Comment – Duck Point
Florida Inland Navigation District clarified the discussion under Objective E.3 regarding Duck Point by requesting two changes: change "dredged spoil material" to "dredged material from the Intracoastal Waterway" and delete the sentence referencing the Indian River County lease at Duck Point for a County park since the lease was never executed.

Service's Response
The Duck Point discussion under Objective E.4 was updated to reflect these changes.

ALTERNATIVES

Comment – Alternative C as Preferred Alternative
Two comments expressed support for Alternative C, the preferred alternative. Alternative C was identified in one of these comments as the alternative providing the most protection for the archaeological resources found on the refuge.

Service's Response
Comments noted. Based on the future needs of the refuge and demands on the refuge and based on the analysis in the Environmental Assessment, Alternative C was selected as the preferred alternative and serves as the basis for the CCP.

Comment – Alternative A as the Preferred Alternative
One comment offered Alternative A (No Action Alternative) as the least objectionable alternative. It stated that the equipment needs to implement alternatives B and C represented good reasons to not implement either alternative.

Service's Response
Comment noted. The Service evaluated three alternatives in the Environmental Assessment and selected Alternative C based on the analysis in the Environmental Assessment and based on its ability to best serve the purposes and goals of the refuge and the mission of the National Wildlife Refuge System.

REFERENCES

Comment – Indian River Lagoon Agencies and Organizations
One comment noted that page 15 referenced the more than 100 agencies and organizations that share responsibility for the Indian River Lagoon system, but that no cite was included in the references.

Service's Response
The CCP was updated to cite the Indian River Lagoon Comprehensive Conservation and Management Plan (Indian River Lagoon National Estuary Program 1996), which references the more than 100 agencies and organizations that share responsibility for the Indian River Lagoon system.

Comment – Missing reference
One comment noted that page 24 referenced Snyder, Herndon, and Robertson 1990, but that this cite was missing from the references list.

Service's Response
The list of references in Appendix II was updated to include the full cite: Snyder, J.R., A. Herndon, and W.B. Robertson, Jr. 1990. Pp. 230-279 *in* Ecosystems of Florida (R.L. Myers and J.J. Ewel, eds.). University of Central Florida Press. Orlando, FL.

Comment – Outdated References
One comment noted that the references cited are extremely old and obsolete. It further stated that some of the bad information shown in the plan comes from using old information such as 1979 information. The comment noted that the world has changed substantially since 1979 and so has the air/water and soil. It requested that the Service use more recent information since global warming, acid rain, and excess carbon dioxide are all impacting what is happening to the U.S. right now.

Service's Response
Comment noted. The Service is committed to using the best available information. The CCP includes references dating from 1891 to 2005. The 1979 wetlands and deepwater habitats classification reference, specifically mentioned in the comment, is from Cowardin et al, which is widely used, accepted, and respected today. As new applicable information becomes available, the Service will adapt management activities accordingly.

VIII. Consultation and Coordination

INTRODUCTION

The Pelican Island National Wildlife Refuge comprehensive planning process involved a wide variety of participants including federal, state, and local governments; universities and other researchers; private non-profit groups; and the friends of the refuge, Pelican Island Preservation Society, as well as a wide variety of local residents, local businesses, concerned citizens from all over the country, local schools, universities, and state and national organizations. At one of the public scoping meetings, a local middle school student even expressed his concerns about the refuge and the future of its resources. Outreach efforts by the refuge and news coverage by the media have spread across the country. The list of participants, beyond those individuals and organizations providing comments during the public scoping process, includes the Core Planning Team, the Wildlife and Habitat Management Review Team, the Public Use Review Team, the Wilderness Review Team, the Intergovernmental Coordination Planning Team, and the Pelican Island Working Group. During the initial phases of this planning process, Pelican Island National Wildlife Refuge was a satellite refuge of the Merritt Island National Wildlife Refuge Complex and heavily involved staff from Merritt Island Refuge. During 2002, Pelican Island and Archie Carr Refuges were separated from the Merritt Island Refuge Complex as a stand-alone complex of two refuges.

Core Planning Team

Consisting exclusively of Fish and Wildlife Service staff, the Core Planning Team involved staff from the Merritt Island National Wildlife Refuge Complex and from the local Ecological Services field office. Key tasks of the team involved defining and refining the vision; identifying, reviewing, and filtering the issues; defining the goals; and outlining the alternatives.

U.S. Fish and Wildlife Service
- Cheri M. Ehrhardt, AICP, Natural Resource Planner, Merritt Island NWR Complex
- Marc Epstein, Refuge Biologist, Merritt Island NWR Complex
- Ron Hight, Project Leader, Merritt Island NWR Complex
- Deborah Jerome, National Wildlife Refuge Planner, Southeast Regional Office
- Ralph Lloyd, Deputy Refuge Manager, Merritt Island NWR Complex
- Evelyn Nelson, Writer/Editor, Southeast Regional Office
- Paul Tritaik, Refuge Manager, Pelican Island NWR
- Jane Tutton, Fish and Wildlife Biologist, South Florida Ecosystem Field Office, Ecological Services
- Dorn Whitmore, Supervisor, Refuge Ranger, Merritt Island NWR Complex

Wildlife and Habitat Management Review Team

Organized by staff at the Merritt Island NWR Complex, the Wildlife and Habitat Management Review Team included a core group of Service staff with invited participants. The invited participants included local and regional experts, researchers, and individuals with intimate knowledge of and expertise in the resources of the refuge. These participants included representatives from: Indian River Mosquito Control District, Indian River Lagoon National Estuary Program (St. Johns River Water Management District), State Parks (Department of Environmental Protection), University of Central Florida, the Florida Fish and Wildlife Conservation Commission, and Service staff from Migratory Birds and State programs.

Core Group
- Jorge Coppen, Refuge Biologist, Ding Darling NWR Complex, USFWS
- Mark Epstein, Refuge Biologist, Merritt Island NWR Complex, USFWS
- Ron Hight, Project Leader, Merritt Island NWR Complex, USFWS
- Paul Tritaik, Refuge Manager, Pelican Island NWR, USFWS
- Kat Royer, Biological Technician, Merritt Island NWR Complex, USFWS

Invited Participants
- Alice Bard, Environmental Specialist II, Division of State Parks, Florida Department of Environmental Protection
- Doug Carlson, Director, Indian River Mosquito Control District
- Robert Day, Environmental Specialist, Indian River Lagoon Program, St. Johns River Water Management District
- Llew Ehrhart, Professor, University of Central Florida
- Grant Gilmore, Senior Fisheries Scientist, Dynamac Corporation, Kennedy Space Center, NASA
- George Heinlein, Mosquito Technician II, Indian River Mosquito Control District
- Chuck Hunter, Wildlife Biologist, Migratory Birds, USFWS
- Steve Rockwood, Supervisor of the South Florida Field Station, Tom Goodwin Wildlife Management Area, Division of Wildlife, Florida Fish and Wildlife Conservation Commission
- Jim Rodgers, Research Biologist, Division of Wildlife, Florida Fish and Wildlife Conservation Commission
- Richard Paperno, Research Administrator, Marine Resources Division, Florida Fish and Wildlife Conservation Commission

Public Use Review Team

The Public Use Review Team consisted of Service staff from the Southeast Regional Office.

U.S. Fish and Wildlife Service
- Frank Podriznik, Outreach/Public Use Specialist, Southeast Regional Office
- Cheryl Simpson, Branch Chief, Division of Visitor Services and Outreach, Southeast Regional Office

Wilderness Review Team

The Wilderness Review Team involved the Refuge Manager and the Planner.

U.S. Fish and Wildlife Service
- Cheri M. Ehrhardt, AICP, Natural Resource Planner, Merritt Island NWR Complex
- Paul Tritaik, Refuge Manager, Pelican Island NWR

Intergovernmental Coordination Planning Team

The Intergovernmental Coordination Planning Team included local, state, and federal governmental field staff representatives involved with the resources at the local level. In addition to the Pelican Island Refuge Manager, this included staff from the Florida Marine Research Institute (Florida Fish and Wildlife Conservation Commission), St. Sebastian River State Buffer Preserve (Florida Department of Environmental Protection), Sebastian Inlet State Park (Florida Department of Environmental Protection), Indian River Lagoon Program (St. Johns River Water Management

District), Community Development Department (Indian River County), Parks Department (Indian River County), County Commission (Indian River County), and Indian River Mosquito Control District.

U.S. Fish and Wildlife Service
- Cheri M. Ehrhardt, AICP, Natural Resource Planner, Merritt Island NWR Complex
- Paul Tritaik, Refuge Manager, Pelican Island NWR

Florida Fish and Wildlife Conservation Commission
- Blair Witherington, Assistant Research Scientist, Florida Marine Research Institute

Florida Department of Environmental Protection
- Brian Proctor, Environmental Specialist, Aquatic Preserve Manager, St. Sebastian River State Buffer Preserve, Florida Department of Environmental Protection
- Steve Williams, Environmental Specialist, Aquatic Preserve Manager, St. Sebastian River State Buffer Preserve, Florida Department of Environmental Protection
- Ron Johns, Resident Park Manager III, Sebastian Inlet State Recreation Area, Florida Department of Environmental Protection
- Terry O'Toole, Parks Services Specialist, Sebastian Inlet State Recreation Area, Florida Department of Environmental Protection

St. Johns River Water Management District
- Robert Day, Environmental Scientist, Indian River Lagoon Program

Indian River County
- Roland DeBlois, Chief, Environmental Planning and Code Enforcement Section, Planning Division, Community Development Department
- Beth Powell, Conservation Lands Manager, Parks Department
- Bob Keating, Director, Community Development
- Ruth Stanbridge, County Commissioner and County Historian
- Terry Thompson, Capital Projects Manager, Public Works Department

Indian River Mosquito Control District
- Doug Carlson, Assistant Director
- George Heinlein, Mosquito Technician II

Pelican Island Working Group

Formed to address issues facing the refuge (e.g., erosion of Pelican Island proper and the Centennial of the National Wildlife Refuge System), the Pelican Island Working Group began as a subcommittee of the South Florida Ecosystem Team. As such, it involves a variety of Service staff, as well as representatives from the U.S. Army Corps of Engineers, Florida Department of Environmental Protection, St. Johns River Water Management District, Florida Inland Navigation District, Indian River County, Indian River Mosquito Control District, Pelican Island Preservation Society, and The Conservation Fund. The membership ebbs and flows, depending on the input and expertise needed to address the issues at hand. Working with the multitude of partners, this group developed the 1999 vision document which guided the comprehensive conservation planning process.

U.S. Fish and Wildlife Service
- Roger Beckham, Supervisory Realty Specialist, Realty, Southeast Regional Office
- Glen Cullingford, Regional Aviation Manager, Southeast Regional Office

- Cheri M. Ehrhardt, AICP, Natural Resource Planner, Merritt Island NWR Complex
- Christine Eustis, ARD, External Affairs, Southeast Regional Office
- Tom Follrath, Chief of Realty, Southeast Regional Office
- Bob Gasaway, Federal Aid, Southeast Regional Office
- George Gentry, Video Productions, National Conservation Training Center
- Kyla Hastie, Regional Centennial Coordinator, Southeast Regional Office
- Ron Hight, Project Leader, Merritt Island NWR Complex
- Louis Hinds, Refuge Supervisor, Southeast Regional Office
- Ricky Ingram, Refuge Supervisor, Southeast Regional Office
- Marsha Isaac, Branch Chief, Contracting and General Services, Southeast Regional Office
- Rick Kanaski, Regional Archeologist, Southeast Regional Office
- Kevin Kilcullen, Service Archaeologist, Arlington Office
- Marilyn Lawal, Federal Aid, Southeast Regional Office
- Mark Madison, Service Historian, National Conservation Training Center
- Richard Mattison, Architect, Southeast Regional Office
- Vicki McCoy, Special Assistant for Strategic Planning and Communications, Regional Director's Office, Southeast Regional Office
- Carol Phillips, former Branch Chief, Division of Information Management, Southeast Regional Office
- Frank Podriznik, Outreach/Public Use Specialist, Southeast Regional Office
- Tom Prusa, Deputy Refuge Supervisor, Southeast Regional Office
- Allison Rowell, Chief, Division of Visitor Services, Arlington Office
- Laurie Shaffer, Centennial Commission Coordinator, Arlington Office
- Cheryl Simpson, former Branch Chief, Division of Visitor Services and Outreach, Southeast Regional Office
- Ruth Slette, former Chief, Division of Contracting and General Services, Southeast Regional Office
- Doug Staller, Acting Chief, Division of Visitor Services and Communications, Washington Office
- Janet Tennyson, Communications Team Leader, Division of Visitor Services and Communications, Washington Office
- Paul Tritaik, Refuge Manager, Pelican Island NWR
- Jane Tutton, Fish and Wildlife Biologist, South Florida Ecosystem Field Office, Ecological Services
- Dorn Whitmore, Supervisor, Refuge Ranger, Merritt Island NWR Complex

U.S. Army Corps of Engineers
- Don Fore, Plan Formulation Branch, Planning Division, Jacksonville District
- Rick McMillen, Don Fore, Plan Formulation Branch, Planning Division, Jacksonville District
- Deborah Peterson, Planning Division, Jacksonville District
- David Schmidt, Chief, Coastal/Navigation Section, Plan Formulation Branch, Planning Division, Jacksonville District
- Steve Traxler, Biologist, Comprehensive Everglades Restoration Program Section, Environmental Branch, Planning Division, Jacksonville District
- Jonas White, Planning Technical Leader, Planning Division, Jacksonville District

Florida Department of Environmental Protection
- Keith Fisher, Manager, St. Sebastian River State Buffer Preserve, Florida Department of Environmental Protection
- Brian Proctor, Environmental Specialist, Aquatic Preserve Manager, St. Sebastian River State Buffer Preserve, Florida Department of Environmental Protection
- Steve Williams, Environmental Specialist, Aquatic Preserve Manager, St. Sebastian River State Buffer Preserve, Florida Department of Environmental Protection

St. Johns River Water Management District
- Robert Day, Environmental Scientist, Indian River Lagoon Program
- Troy Rice, Indian River Lagoon Project Office Director

Florida Inland Navigation District
- George Bunnell, Commissioner
- Mark Crosley, Assistant Executive Director

Indian River County
- Roland DeBlois, Chief, Environmental Planning and Code Enforcement Section, Planning Division, Community Development Department
- Beth Powell, Conservation Lands Manager
- Ruth Stanbridge, County Commissioner and County Historian

Indian River Mosquito Control District
- Doug Carlson, Assistant Director
- George Heinlein, Mosquito Technician II

Pelican Island Preservation Society
- Walt Stieglitz, President

The Conservation Fund
- Matt Sexton, Florida Representative

The Environmental Learning Center
- Holly Dill

Consultants
- Joe Carroll, Carroll and Associates (Indian River Lagoon Habitats)
- Robin Lewis, Lewis Environmental Services (Habitat Restoration and Shoreline Stabilization)
- Brad Smith, Brad Smith Associates (Public Use Planning)

Congressional Representatives
- Pam Gillespie, Congressman Dave Weldon's District Office
- Michelle McGovern, Senator Bill Nelson's Palm Beach Office

IX. Finding of No Significant Impact

Pelican Island National Wildlife Refuge
Comprehensive Conservation Plan
Indian River County, Florida

Introduction

The U.S. Fish and Wildlife Service (Service) prepared an Environmental Assessment (EA) to inform the public of the possible environmental consequences of implementing the Comprehensive Conservation Plan (CCP) for Pelican Island National Wildlife Refuge (Refuge) in Indian River County, Florida. A description of the alternatives, the rationale for selecting the preferred alternative, the environmental effects of the preferred alternative, the potential adverse effects of the action, and a declaration concerning the factors determining the significance of effects, in compliance with the National Environmental Policy Act of 1969, are outlined. The supporting information can be found in the EA.

Alternatives

In developing the CCP for Pelican Island National Wildlife Refuge, the Fish and Wildlife Service evaluated three management alternatives, carefully considering their impacts on the environment and their potential contributions to the purposes of the Refuge and to the mission of the National Wildlife Refuge System:

- Alternative A – Continue Current Refuge Management (No Action Alternative),
- Alternative B – Minimally Expand Refuge Programs, and
- Alternative C – Moderately Expand Refuge Programs (Preferred Alternative).

During the planning process, additional future management alternatives were discussed in a limited fashion, but were not fully developed due to their inabilities to meet mission requirements, purposes and goals of the Refuge, and conservation goals established for the ecosystem. One alternative to increase the size of the Refuge by over five times was abandoned in an effort to build consensus amongst the public and partners and within the Service.

The Draft CCP and EA were distributed for a 60-day public review and comment period from July 25, 2005 to September 26, 2005. After consideration of all the public comments, the Service adopts Alternative C as the preferred alternative to guide the direction of the refuge for the next 15 years. The overriding concern reflected in this plan is that wildlife conservation assumes first priority in refuge management and that wildlife-dependent recreational uses are allowed only if they are determined to be appropriate and compatible with the purposes of the refuge and the mission of the National Wildlife Refuge System. For Pelican Island National Wildlife Refuge several wildlife-dependent recreation uses will be emphasized and encouraged, when and where appropriate and compatible (e.g., fishing, wildlife observation, wildlife photography, and environmental education and interpretation).

Alternative A. Continue Current Refuge management (No Action Alternative)
The No Action Alternative continues current management activities. Recent refuge management activities have included stabilizing the Pelican Island proper rookery; conducting occasional patrols; occasionally removing monofilament line and other trash from Pelican Island proper; occasionally removing moon vine and Brazilian pepper; conducting 2-3 annual colonial bird surveys; conducting 2-3 annual roost counts; and participating in Audubon's annual Christmas Bird Count. The refuge is working with the Florida Department of Environmental Protection and other partners to restore

perennial and ephemeral wetlands and maritime hammock along Jungle Trail in the refuge. As funding becomes available and as willing sellers are identified, the refuge is working to complete the acquisition boundary on the barrier island. However, development pressures in this area are high with small tracts selling for millions of dollars. Much of the refuge is covered by a lease agreement with the State of Florida, which allows traditional uses. The refuge relies on the volunteers and partners for environmental education activities. Otherwise, the refuge is open to fishing, as well as to wildlife observation, photography, interpretation, and environmental education. The historic lack of staff has helped to limit refuge management activities, including little or no management activities addressing the Wilderness Area, other special designations, cultural resources, contaminants, research activities, and commercial activities.

Alternative B. Minimally expand refuge programs
This alternative adds biological and public use activities to increase the functionality of the refuge. Proposed management to protect wildlife and habitats includes stabilizing and restoring the Pelican Island proper rookery, implementing an expanded buffer for the Pelican Island rookery, conducting regular patrol and enforcement activities, conducting habitat restoration activities on the barrier island, developing baseline data, implementing a litter removal program, increasing awareness of issues related to threatened and endangered species, increasing coordination with the State of Florida, working with the partners to limit wildlife and habitat disturbance, and working with the partners to address the loss and decline of seagrass beds. As willing sellers are identified, the refuge is working to complete the acquisition boundary on the barrier island, with several priorities identified. The refuge would continue to operate under the current lease agreement with the State of Florida. The refuge would provide opportunities for bank fishing, develop new boardwalks and trails, coordinate with the environmental education partners to increase awareness and understanding of the refuge and the resources protected, expand outreach activities, and require permits for commercial operations on the refuge. Further, the refuge would work with Indian River County to have the refuge's shell middens included on the State of Florida Master Site File and the refuge would provide patrol and enforcement for these sites. To accomplish the outlined activities, the staff is proposed to be increased to nine by adding three staff: Refuge Officer, Maintenance Worker, and Supply Technician.

Alternative C. moderately expand refuge programs (preferred alternative)
The preferred alternative, Alternative C, is considered to be the most effective management action for meeting the purposes, vision, and goals of the refuge. Proposed management to protect wildlife and habitats includes stabilizing and restoring the Pelican Island proper rookery, implementing an expanded buffer for the Pelican Island rookery, conducting regular patrol and enforcement activities, conducting habitat restoration activities on the barrier island, developing baseline data, implementing a litter removal program, increasing awareness of issues related to threatened and endangered species, increasing coordination with the State of Florida, working with the partners to limit wildlife and habitat disturbance, working with the partners to address the loss and decline of seagrass beds, expanding the refuge's role and activities in recovering threatened and endangered species, developing comprehensive wildlife and habitat management plans, developing and implementing surveying and monitoring programs, developing disturbance free zones, and providing technical assistance to partners for off-refuge habitat restoration efforts. As willing sellers are identified, the refuge is working to complete the acquisition boundary on the barrier island, with several priorities identified. The refuge would work with the State of Florida to modify the lease agreement to enable the enforcement of Service regulations on all refuge-managed lands and waters to better protect wildlife and habitat. The refuge would provide opportunities for bank fishing, develop new boardwalks and trails, coordinate with the environmental education partners to increase awareness and understanding of the refuge and the resources protected, expand outreach activities, require permits for commercial operations on the refuge, and develop a modest visitor center. And, the refuge would work with the partners to eliminate those uses not determined to be wildlife-dependent and

appropriate for the refuge. Further, the refuge would work with Indian River County to have the refuge's shell middens included on the State of Florida's Master Site File. The refuge would work with the partners to acquire and manage the Kroegel Homestead and pursue addition of the Kroegel Homestead to the National Register. The refuge would also provide patrol and enforcement for the cultural resource sites. To accomplish the outlined activities, the staff is proposed to be increased to eleven by adding five staff: Refuge Officer, Maintenance Worker, Biological Science Technician, Refuge Ranger, and Supply Technician.

Selection Rationale

Alternative C is selected for implementation because it directs the development of programs to best achieve the purposes and goals of the refuge and ensures long-term achievement of refuge and Service objectives. At the same time, these management actions provide balanced levels of compatible public use opportunities consistent with existing laws, Service policies, and sound biological principles. It provides the best mix of program elements to achieve desired long-term conditions and to respond to the growing human population and the impacts associated with development near and adjacent to the refuge.

Environmental Effects

Implementation of the Service's management action is expected to result in environmental, social, and economic effects as outlined in the CCP and EA. The wildlife and habitat, land protection and conservation, visitor services, refuge administration, and cultural resources management activities outlined in the CCP are anticipated to result in net positive environmental benefits, increasing wildlife and habitat knowledge, management, and protection; decreasing the numbers and spread of exotic, invasive, and nuisance species; ensuring the compatibility of all uses of the refuge; expanding awareness and opportunities for public use of the refuge; and increasing research and information to enable better decision-making.

- Stabilization and accretion of Pelican Island proper are anticipated to increase nesting and resting use of the rookery by wading birds and shorebirds.
- Increased protection and management and decreased disturbance are anticipated to increase the populations of federally listed species using the refuge.
- Habitat restoration and management are anticipated to increase the use of the refuge by neotropical migratory birds, shorebirds, wading birds, and waterfowl.
- Although increased human use of the refuge is anticipated, monitoring is proposed and management will be adapted as necessary to ensure that all activities are wildlife-dependent, appropriate, and compatible.
- Implementing the CCP is not expected to have any significant adverse effects on wetlands and floodplains, pursuant to Executive Orders 11990 and 11988, nor would implementation result in irrevocable, long-term adverse impacts.

Potential Adverse Effects and Mitigation Measures

Wildlife Disturbance

Disturbance to wildlife at some level is an unavoidable consequence of any public use program, regardless of the activity involved, as well as an unavoidable consequence of many management and restoration activities. Obviously, some activities innately have the potential to be more disturbing than others. The management actions to be implemented have been carefully planned to avoid unacceptable levels of impacts. Further, the habitat management and restoration activities are anticipated to result in net positive benefits, despite any minor short-term negative impacts.

As currently proposed, the known and anticipated levels of disturbance of the management action are considered minimal and well within the tolerance level of known wildlife species and populations present in the area. Implementation of the public use program would take place through carefully controlled time and space zoning, such as expanding the closed area buffer around the Pelican Island proper rookery, considering potential seasonal closures around fish spawning and settlement sites, and limiting access to only daylight hours for the barrier island portion of the refuge. Further, the pro-active efforts to increase user awareness and understanding will also help limit wildlife and habitat disturbance. Monitoring activities will help ensure that all public use activities minimize disturbance to wildlife and habitat. Public use programs will be adjusted as necessary to limit disturbances to ensure compatibility. Orientation of staff, volunteers, and contractors regarding avoiding impacts will help to minimize wildlife and habitat disturbance.

User Group Conflicts
As public use visitation increases over time, some conflicts between user groups may occur. Programs would be adjusted, as needed, to eliminate or minimize these problems and provide high quality wildlife-dependent recreational opportunities. Experience has proven that time and space zonings, such as establishing separate use areas and use periods and restricting the numbers of users, are effective tools in eliminating conflicts between user groups.

Effects on Adjacent Landowners
Implementation of the management action is not anticipated to negatively impact adjacent or inholding landowners. Further, living next to a national wildlife refuge is touted as a selling point in this area. Future land acquisition will continue to occur on a willing seller basis. Lands are acquired through a combination of fee title purchases, donations, and less-than-fee title interests (e.g., conservation easements, cooperative agreements, and management agreements) from willing sellers.

Land Ownership and Site Development
Proposed acquisition efforts by the Service would result in minor to no changes in land and recreational use patterns, since few inholdings remain and since all uses on national wildlife refuges must meet compatibility standards. Land ownership by the Service precludes any future economic development by the private sector.

Potential development of access roads, trails, kiosks, and visitor parking areas could lead to minor short-term negative impacts on plants, soil, and some wildlife species. When site development activities are proposed, each activity will adhere to all applicable permit requirements and will strive to minimize impacts. At that time, any required mitigation activities will be incorporated into the specific project to reduce the level of impacts to the human environment and to protect fish and wildlife and their habitats.

As indicated earlier, one of the direct effects of site development is increased public use. This increased use may lead to increased littering, noise, and vehicle traffic. While funding and personnel resources will be allocated to minimize these effects, such allocations make these resources unavailable for other programs. Increasing awareness and understanding will help limit impacts associated with public use of the refuge. Further, orientation and preliminary site assessments will help staff, volunteers, and contractors to minimize impacts to wildlife and habitats.

The management action is not expected to have significant adverse effects on wetlands and floodplains, pursuant to Executive Orders 11990 and 11988.

Coordination
The management action has been thoroughly coordinated with all interested and/or affected parties. Parties contacted include those listed.

> Interested Members of the Public (i.e., through the CCP mailing list)
> U.S. Army Corps of Engineers
> Florida Fish and Wildlife Conservation Commission
> Florida Department of Environmental Protection
> Florida Department of Agriculture and Consumer Services
> Florida Department of Transportation
> State Historic Preservation Office
> Florida Inland Navigation District
> St. Johns River Water Management District
> Treasure Coast Regional Planning Council
> Indian River County
> Indian River Mosquito Control District
> City of Sebastian
> Conservation Organizations
> Local Businesses
> Congressional Representatives

Findings
It is my determination that the management action does not constitute a major federal action significantly affecting the quality of the human environment under the meaning of Section 102(2)(c) of the National Environmental Policy Act of 1969 (as amended). As such, an environmental impact statement is not required. This determination is based on the listed factors (40 C.F.R. 1508.27), as addressed in the EA for the Pelican Island National Wildlife Refuge.

1. Both beneficial and adverse effects have been considered and this action will not have a significant effect on the human environment. (See the EA, pages 115-133.)

2. The actions will not have a significant effect on public health and safety. (See the EA, page 117.)

3. The project will not significantly affect any unique characteristics of the geographic area such as proximity to historical or cultural resources, the Wilderness Area, or ecologically critical areas. (See the EA, pages 87, 115-117, 117-123, and 125-133.)

4. The effects on the quality of the human environment are not likely to be highly controversial. (See the EA, pages 86, 121-123, and 125-133.)

5. The actions do not involve highly uncertain, unique, or unknown environmental risks to the human environment. (See the EA, pages 87, 115-117, 117-123, and 125-133.)

6. The actions will not establish a precedent for future actions with significant effects nor do they represent a decision in principle about a future consideration. (See the EA, pages 87, 115-117, 121-123, and 125-133.)

7. There will be no cumulatively significant impacts on the environment. Cumulative impacts have been analyzed with consideration of other similar activities on adjacent lands, in past action, and in foreseeable future actions. (See the EA, pages 87, 115-117, 121-123, and 125-133).

8. The actions will not significantly affect any site listed in, or eligible for listing in, the National Register of Historic Places, nor will they cause loss or destruction of significant scientific, cultural, or historic resources. (See the EA, pages 85, 87, 115, 121-123, 125, 127, and 133.)

9. The actions are not likely to adversely affect threatened or endangered species, or their habitats. (See the EA, pages 85, 94, 115, 121-123, and 125-133.)

10. The actions will not lead to a violation of federal, state, or local laws imposed for the protection of the environment. (See the EA, pages 86-87.)

Supporting References
U.S. Fish and Wildlife Service. 2005. Draft Comprehensive Conservation Plan and Environmental Assessment for Pelican Island National Wildlife Refuge, Indian River County, Florida. U.S. Department of the Interior, Fish and Wildlife Service, Southeast Region. Atlanta, GA. 183 pp.

Document Availability
The Environmental Assessment was Section B of the Draft CCP and EA for Pelican Island National Wildlife Refuge and was made available in July 2005. Additional copies are available by contacting: Pelican Island National Wildlife Refuge, 1339 20th Street, Vero Beach, FL 32960; 772.562.3909 extension 275; or PelicanIsland@fws.gov.

for Signed _____   August 31, 2006
Sam D. Hamilton   Date
Regional Director